The Inter-War Crisis 1919–1939

The Inter-War Crisis
1919–1939

Second revised edition

Richard Overy

Longman
is an imprint of

Harlow, England • London • New York • Boston • San Francisco • Toronto • Sydney • Singapore • Hong Kong
Tokyo • Seoul • Taipei • New Delhi • Cape Town • Madrid • Mexico City • Amsterdam • Munich • Paris • Milan

PEARSON EDUCATION LIMITED

Edinburgh Gate
Harlow CM20 2JE
United Kingdom
Tel: +44 (0) 1279 623623
Fax: +44 (0) 1279 431059
Website: www.pearsoned.co.uk

First edition published 1994
Second edition published 2007
Second revised edition published in Great Britain in 2010

© Pearson Education Limited 1994, 2007, 2010

The right of Richard Overy to be identified as author of this work has been
asserted by him in accordance with the Copyright, Designs and Patents Act 1988.

ISBN: 978-1-4082-2317-8

British Library Cataloguing in Publication Data
A CIP catalogue record for this book can be obtained from the British Library

Library of Congress Cataloging-in-Publication Data
Overy, R. J.
    The inter-war crisis 1919–1939 / Richard Overy. – 2nd rev. ed.
        p. cm.
    Includes bibliographical references and index.
    ISBN 978-1-4082-2317-8 (pbk.)
    1. History, Modern – 20th century.   I. Title.
    D723.O98 2009
    909.82′2—dc22
                                                                    2009030096

10   9   8   7   6   5   4   3   2   1
13   12   11   10   09

Set in 10/13.5pt Berkeley Book by 35
Printed and bound in China (SWTC/01)

The Publisher's policy is to use paper manufactured from sustainable forests.

Introduction to the series

History is a narrative constructed by historians from traces left by the past. Historical enquiry is often driven by contemporary issues and, in consequence, historical narratives are constantly reconsidered, reconstructed and reshaped. The fact that different historians have different perspectives on issues means that there is also often controversy and no universally agreed version of past events. *Seminar Studies in History* was designed to bridge the gap between current research and debate, and the broad, popular general surveys that often date rapidly.

The volumes in the series are written by historians who are not only familiar with the latest research and current debates concerning their topic, but who have themselves contributed to our understanding of the subject. The books are intended to provide the reader with a clear introduction to a major topic in history. They provide both a narrative of events and a critical analysis of contemporary interpretations. They include the kinds of tools generally omitted from specialist monographs: a chronology of events, a glossary of terms and brief biographies of 'who's who'. They also include bibliographical essays in order to guide students to the literature on various aspects of the subject. Students and teachers alike will find that the selection of documents will stimulate discussion and offer insight into the raw materials used by historians in their attempt to understand the past.

Clive Emsley and Gordon Martel
Series Editors

Contents

Acknowledgements

We are grateful to the following for permission to reproduce copyright material:

Plates 1 and 8 courtesy of the Mary Evans Picture Library; plate 2 © The Galton Institute, London, image L0030836 held in the Wellcome Library, London; plate 3 © Stefano Bianchetti/ Corbis; plate 4 courtesy of Bob Thomas/ Popperfoto/ Getty Images; plates 5 and 9 courtesy of the Bridgeman Art Library; plate 6 © Minnesota Historical Society/ Corbis; plate 7 © Hulton-Deutsch Collection/ Corbis; plate 10 courtesy of Popperfoto/ Getty Images.

Extract on p. 92 from David Gascoyne's 'Farewell Chorus' is from his *Selected Poems* (Enitharmon Press, 1994). Text of Document 24 from Jahoda, M., Lazarsfeld, P. and Zeisel, H., *Marienthal: The Sociography of an Unemployed Community* (Transaction Publications, 2002; reprinted from *Die Arbeitslosen von Marienthal*, 1933).

In some instances we have been unable to trace the owners of copyright material, and we would appreciate any information that would enable us to do so.

Chronology

1914

28 July–4 August   Outbreak of First World War.

1917

23 February   Demonstrations in Petrograd provoke revolutionary crisis.
2 March   Tsar Nicholas II abdicates.
25 October   Bolshevik seizure of power in Russia.

1918

3 March   German–Russian Treaty of Brest-Litovsk.
9 November   Kaiser Wilhelm II abdicates.
11 November   Armistice on Western Front ends First World War.
November–December   Communist seizure of power in Bavaria.

1919

15 January   Murder of Rosa Luxemburg and Karl Liebknecht.
21 March   Bela Kun leads Communist takeover in Hungary.
28 June   Signing of the Versailles Treaty.

1920

10 January   League of Nations Organization begins its operations.

1921

17 March   Marie Stopes opens first Birth Control Clinic.

1922

6 February	Washington Naval Treaty signed.
May	Stalin appointed General Secretary of the Central Committee of the Russian Communist Party.
28 October	March on Rome by Italian Fascists.

1923

3 September	Primo de Rivera becomes Spanish dictator.
9 November	Hitler *Putsch* in Munich ends in his arrest.
15 November	German mark collapses at end of hyperinflation.

1925

1 December	Locarno Treaty signed by Britain, Germany, Italy, France and Belgium.

1926

12–14 May	Marshal Pilsudski assumes power in Poland.
28 May	Parliamentary rule overthrown in Portugal.

1928

29 August	Kellogg–Briand Pact signed in Paris.

1929

29 October	Start of 'Great Crash' on US Stock Exchange.

1930

17 June	Hawley–Smoot Tariff Act.
14 April	Founding of Second Spanish Republic.

1931

September	Japanese Kwantung army seizes Manchuria.
11 December	Statute of Westminster gives dominions right to declare war.

1932

6 March	US 'Bank Holiday' to prevent collapse of banking system.

1932

9 July	End of Lausanne Conference on reparations.
July/August	British Commonwealth Ottawa Conference.
July	NSDAP wins 37% of the popular vote in German election.

1933

30 January	Hitler appointed German chancellor.
2 May	German trade unions dissolved.
June	World Economic Conference, London.
July	US Dow Jones share index reaches lowest point.
16 October	Germany withdraws from League of Nations and from Disarmament Conference.

1934

6 February	Riots in central Paris.
15 May	Konstantin Ulmanis declares dictatorship in Latvia.
19 May	King Boris III and the army stage coup in Bulgaria.
30 June	Hitler orders murder of former opponents and SA leaders on 'Night of the Long Knives'.
2 August	Hitler proclaimed Führer by German parliament.
September	Hjalmar Schacht becomes German Economics Minister.
19 September	USSR joins League of Nations.

1935

13 January	Saar plebiscite returns territory to Germany.
5 July	Salazar becomes dictator of Portugal.
August	Provisional Neutrality Act passed in the United States.
2/3 October	Italian forces attack Ethiopia (Abyssinia).

1936

13 March	German forces remilitarize the Rhineland provinces.
17 July	Nationalist forces stage attempted coup, start of Spanish Civil War.

1937

26 April	German and Italian aircraft bomb Basque city of Guernica.

9 July	Start of Sino-Japanese war.
13 December	Japanese capture Chinese capital of Nanking.

1938

12 March	Germany concludes 'Anschluss' with Austria.
30 September	Partition of Czechoslovakia agreed at Munich Conference.

1939

15 March	German forces occupy Bohemia and Moravia.
30 March	Chamberlain gives guarantee to Poland.
23 August	Signing of German-Soviet Pact of Non-Aggressioin.
25 August	Anglo-Polish Treaty signed.
1 September	Germany attacks Poland.
3 September	Britain and France declare war on Germany.

Who's who

Alexander I (of Yugoslavia) *(1888–1934)* Succeeded to the Yugoslavian throne in 1921, and played an important part in subverting federal democracy from 1929. He was assassinated at Marseilles in 1934.

Antonescu, Ion *(1882–1934)* Romanian army marshal who overthrew the rule of King Carol in 1940 and declared his solidarity with Hitler. He suppressed the native Iron Guard fascist movement, and in 1944 was in turn overthrown by other pro-German forces shortly before the Soviet conquest of Romania.

Ataturk, Kemal *(1881–1938)* Turkish soldier who after the First World War played a leading part in transforming the former Ottoman Empire into the modern Turkish state. He became Turkish President in 1920 and suppressed both Communism and Islamic fundamentalism.

Attlee, Clement *(1883–1967)* Labour politician who led the party after it split in 1931 when Ramsay Macdonald set up a National Government. He joined Churchill's war cabinet in 1940 and became prime minister in July 1945. He presided over the introduction of the NHS and the widespread nationalization of British industries. Defeated in the 1951 election, he retired in 1955.

Carr, E.H. *(1892–1982)* British international historian best known for his multivolume study of the Bolshevik Revolution.

Chamberlain, Housten Stewart *(1855–1927)* British race theorist who settled in Germany where he wrote popular and influential books on the superiority of the 'Aryan' race. His work was read and absorbed by *Adolf Hitler*.

Chamberlain, Neville *(1873–1940)* Conservative politician from a prominent Birmingham political family. He was a successful minister in the 1920s, Chancellor of the Exchequer in 1934 (when he oversaw the programme of British rearmament), and from June 1937 prime minister. He is seen as the architect of the policy of 'appeasement', but declared war on Hitler in September 1939. He resigned in May 1940.

Chiang Kai-shek *(1887–1975)* Chinese army officer who rose to power in China in the 1920s and fought a long civil war against Chinese Communists and native warlords. He led Chinese resistance to Japanese invasion in the 1930s and 1940s but was defeated by Communist insurgents in 1949 and retired to the island of Taiwan which he ruled until his death.

Churchill, Winston *(1874–1965)* English politician, soldier and writer. He held high office before 1914 as a Liberal minister, saw service on the Western Front in 1916, before becoming Minister of Munitions. In the 1920s he became a Conservative and served as Chancellor of the Exchequer from 1926 to 1929. In the 1930s he was on the political fringes until the coming of war in 1939 when he took over the Admiralty. In May 1940 he became prime minster, a post which he held until 1945, and again from 1951 to 1955.

Citroën, André *(1878–1934)* Prominent French car manufacturer who helped to pioneer mass motoring in the 1920s. He was well known for his flamboyant lifestyle and advertising gimmicks. In 1934 he produced the first front-wheel drive car.

Clemenceau, Georges *(1841–1929)* French statesman and politician nicknamed 'the tiger' because of his pugnacious character. He was prime minister of France from 1917 to 1920 and played a key role in negotiating the *Versailles Settlement*.

Darré, Walther *(1895–1953)* National Socialist politician appointed by Hitler to lead the campaign to convert the German peasantry to the move-ment in 1931 and subsequently appointed leader of the Reich Food Estate in 1933 set up to coordinate all aspects of German agriculture. He was arrested in 1945 and sent to prison in 1949.

Dollfuss, Engelbert *(1892–1934)* Austrian Catholic politician who estab-lished a semi-authoritarian regime in 1933. He was hostile to the Austrian National Socialist Party and suppressed it in 1934, but was assassinated by a group of Nazis the same year.

Dorgères, Henri *(1897–1985)* Radical right-wing politician who championed the cause of the French peasantry in the 1930s along quasi-fascist lines. A keen supporter of the Vichy regime, he was arrested and imprisoned in 1944.

Douhet, Giulio *(1869–1930)* Italian general who pioneered the strategy of modern air power. His book *The Command of the Air* (1921) became a classic statement of the capacity of aircraft to act independently of the army and navy by pursuing the defeat of the enemy nation by bombing.

Ebert, Friedrich *(1871–1925)* German trade unionist and politician, who rose to become leader of the German Social-Democratic Party in 1913 and later the first President of the Weimar Republic.

Franco, Francisco *(1892–1976)* A career soldier from the region of Galicia, Franco fought in Spain's Moroccan wars in the 1920s and rose to be army chief-of-staff by 1935 under the new Republican regime. Fearing an imminent Communist coup, Franco led a military coup in July 1936 that resulted in a bloody three-year civil war. In March 1939 he became dictator of all Spain and established a brutal regime of repression which lasted until his death in 1976.

Freud, Sigmund *(1856–1939)* A Viennese doctor who became the founding father of modern psychoanalysis. He is best remembered for his pioneering books *Interpretation of Dreams* (1900) and *The Ego and the Id* (1923). He argued that most psychological disorders were related to problems of early sexuality, which were suppressed in the unconscious portion of the mind but later manifested themselves in neurotic behaviour. When Germany occupied Austria in 1938, Freud, who was Jewish, emigrated to London.

Fukuyama, Francis *(1952–)* American State Department official who became famous in 1989 when he published *The End of History* in which he claimed that liberal capitalism had triumphed worldwide and that there was no necessity for further historical development. He has since written other books on the state of the world which have modified his original claims.

Goebbels, Joseph *(1897–1945)* An enthusiastic and radical National Socialist in the 1920s, Goebbels rose to be first party propaganda chief, then Minister for Propaganda and Popular Enlightenment in Hitler's regime. In 1944 he was made Plenipotentiary for Total War, but following German military failure he committed suicide in Hitler's bunker in Berlin in May 1945.

Haile, Selassie *(1892–1975)* Emperor of Ethiopa (Abysinnia) who succeeded to the throne in 1930. He was overthrown by Italian forces in 1936, fled to London and returned as emperor in 1941 when Italy was expelled in turn by British Empire forces. He was forced from the throne a second time in 1974.

Himmler, Heinrich *(1901–1945)* Fanatical member of the German National Socialists in the 1920s, he was appointed head of the SS in 1929, and police chief in Bavaria when Hitler came to power. In 1936 he took over the whole police and security network and ran the concentration camps. He organized the genocide of the European Jews and committed suicide when captured in 1945.

Hindenburg, Paul von *(1847–1934)* German soldier who fought in the Franco-German War of 1870 as a young officer and became by the First World War one of a coterie of senior officers who dominated the German war effort. In 1916 he became commander-in-chief of the German armies. In

1925 he was elected President, a position which he used to encourage a revival of German nationalism. He agreed to make Hitler Chancellor in January 1933.

Hitler, Adolf *(1889–1945)* Austrian-born politician who came to Germany in 1913, served in a Bavarian regiment in the First World War and joined the tiny German Workers' Party in 1919. The party became the National Socialist Party two years later with Hitler at its head. He attempted a coup in 1923 and was imprisoned. He took control of the party again in 1926, and seven years later was appointed German Chancellor. He became dictator of Germany and embarked on a programme of rearmament, territorial expansion and anti-Semitism. He attacked Poland in 1939 and launched world war. In 1941 he initiated what became the Holocaust and in April 1945 committed suicide in the ruins of Berlin.

Ho Chi Minh *(1890–1969)* Vietnamese nationalist politician who led the struggle against French rule in Vietnam in the 1930s and established the Communist state of North Vietnam in 1954. He became a symbol of popular defiance of imperialism in the youth revolt of 1968.

Horthy, Nicholas *(1868–1957)* An admiral in the Austro-Hungarian navy during the First World War, he led Hungarian and Romanian forces in the summer of 1919 in a counter-revolutionary civil war against Hungarian Communism. He declared himself Regent in 1919 in place of the exiled Habsburgs, and ruled Hungary until 1944 when he was deposed by German intervention.

Jung, Carl *(1875–1961)* Swiss psychologist who at first supported Freud's discoveries but broke with him over what he saw as excessive emphasis on sexuality. Jung is best remembered for the idea that people are divided into extrovert or introvert personalities. He accepted the idea of the unconscious, but suggested that it was a product of a collective entity shaped by the whole experience of early human development.

Jünger, Ernst *(1895–1998)* German soldier in the First World War who became a leading radical nationalist writer in the 1920s. Most famous for his depiction of war in *Storm of Steel* (1921), he was hostile to Hitler and lived a long life after 1945 as a conservative philosopher and writer.

Kun, Bela *(1886–1937)* Hungarian Communist who led the Hungarian revolutionary government in the summer of 1919 until its overthrow by force in July. He lived in exile in the Soviet Union where he was accused of spying and executed in 1937.

Lenin (Vladimir Ulyanov) *(1870–1924)* Chairman of the Russian Social Democratic Party (Bolsheviks) and the most influential theoretical Marxist of his generation. He encouraged the party to launch the revolution in October 1917 and became leader of the new government until illness in 1922 forced him to withdraw from active politics.

Levine, Eugen (*1883–1919*) Radical socialist politician who led the Bavarian Communist uprising in 1919 and was assassinated that same year.

Liebknecht, Karl (*1871–1919*) German social democrat politician who is best known for arguing against war in August 1914. He founded the radical Marxist Spartacist League in November 1914, took part in the Communist revolt at the end of the war and was murdered in January 1919 by nationalist soldiers.

Luxemburg, Rosa (*1870–1919*) Polish Marxist philosopher who played a prominent role in the German Social Democratic Party before 1914. She was hostile to Lenin's view of the revolutionary party and favoured reliance on the working masses. Imprisoned during the First World War, she became a leader of the German revolutionary movement in late 1918 and was murdered by nationalist soldiers in January 1919.

Mussolini, Benito (*1883–1945*) Radical socialist politician from the Romagna who became a nationalist during the First World War, fought at the front and returned to found the Italian Fascist movement. In October 1922 he was appointed prime minister, established a single-party dictatorship by 1926 and led Italy into wars in Ethiopia (1935), Spain (1936–39), and against the Western powers (1940–43). He was overthrown by a military coup in 1943, and killed by Italian partisans at the end of the war in 1945.

Nicholas II (*1868–1918*) Tsar (emperor) of Russia from 1894 until his abdication in March 1917. He and his family were assassinated by the Bolshevik regime in July 1918.

Nietzsche, Friedrich (*1844–1900*) German writer and philosopher whose work undermined conventional moral beliefs and celebrated strenuous self-expression. He is best known for his assertion in *Thus Spake Zarathustra* that 'God is dead'.

Nye, Gerald (*1892–1971*) American Republican senator from Illinois who campaigned in the 1930s against armaments manufacture and promoted American *isolationism*.

Orwell, George (*1903–1949*) British author and journalist who fought in the Spanish Civil War in the International Brigades. His disillusionment with Communism produced the classic satire *Animal Farm* (1945) and the futuristic *1984* (1949), best remembered for the idea that 'Big Brother' is always watching you.

Primo de Rivera, Miguel *(1870–1930)* Spanish general who took over power in Spain in 1923. He established a dictatorship but alienated his army supporters and was forced out of office in 1930.

Röhm, Ernst *(1887–1934)* A German soldier who became prominent in radical nationalist circles in the early 1920s before joining the Hitler movement. He was made chief-of-staff of the *SA* in 1931 and murdered on 1 July 1934 on the 'Night of the Long Knives' for allegedly plotting to overthrow Hitler.

Roosevelt, Franklin Delano *(1882–1945)* A prominent Democrat politician who served under Woodrow Wilson as Assistant Secretary for the Navy in the First World War. After struggling against polio in the 1920s, he became first Governor of New York State in 1928 and four years later was elected US President. He held the office for an unprecedented four terms, and played an important role in holding together the wartime Grand Alliance with Britain and the USSR.

Salazar, Antonio de *(1889–1970)* Portuguese politician who became finance minister in 1928 and prime minister in 1932. He established a 'New Order' along authoritarian lines but Portugal became a backward and impoverished state. He was influential in refusing independence to Portugal's African colonies.

Schacht, Hjalmar *(1877–1970)* German banker who was chosen to help solve the inflation crisis in Germany in late 1923, then to head the German Central Bank until his resignation in 1929 in protest at reparation payments. In 1933 Hitler appointed him to head the Central Bank again and in 1934 he also became Economics Minister. He helped to supply the finance for German rearmament, but argued with Hitler over its extent and was forced to resign his posts. He was put on trial at Nuremberg but acquitted.

Spengler, Oswald *(1880–1936)* German philosopher whose book on the decline of the west published in English in 1928 had enormous influence in the inter-war years.

Stalin (Joseph Dzhugashvili) *(1879–1953)* Georgian Marxist who joined the Russian Social Democratic Party, followed Lenin when the party split in 1904 and became Commissar for Nationalities when the Bolshevik government was set up in November 1917. In 1922 he was appointed General Secretary of the party and used this position to help him establish a personal dictatorship in the Soviet Union from the 1930s to the 1950s. He was prime minister from 1941 until his death in 1953, and commissar for defence from 1941 to 1946.

Webb, Sidney and Beatrice *(1859–1947) (1858–1943)* Campaigning British socialists who helped to launch the Fabian Society in 1884 and pioneered ideas about welfare reform and effective local government. In 1935 they published a study of the Soviet Union as a new civilization which helped to persuade many western intellectuals that Stalin's Russia was progressive and enlightened.

Wilson, Woodrow *(1856–1924)* President of the United States from 1913 to 1921 who played a major part in shaping the post-war peace settlement in Europe through his campaign for the 'self-determination of peoples'.

Glossary

Words which appear in the glossary have been emboldened in the main text of the book.

Anschluss: The 'joining on' of Austria to Germany when German troops occupied the country on 12 March 1938.

Artisan: Skilled worker, usually independent, producing specialised hand-crafted goods.

Aryan: Term originally applied to languages derived from an Indian root, but later taken to mean a particular race with a distinctive physical appearance and cultural level. The word was applied under National Socialism to distinguish Nordic Europeans from Jews and Slavs.

Autarky: Term used in the 1930s to describe a policy of economic self-sufficiency at the expense of international trade.

Bolsheviks: One of two factions of the Russian Social Democratic Party when it split in 1904 into majority socialists (Bolsheviks) and minority socialists (Mensheviks) over issues of revolutionary practice.

Bourgeoisie: Originally a term defining the non-noble 'burghers' of European cities whose status and wealth gave them particular privileges. Later used indiscriminately to describe the wealthier middle classes.

Centre Party: Name of the main Catholic political party in Germany, founded in 1870, dissolved under Hitler in 1933.

Cheka: The so-called Extraordinary Commission set up by the Bolshevik revolutionary government in November 1917 to combat all political enemies of the regime. It operated as a political police force until superseded by the GPU (State Political Directorate) in 1922.

Collectivization: The policy adopted by the Soviet regime in 1928 to force the Russian peasantry to abandon private farming and create large co-operative farms on which they would work as paid employees of the 'collective'.

Communism: A political movement from the early years of the nineteenth century in favour of democratic societies based on common ownership of property and the abolition of privilege. Marx adopted Communism in the 1840s and gave it a firm theoretical foundation.

Concert of Europe: Term used to describe the usually informal agreement of the European great powers to act together to maintain the peace during the century from the Napoleonic Wars to the First World War.

Corporatavism: The concept of corporate organization of industrial workers and employers. Adopted in Mussolini's Italy in the late 1920s and copied by fascist movements everywhere as an alternative model to class conflict.

Dadaism: Radical art movement in Italy in the 1910s which applauded violence and the capacity of art to engage with politics.

Democratic centralism: Concept used to describe the operation of the Bolshevik party in Russia. Decisions were taken by the central authority, but only after 'consultation' with the voice of the people. In practice the centralism always triumphed over the democratic principle.

Diktat: Term used in Germany to describe the 'dictated' Peace Settlement of 1919.

Duma: The Russian parliament established by the Tsar's 'manifesto' of 1906 following the 1905 revolution.

Eugenics: First developed as a science in the 1880s, eugenics was the study of scientific improvement of the human race through a combination of genetic manipulation and social reform.

Fin-de-siècle: Literally 'end of an age', a term used to describe the widespread sense at the end of the nineteenth century of an imminent period of crisis and transformation.

Five-Year Plans: A series of economic plans drawn up in the Soviet Union from 1928 onwards to provide targets for industrial and agricultural development. There were three plans in the 1930s and 1940s before the coming of war.

Fordism: A term derived from the efforts of the American car manufacturer Henry Ford to create large, efficient and modern factories and the rational exploitation of labour through mass-production methods.

Four-Year Plan: Name given to the planning organization created for Hermann Goering in Germany in October 1936 to prepare the armed forces and the economy for war. It was the second four-year plan following the plan for re-employment and recovery launched in 1933.

Freikorps: Name given to the irregular units of returning soldiers in Germany in 1919 who acted as an anti-Communist militia to suppress political radicalism.

Gestapo: Secret State Police set up in Prussia in April 1933 to combat resistance to the Hitler regime, and the heart of the security police organization later set up in 1936 under Heinrich Himmler. The head of the Gestapo from 1935 to 1945 was a career policeman, Heinrich Müller.

Gold Standard: A system of fixed currencies pegged to the value of gold. First used in Britain in 1821 it was adopted by most major states before 1914. Like the Euro, a common standard helped to ease international trade and currency exchange.

Have-not states: Term used to describe those major powers who lacked a large empire and/or secure access to adequate supplies of food and raw materials.

Hyperinflation: The point at which a currency becomes valueless because of an absolute loss of confidence in its purchasing power. Experienced in the USSR in 1919–20, Germany in 1922–23, Austria and Hungary in 1923–24.

Imperial Preference: (see *Ottawa Conference*)

Institute for Industrial Reconstruction: Organization set up in Italy in 1933 to direct investment and resources into key areas of production.

Isolationism: Name given to that strand of American opinion hostile to foreign commitments and unwilling to endorse the League of Nations.

Italian Fascist Party: Founded in 1921, the Fascist Party became the only permitted party in 1926. The party's Grand Council played an important part in the politics of the regime until its collapse in 1943.

Johnson Act: Legislation introduced in the United States in 1934 prohibiting the export of American capital to any state that still owed war debts or commercial debts. Only Finland was exempt from the ban.

Kellogg–Briand Pact: Agreement signed between 68 states, including Germany, to outlaw war as a means of settling disputes between them. The Pact was used at the *Nuremberg Trials* as a basis on which to accuse German leaders of crimes against peace.

Kulak: Name applied to alleged rich peasants in the Soviet Union in the 1920s. Those identified as kulaks were often sent to labour camps during the period of *collectivization*.

Kwantung Army: The name given to the portion of the Japanese army stationed in northern China, which staged a coup and seized Manchuria in 1931.

Laissez-faire: Literally 'to leave alone', the term was used to describe an economy in which the self-regulation of the market replaced state control or regulation of economic activity.

League of Nations: Set up in 1919 under the terms of the international agreements at Versailles, the League was responsible not only for keeping the peace but also for international collaboration on labour conditions, refugees, drugs, intellectual collaboration and culture. It was based at Geneva in Switzerland.

Lebensraum: Term commonly used in Germany in the 1920s to describe that amount of territory thought to be necessary to allow a nation to feed and provision itself to a reasonable standard. 'Living space' became the excuse for programmes of territorial expansion.

Locarno Treaty: Agreement signed in October 1925 between Britain, Germany, France, Italy and Belgium to guarantee the frontiers of western Europe drawn up in 1919.

Maginot Line: A series of defensive fortifications along France's eastern border, begun at the inspiration of the Defence Minister, André Maginot, in 1929, and still incomplete ten years later.

Managed economy: Term used to describe an economy that was not owned by the state but was subject to state regulation and planning to maintain economic equilibrium.

National Socialist German Workers' Party: Better known as the Nazi Party, the NSDAP was founded in 1920 and by the 1940s had more than 8 million members. Hitler led the party from 1921 until its collapse in 1945.

Neutrality Acts: A series of legislative acts passed in the United States between 1935 and 1937, when a permanent state of neutrality was secured. Under the terms of the 1937 Act the United States could not ship arms or give financial assistance to the combatant powers.

New Deal: General term to describe the package of reform measures introduced by American president Franklin Roosevelt in 1933/4 to cope with the impact of the economic recession.

New Order: Term widely used in the 1930s to describe a politics of national rebirth. Usually used to describe the political system set up in Europe under German occupation.

Night of the Long Knives: The night of 30 June 1934 when the SS at Hitler's order murdered the leaders of the paramilitary SA (including Ernst Röhm) and a number of other political opponents.

Nuremberg Laws: A series of laws passed in a special Reichstag session at the National Socialist party rally in Nuremberg in September 1935. The laws prohibited marriage or sexual relations between Jews and Germans, and conferred German citizenship only on those of so-called German blood, excluding German Jews.

Nuremberg Trials: A series of trials of senior German political and military leaders which began in November 1945 with the Trial of the Major War Criminals, but also included later trials against businessmen, officials, SS officers and concentration camp personnel.

Orthodox Christianity: Following the division of the Catholic Church in the eleventh century into Western Catholicism and Eastern Orthodoxy, the Orthodox Church survived in the Balkans and Russia, divided in its turn between Greek and Russian Orthodoxy.

Ottawa Conference: Conference of the major British Empire states in Canada in July/August 1932 to agree on a system of so-called Imperial Preference under whose terms Britain agreed to take raw materials and food from Empire states who in return bought industrial goods from Britain.

OVRA: Italian political police organization established in 1927 to combat the enemies of Fascism at home and abroad.

Peace Pledge Union: Anti-war organization founded in 1934 by the British clergyman Richard Sheppard, which became the largest of its kind in the 1930s.

Planisme: Term used in France to describe the idea that every aspect of modern life, but particularly the economy and environment, was capable of rational planning.

Popular Front: Term used in 1935 to describe a political alliance between progressive political forces to combat the threat of Fascism. Usually applied to the alliance of social democrats and Communists in France and Spain in the mid-1930s.

Protectionism: Policy of erecting tariff walls to protect domestic industry from foreign competition.

Reich Food Estate: National organization for agriculture and food production set up in Germany in 1933 under Walther Darré.

Reichstag: German parliament, established with the founding of the German Empire in 1871.

Reparations: Term used to describe the payment in goods or money from the defeated states in the First World War to the Western Allies in compensation for war damage.

Russian Civil War: Conflict between the Bolshevik-controlled 'Red Army' and counter-revolutionary, nationalist and anarchist forces in Russia from 1918–21.

SA: The 'Sturmabteilung' were the shock troops of the NSDAP. Founded in 1922, the SA grew to be more than 2 million men by 1934. Their role was to fight the enemies of the movement. During the 1920s they murdered hundreds of political enemies.

Self-determination: The right of all nationalities to find expression through the creation of a national state.

Soviet: Literally 'council'. The term used to describe the popular committees of revolutionaries set up during the 1905 revolution in Russia, and later applied to all local and national assemblies set up to administer Russia after the revolution of 1917.

Spanish Civil War: Conflict between rebel nationalist forces led by General Franco and the armed forces and irregular socialist and anarchist militia in support of the Second Spanish Republic. The nationalist revolt began in July 1936 and ended with Franco's victory in March 1939.

Spartacist League: Communist organization set up in Germany in 1918 to unite all those committed to radical revolution. Violently suppressed in 1919.

SS: The 'Schutzstaffel' elite guard in Hitler's Germany. Founded in 1929 the SS under Heinrich Himmler grew to be the most feared and powerful institution in the Third Reich.

Sudeten Germans: German-speaking inhabitants of northern Bohemia, former subjects of the Habsburg Empire who formed a hostile minority in the post-1919 Czechoslovak state until they were incorporated into Germany in October 1938.

Totalitarianism: Political concept first coined in the early 1920s to describe the aspirations of the Italian Fascist Party to control the totality of society. More commonly misused to describe authoritarian systems with a 'total' control over the population.

Total war: Term usually associated with the German general Erich Ludendorff, who in 1919 described the First World War as a 'total war' because it had demanded the total commitment of the economic, social and moral resources of the nation. The term was also understood to describe a war in which civilians as well as soldiers were part of the war effort and a legitimate target of attack.

Versailles Settlement: Name given to the set of treaties drawn up by the victorious powers at Versailles, outside Paris. They included the Paris Treaty with Germany, the St Germain Treaty with Austria and the Trianon Treaty with Hungary.

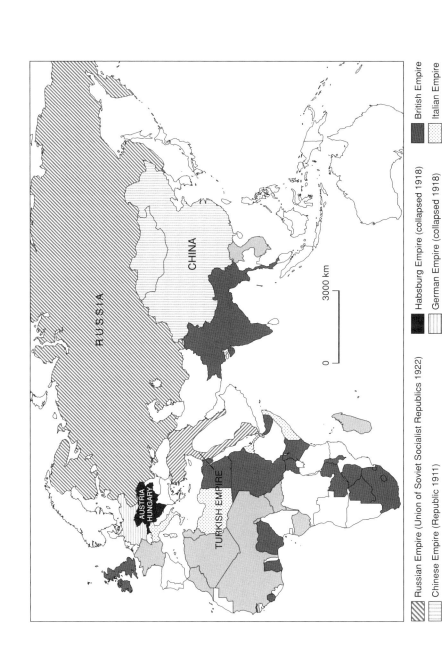

Map 1   The main empires in 1900

Map 2 The post-war territorial settlement

Part 1

THE BACKGROUND

1

What Kind of Crisis?

In 1939 the historian **E.H. Carr** published a widely read and challenging book. He called it *The Twenty Years' Crisis*, and his subject was the long period of political and economic instability which ran from the end of the Great War, in November 1918. The book was written before the coming of the Second World War, which turned the crisis years into a mere *entr'acte*, the 'inter-war years', between two periods of violent upheaval. Carr's title reflected a widespread view in the 1930s that ever since the Great War transformed the established political and international structure, the populations of Europe (and beyond) had lived in the shadow of almost permanent crisis (Carr, 1939).

How is a crisis defined in historical terms? It is clearly not enough simply to recount a record of revolution, armed conflict or business decline, for this is the stuff of much of modern history. Nor is crisis quite the same as an age of rapid, even radical, change. We have all lived with an accelerated rate of change since 1945 – economic, technical, political – without the sense that the world is in perennial crisis. Quite the opposite. The great economic boom since 1945, and the bipolar world system built around American and Soviet power created a growing sense of stability, of change that was managed more or less effectively. Only in the last decades has the post-war order itself begun to dissolve, amidst renewed anxieties about an age of 'crisis'.

When historians use the word 'crisis' they usually employ it with hindsight, taking all the facts together and imposing on them greater coherence or significance than was perceived by contemporaries. The 'Great Crisis' in the seventeenth century occasioned by the Thirty Years War may well describe the sum of its parts, but this is not how Europeans described it themselves at the time. The period of the French Revolutionary and Napoleonic Wars was one of intense crisis on any scale of historical judgement, but it was difficult to perceive at the time with any coherence. In an age before mass newspapers, telegraph and telephone, or even an effective postal service, most Europeans had little idea about what was going on. The inter-war crisis differed from

Carr, E.H. (1892–1982): British international historian best known for his multi-volume study of the Bolshevik Revolution.

earlier upheavals because people were conscious of living through a crisis, aware, as populations had not previously been, that they confronted an age of unstable transformation. Carr's title was meant to convey that sense, and historians have not scrupled since to accept it at face value.

Why, then, did contemporaries feel they were living through an age of crisis? Or, to put it another way round, what did they regard as stability, and why did they see it under threat? Part of the answer can be found in the expectations of the post-1918 world. After the war, there existed a wide-spread desire to return to what Americans called 'normalcy'. The world before the conflict, the world of *belle époque*, seemed rosier than ever now that it was lost. Europeans yearned for the life immortalized in countless Impressionist paintings, of dreamy warm summers, of picnics in the country, of bars and terraces thronged with the prosperous middle classes, and the gaiety of youth. Life was not like that, of course, for most Europeans before 1914, but it was a seductive illusion.

So, too, was the other great expectation in 1919, that after 'the war to end all wars' it might prove possible to construct a new world order based on the liberal outlook of the winners. When the American President, **Woodrow Wilson**, addressed Congress in January 1918 on American war aims, he out-lined his vision of a brave new world 'made safe and fit to live in . . . made safe for every peace-loving nation'. He saw in this vision 'the moral climax of this culminating and final war for human liberty'. There was a widespread yearning for peace by 1918; there was much idealism too, a sense that the war had in some way purged Europe and that it could now once again step out, collectively, along the path of peace and prosperity from which a moment of historical madness had distracted it. The primary aim of the Peace Settle-ment finalized at **Versailles** in June 1919 was 'to achieve international peace and security' by renouncing war, respecting international agreements and establishing 'open, just and honourable relations between nations'.

Against this weight of idealism and illusion, the reality of the post-war world was a grave disappointment. Social unrest, economic stagnation and international political conflict were measured against the hopes for peace abroad and stability at home, and found sadly wanting. These disappoint-ments helped to produce a growing mood of pessimism, a belief that what-ever efforts were made to restore the pre-war golden age, or to build a new order rooted in justice and respect for others, Europe or western civilization was in some sense doomed. This was nothing new, of course. Even before the war there had been gathering force for twenty years a profound sense of *fin de siècle*, of the end of an age. Writers and artists expressed this in a num-ber of ways, but they were united in a sense of loss – of innocence, of moral certainty, of social values, of cultural confidence. The Europe which aston-ished the nineteenth century with its wealth, inventiveness and power was

Wilson, Woodrow (1856–1924): President of the United States from 1913 to 1921 who played a major part in shaping the post-war peace settle-ment in Europe-through his campaign for the 'self-determination of peoples'.

Versailles Settlement: Name given to the set of treaties drawn up by the victorious powers at Versailles, outside Paris. They included the Paris Treaty with Germany, the St Germain Treaty with Austria and the Trianon Treaty with Hungary.

Fin-de-siècle: Literally 'end of an age', a term used to describe the widespread sense at the end of the nineteenth century of an imminent period of crisis and transformation.

prey to growing self-doubt and fears for the future. The Great War only served to heighten this sense of passing from an age of certitude to an age of fearful instability [Doc. 1]. **Georges Clemenceau**, the fiery Frenchman who led his country to victory in 1918, pondered gloomily the frailty of human nature exposed by the war:

> Human beings are like apes who have stolen Jupiter's thunder. It's easy to foresee what will happen one of these days; they will kill one another to the last man. At most some dozen will escape, some negroes in the Congo. Then they'll begin the whole story again. The same old story!
>
> (Schwarzschild, 1943: 47)

Clemenceau, Georges (1841–1929): French statesman and politician nicknamed 'the tiger' because of his pugnacious character. He was prime minister of France from 1917 to 1920 and played a key role in negotiating the Versailles Settlement.

The collapse of confidence in European civilization and progress can be traced back to the German philosopher **Friedrich Nietzsche**, who mounted a powerful attack on the stolidly bourgeois, Christian culture of late nineteenth-century Europe. His rejection of God and organized religion, his profound scepticism about all things modern, his scornful rejection of contemporary morality and values, and his hatred of the masses ('the superfluous ones'), were an inspiration to a whole generation of educated young westerners who despised the self-satisfied, materialistic world around them [Doc. 2]. In Nietzsche they found a prophet of decadent decline, and of strenuous, spiritual renewal. A great many young men went off to war in 1914 with Nietzsche in their rucksack (the German Army even ordered thousands of copies of Nietzsche's *Thus Spake Zarathustra* to distribute to officer recruits). The war turned out to be grim, dirty and brutalizing, a moral desert for those who lived through it. But it did signify Nietzsche's premonition of decline, of negative evolution. Many intellectuals regarded 'crisis' as a welcome purification, before a period of moral and social renewal.

Nietzsche, Friedrich (1844–1900): German writer and philosopher whose work undermined conventional moral beliefs and celebrated strenuous self-expression. He is best known for his assertion in *Thus Spake Zarathustra* that 'God is dead'.

The most famous exponent of European crisis and decline was another German, **Oswald Spengler**, whose *Decline of the West* [*Der Untergang des Abendlandes*] was published in Germany in two volumes in 1918 and 1922. Although Spengler began writing before 1914, its publication at the end of the war gave it a fortuitous prominence. The book was an international bestseller and won Spengler a worldwide reputation. In it he argued that all civilizations have a natural life cycle of growth, flowering and decay, and that European culture, absorbed with narrow materialism and urban chaos, was in the last stage, the winter of a once fruitful world. Unless Europe could cleanse itself and rebuild its spiritual values and racial stock, it would become prey to primitive politics and wars of extermination (Spengler, 1932). The cycle of rise and decline seemed to many Europeans to express what they had experienced across the period of the Great War. The horrors of war – the gassing, bombing, starvation – demonstrated what a shallow veneer civilization was.

Spengler, Oswald (1880–1936): German philosopher whose book on the decline of the west published in English in 1928 had enormous influence in the inter-war years.

Of course Spengler was not thinking just of the war, although the conflict confirmed what *fin-de-siècle* writers had been saying for years. The powerful sense of imminent doom had a great many causes. In the first place it expressed a reaction against the rapid industrialization and urbanization which transformed European society in the last third of the nineteenth century. When Bismarck founded the new German Reich in 1871, two out of every three Germans worked and lived on the land. Between 1871 and 1911 the population of Germany rose from 40 million to 65 million; when war broke out in 1914 two out of every three Germans lived in cities. The sheer speed of this transformation left traditional European society – peasants, craftspeople, gentry – stranded in a bustling world of sprawling, poorly managed cities, dominated by a new wealthy **bourgeoisie**. In the middle of the nineteenth century European states had been in the main still run by aristocrats, relying on social prestige and customary allegiance, aided by a small bureaucratic class and army. By the end of the century the state, too, was transformed: central and local government were modernized and their powers greatly extended. State interests were enforced by an army of bureaucrats and officials and were defended by vast conscript armies; politics were run by a loose alliance of modernizing gentry and ambitious, educated bourgeois drawn from both left and right.

Bourgeoisie: Originally a term defining the non-noble 'burghers' of European cities whose status and wealth gave them particular privileges. Later used indiscriminately to describe the wealthier middle classes.

With industrialism came mass politics. The intellectual pessimist's nightmare was the rise of new political forces representing the interests of the vast under-class of workers and clerks thrown up by economic change. During the 1880s and 1890s socialist parties and trade unions were founded worldwide. Demands for social reform and political freedom expressed by middle-class liberals were increasingly usurped by talk of revolution and social transformation. Karl Marx, the German social theorist who lived and worked for most of his life in London, exposed what he saw as the alienating, self-serving character of bourgeois society and private property, and offered the promise of revolutionary transition, through the efforts of the new urban proletariat, to a golden age of shared property and creative labour. Even though only a fraction of Europe's working classes was actually Marxist by 1914, the fear of violent overthrow, and the economic levelling and mass culture that was supposed to follow, was enough on its own to create a climate of insecurity and uncertainty for property-holders big and small.

Industrialization, and the modern state-building to which it gave rise, profoundly affected the balance of power between states as well. For much of the nineteenth century European states had collaborated loosely to maintain a **Concert of Europe** and international peace. But the very idea of a European concert was rendered increasingly obsolete by the rise of new industrial powers overseas, in particular Japan and the United States, and by the spread of European interests worldwide through trade and colonialism.

Concert of Europe: Term used to describe the usually informal agreement of the European great powers to act together to maintain the peace during the century from the Napoleonic Wars to the First World War.

Within Europe the concert was undermined by the changes in the relative economic and military power of the major states. In the 1850s, Britain and France were the largest industrial powers and the leading colonists; by 1914 both had been overtaken as industrial producers by the United States and Germany, and Tsarist Russia, after a short burst of state-led industrialization, was hard on their shoulder. Italy, Germany and Belgium had joined the ranks of the colonial powers, and imperial rivalry produced serious squabbles between the European states. The rapid realignment of the powers ended the spirit of collaboration and self-restraint characteristic of much pre-1900 diplomacy. Economic and imperial rivalry spawned popular nationalism at home, which forced the traditional ruling elite to pay greater attention to public opinion, while it sharpened antagonisms between the powers. Both at home and abroad, the sources of stability were in full retreat.

Nowhere was this sense of uncomfortable disorder more evident than in the remarkable cultural upheavals of the early twentieth century. In art, music, literature, science, the frontiers were suddenly and excitingly pushed back, both reflecting and stimulating the urgent changes in society and politics. Only a matter of a few years separated the conventional portraits and landscapes of European high art from the creative experiments of Picasso, Kandinsky or the **Dadaists**. While Vienna danced to the traditional waltzes of Johann Strauss, another Austrian, Arnold Schoenberg, was taking the first steps towards a revolution in composition that laid the foundation for the contrapuntal, atonal music of the twentieth century. Science produced the motor car and the aeroplane which transformed communications and war. Engineers and architects turned their backs on bricks, tiles and slates and began to experiment with steel, concrete and glass, the materials of the modern landscape. The order of the day was experiment and challenge. The comfortable culture of well-off Europeans and Americans was confronted with the 'shock of the new', and shock it often was.

Dadaism: Radical art movement in Italy in the 1910s which applauded violence and the capacity of art to engage with politics.

If the cultural flowering was exhilarating, liberating, for young artists and intellectuals, it was taken by many as a symbol of degeneration, of chaos confronting order. When in the 1930s Hitler ordered an exhibition of 'degenerate art' to be set up in Munich, he filled it with the fruits of this early modernism. He ordered the German Chamber of Culture to compel artists to paint objects only in their natural colours and natural forms. For Hitler, and, we can assume, for many of his respectable middle-class followers, 'Modern Art' came to express all that seemed distorted and decadent about modernity itself.

The revolution in culture – the core of the pre-1914 *fin de siècle* – produced a more sinister response. It came to be regarded as evidence of a more fundamental degeneration, not just of art, but of race. 'What does it all mean?' demanded one outraged critic of modern culture. 'It simply means one more phase of the worldwide *revolt against civilization* by the unadaptable, inferior, and degenerate elements, seeking to smash the irksome framework of modern society, and revert to the congenial levels of chaotic barbarism and savagery' (Stoddard, 1922: 128). From at least the 1890s onwards, there were widespread fears expressed in Europe and the United States that unchecked population growth, both at home and overseas, might lead to a biological weakening of the white race and the undermining of white civilization. Attention was drawn to the physically damaging effects of urbanization and industrial labour, which threatened to produce a vast under-class of cretinous, deformed individuals who would, through sheer numbers, swamp the healthy elements of the species and produce racial degeneration. Modern science was marshalled in defence of such views. A long list of respectable academics and doctors subscribed to the idea that the race could somehow be engineered through breeding to become biologically sound. The science was known as '**eugenics**', and its champions included figures on both the political right and left. The object of eugenic study was to find ways – through improved medical care, or compulsory sterilization, or contraception – to limit the reproduction of the allegedly poorer physical specimens in a population. In this way the crisis of racial decline would be averted, and the white race retain its supremacy [**Doc. 3**].

Views on race were certainly not confined to the extreme nationalist fringe in European politics, and were anything but exclusively German. The inspiration for much of pre-1914 race theory came from a Frenchman, Count Arthur de Gobineau, and an Englishman, **Houston Stewart Chamberlain**. The racism of Hitler's **National Socialists** was one fragment of a much broader concern with race, evident throughout the western world, and which pre-dated Nazism by a generation. Nowhere was that concern more energetically displayed than in the sprawling Habsburg Empire, which became before 1914 an inflammable cauldron of racial conflict between Germans, Magyars, Jews and a dozen Slavic nationalities. It is perhaps no coincidence that Habsburg Austria, wilting before the onslaught of mass politics, popular nationalism and economic transformation, was home to the worst excesses of European racism and the most self-consciously *fin-de-siècle* culture. Vienna was a microcosm of the wider tensions generated by rapid political and social change, and of the disintegrative effects of modern culture and sceptical philosophy. The reaction of the Emperor and the Austrian ruling class was to confront the forces making for change, rather than ride with them. At home the empire rejected moves to greater democracy and remained an aristocratic state. The regime sought ways to limit domestic nationalist agitation, and opted in the first decade of the twentieth century for an aggressive, expansionist foreign policy to reverse the long decline in the empire's international position. In the course of this final rallying of traditional Europe, crisis turned into disaster. Attempts to compel Serbia, chief ally of the movement

Eugenics: First developed as a science in the 1880s, eugenics was the study of scientific improvement of the human race through a combination of genetic manipulation and social reform.

Chamberlain, Houston Stewart (1855–1927): British race theorist who settled in Germany where he wrote popular and influential books on the superiority of the 'Aryan' race. His work was read and absorbed by *Adolf Hitler.*

National Socialist German Workers' Party: Better known as the Nazi Party, the NSDAP was founded in 1920 and by the 1940s had more than 8 million members. Hitler led the party from 1921 until its collapse in 1945.

for Slav independence from Habsburg rule, to accept domination from Vienna and end racial agitation, ended in a war between the two states in late July 1914 which dragged in the other great powers, one by one.

The Great War which resulted was not directly caused by the growing sense of crisis before 1914, although the fatalism it engendered made war seem unavoidable. But even if the war had not broken out in 1914, mass politics and national rivalry would almost certainly have dissolved the old social order and international system sooner or later. What the war *did* do was to magnify and accelerate those changes. The armies that marched to the battlefield in 1914 garlanded with flowers from the flag-waving crowds that saw them off, expected the war to be 'over by Christmas', like the wars of 1866 or 1870. Instead, the conflict, fuelled by vast financial wealth and industrial muscle, prolonged by a new military technology that favoured entrenched defences, became a slugging match which consumed 7 million lives, devastated large tracts of Europe, and impoverished the states that fought it. A whole generation of young Europeans was embittered and brutalized by the experience. Thirteen million of them carried the scars of war. Twenty years later half of the French budget was still devoted to paying off war debts and providing pensions for crippled veterans. No family was left untouched; the war became etched in the modern memory.

The war fulfilled the worst of expectations. At its end the political landscape of Europe and beyond was transformed. In 1900 the world was dominated by large territorial empires, ruled, except for France, by hereditary monarchs. In 1920 only two major ones remained – the British and the French empires – and they too were subject to increasing pressure for reform from nationalist groups throughout their far-flung territories. The other major empires all disappeared. The huge Chinese Empire, ruled for centuries by the Manchus, was overthrown by revolution in 1911 and descended into political chaos as rival warlords vied for power. The Ottoman Empire, the sick man of Europe for much of the previous century, finally died. In 1908 the Ottoman Sultanate was challenged by the so-called Young Turks bent on modernizing the ramshackle imperial structure. The war brought the defeat of Turkey at Germany and Austria's side, and the end of Ottoman rule throughout much of the Middle and Near East. The great empires of Europe collapsed through the sheer effort of waging war on such a colossal and damaging scale. The Russian Romanov dynasty was overthrown by popular revolution in February 1917, and eight months later a **communist** revolution destroyed what was left of the Tsarist Empire. Defeat for Germany and Austria–Hungary in 1918 brought the fall of the Hohenzollern and Habsburg rulers and the physical dismemberment of both states. In eastern Europe a whole necklace of new states sprang up which reflected more closely the racial divisions of the region. In the Middle East the modern states were defined – Iraq,

Communism: A political movement from the early years of the nineteenth century in favour of democratic societies based on common ownership of property and the abolition of privilege. Marx adopted Communism in the 1840s and gave it a firm theoretical foundation.

Syria, Lebanon – and a foothold granted to the Jewish population in Palestine in what became, a generation later, the new state of Israel (see **Map 1**).

A mere recital of these changes hardly does justice to the sheer speed and completeness with which the political map of the world was redrawn. The great dynastic houses of central and eastern Europe, and of Asia, had been facts of political life for centuries. They disappeared in a year. With them went a vast army of officials, soldiers and landlords who had run the old regime but were now redundant, stranded in a no man's land, like the secret policemen and Communist functionaries left high and dry by the collapse of the Soviet bloc in 1989. In their place came new political classes committed to democracy and social reform, or more modern forms of authoritarianism. The collapse of the political structure of empire went hand in hand with the collapse of the traditional social and political order which had run it. A third victim of the war was the international economy. The war ended the long period of economic growth and stability built on the foundation of international collaboration in constructing and regulating the world market. The war brought financial disaster, vast war debts and high inflation – the first since the Napoleonic Wars – and heavy taxation. Trade was massively disrupted and never recovered to the heady growth rates before 1914 throughout the inter-war years. For many Europeans these were years of relative poverty and economic stagnation.

The war did more than any other single event to reinforce the impression of crisis, of forces out of control, of a world lost for ever. For all the popular expectations of a new order based on democracy at home and responsible collaboration abroad, the war left too many loose ends, too many bitter legacies. Beside the hopes of pacifist internationalism there stood outraged nationalism; beside confidence in democracy and social justice stood a yearning for harsh, counter-revolutionary authority; beside the indulgent materialism of the age of jazz and fast cars could be found a conservative intelligentsia which despaired of reviving traditional spiritual values and arresting racial impoverishment. The post-war world was full of unresolved disputes and manifest ambiguities. The very fact that the war had even happened, that the populations which regarded themselves as the bearers of modern civilization had indulged in such an orgy of blood-letting and destruction, called in question the ability of those same states to rebuild the world they had destroyed. The claim to the moral high ground expressed so confidently by Europeans before 1914 looked hollow indeed four years later. The idea of progress as somehow irresistible and preordained was morally bankrupt in the 1920s. 'What are the roots that clutch, what branches grow Out of this stony rubbish?' asked the poet T.S. Eliot in *The Waste Land*, written in 1922. For Eliot, like so many of his generation, there was no answer, 'only a heap of broken images'.

Part 2

ANALYSIS

2

Revolution and Counter-Revolution

THE RUSSIAN REVOLUTION

On 23 February 1917, in protest at the growing hardships and hunger of war, 80,000 workers marched through the streets of the capital of the Russian Empire, Petrograd (St Petersburg). It was a modest enough start to what became the Russian Revolution, an event that overshadowed the post-war world, like the war itself, as a persistent reminder of crisis past and crisis to come. Within three or four days the Russian capital was in turmoil. Troops in the city fraternized openly with the protesters. On 27 February the President of the Russian parliament, or **Duma**, called on the Tsar to give way to demands for popular government. The leaders of Russia's vast army, fighting a desperate retreat against German forces, supported parliament against the Emperor. On 2 March **Nicholas II**, last of the Romanovs, bowed to reality and abdicated. A day later a Provisional Government was set up under the liberal politician, Prince Lvov.

The Russian Empire, with 8 million men under arms, was overthrown in just a week by a series of uncoordinated, angry demonstrations. Thirteen hundred Russians were the only casualties, in a country of 140 million. Yet appearances were deceptive. The roots of the revolution lay well before the war, in growing disillusionment with autocratic rule. The attempts by Nicholas to rule in the old ways, oblivious to demands for more popular forms of government, or for civil rights and social reforms, bankrupted support for the Tsar even among sections of the upper classes. The rush for industrialization and military power, initiated at great pace from the 1890s, produced an impoverished, badly housed working class, facing conditions much worse than anywhere else in industrial Europe, a peasantry resentful at high taxation and the pressures of modern commerce, and a state that tottered on the edge of actual bankruptcy until rescued by loans from Russia's ally, France. Popular hostility spilled over in a wave of violent protest in 1905, following Russia's defeat at the hands of Japan in the Far East. The regime survived only because of the fragile loyalty of the army. In 1914

Duma: The Russian parliament established by the Tsar's 'manifesto' of 1906 following the 1905 revolution.

Nicholas II (1868–1918): Tsar (emperor) of Russia from 1894 until his abdication in March 1917. He and his family were assassinated by the Bolshevik regime in July 1918.

Russia was seething with social unrest and rumours of revolution, and only the war crisis in July, at the height of a general strike in St Petersburg, prevented more serious unrest. After an initial burst of patriotic enthusiasm, the war went badly wrong. In three years Russia suffered 8 million casualties; an army of new workers crowded into the cities to build armaments, making intolerable conditions impossibly worse. The countryside, where Russia's vital food supplies were generated, lost most of the young male workers, and two-thirds of the draft animals needed for ploughing. By 1916 one-third of the soil in western Russia went untilled, and peasants turned their grain into vodka rather than sell it at the low prices fixed by the state. The food supply for the cities and the front declined dangerously. The war effort itself was a shambles. The creaky Tsarist bureaucracy, pierced through with corruption and incompetence, simply failed to cope with the huge problems of supply, of refugees and of medical services which were thrown up by the conflict. Voluntary associations, staffed by bourgeois critics of the regime, set up their own organizations to run services on the home front. Confidence in the Tsar ebbed away. By the spring of 1917 Nicholas enjoyed support only among the most diehard monarchists. The British ambassador in Petrograd reported back that it was 'as certain as anything can be that emperor and empress are riding for a fall' (Kochan, 1967: 190).

The first revolution was, at first, widely welcomed. The government was dominated by moderate bourgeois and liberal gentry, and although the revolution was committed to popular rule and civil rights, there was no call for a complete social transformation, and, to the relief of Russia's western allies, no call to end the war. Political parties of all colours, with one exception, saw the revolution as an opportunity for a patriotic rallying to drive Germany from Russian soil and to begin the process of moderate democratic reform stifled by Tsardom. That exception was, of course, a telling one. On the extreme left there existed a small splinter group of Russian Marxists, who styled themselves **Bolsheviks**, which saw the overthrow of the Tsar as the chance to create a genuine socialist revolution. Opinions differed inside the party about exactly what that was, but most Bolsheviks knew what they were against – landlords, factory owners, generals – and called for an end to the war, a workers' state and land redistribution, so to wrest power from the gentry and the bourgeoisie. As Bolshevik leaders were released from gaol, and returned from exile abroad or in Siberia, the nucleus of an organization could be set up. In April their chief spokesman, Vladimir Ulyanov, better known as **Lenin**, returned from Switzerland, calling on his party to make common cause with poor peasants, soldiers and factory workers to mount a second revolution against the Provisional Government, which would usher in the dawn of Russian Communism.

If the Provisional Government had worked, and won mass approval for its strategy of fighting the war first and reforming later, the Bolshevik movement

Bolsheviks: One of two factions of the Russian Social Democratic Party when it split in 1904 into majority socialists (Bolsheviks) and minority socialists (Mensheviks) over issues of revolutionary practice.

Lenin (Vladimir Ulyanov) (1870–1924): Chairman of the Russian Social Democratic Party (Bolsheviks) and the most influential theoretical Marxist of his generation. He encouraged the party to launch the revolution in October 1917 and became leader of the new government until illness in 1922 forced him to withdraw from active politics.

might well have remained a fringe group of noisy activists. It was the failure of the first revolutionary regime, and the progressive disillusionment of broad sections of Russian society, that provided the opportunity. The war continued to go badly. The new summer offensive planned for June came to nothing. The war economy became the victim of a crumbling transport system, shortages of raw materials and machine tools, and an angry, hungry and dispirited workforce. Wages chased vainly after prices. By the autumn of 1917 real wages had declined by a third from the level at the start of the year, food supplies to the main cities, Moscow and Petrograd, were down to just a few days' supply, inflation was out of control, and many factory owners, frightened of truculent workers and anxious to save what they could, closed factories down and fled. Unemployment in Petrograd rose sharply during the summer months. The social and economic crisis which had created the revolution in the first place became worse rather than better, and swelled a rising tide of radical anger in the cities. In the countryside the peasants, who thought the revolution would give them the land, became restless at the failure of the government to address rural grievances seriously. During the course of 1917 they seized the land for themselves, often violently, and reformed it into traditional communes, with small plots of land divided up among the village population. The ability of the cities to force the peasant farmers to part with their produce declined disastrously. By October Petrograd was close to starvation.

The Bolsheviks profited from this crisis in a number of ways. They had never been identified with the Provisional Government in the first place, and stood as an attractive radical option outside the party squabbles of the Duma. Secondly, Lenin insisted that Bolsheviks should take the lead at grassroots level in agitating for change, spurring on disorder and disillusionment, spreading effective propaganda through newspapers, broadsheets and local meetings. When the popular mood turned against the government, all the local political activity paid off. Bolshevism came to be identified with demands for real change, for peace, employment, land. Finally, the Bolsheviks made common cause with the popular committees – the **Soviets** – which sprang up all over Russia in factories, villages and military units. The Soviet was the authentic voice of popular politics. So powerful was the spontaneous eruption of Soviets in the spring of 1917 that a central body was established in Petrograd representing the local committees, which shared power with the Provisional Government by virtue of the fact that workers and soldiers did what the Soviet said, but distrusted the Duma. Even when the Provisional Government swung more to the left in July 1917, under the Social-Revolutionary minister, Alexander Kerensky, in response to the rising tide of radicalism and protest, it made little difference. By October the government was fast losing credibility, while the Bolsheviks had 200,000 members and were drawing more, daily, from the other political parties. In October the

Soviet: Literally 'council'. The term used to describe the popular committees of revolutionaries set up during the 1905 revolution in Russia, and later applied to all local and national assemblies set up to administer Russia after the revolution of 1917.

Bolshevik leadership began an agonized debate about whether the moment had arrived for the 'historically necessary' step of seizing state power. Lenin, recently returned from another enforced exile, this time in Finland, following an abortive Bolshevik coup in July, argued powerfully and persuasively that now was the time. On 25 October, to coincide with the calling of the All-Russian Congress of Soviets, popular militia in Petrograd seized the Winter Palace and disbanded the Provisional Government that sat there. The following day the All-Russian Congress installed a Bolshevik government, and the almost bloodless 'second revolution' was established (Ferro, 1980; Figes, 1996).

The new leaders knew that they had come to power almost by default. Most of the army was stuck out in Poland still fighting the Germans and Austrians. The peasantry had retreated into self-imposed isolation, and the Bolsheviks had very little active support among them. The task of consolidating power was a daunting one. Lenin remembered that revolutions devour their children; instead, he devoured the revolution. In the first months of power the party set up what Lenin called 'the dictatorship of the proletariat', a phrase first used by Marx to describe the period of transition from bourgeois society to Communism. In his pamphlet 'State and Revolution', written in August 1917, he called for the '*strictest* control by society *and by the state*', which would be run by the Bolsheviks as a revolutionary vanguard working on behalf of, although not elected by, the working people of Russia. Democracy was torn up. When a Constituent Assembly was elected in January 1918 to draft a democratic constitution, only one-fifth of the seats were held by Bolsheviks. Lenin dissolved it like any tsar. When democratic movements emerged in the armed forces and among the big-city factory workers, they were suppressed by force. To keep the Bolsheviks in power, the secret police force was revived, the army was reorganized to stamp out the loose discipline and democratic practices inherited from the first revolution. A rigid authority was exercised over the Soviet people, forced labour was extracted when it was needed and all vestiges of 'bourgeois' culture and institutions assaulted. Most industry and banking was nationalized; landed estates were broken up; a stream of the rich and dispossessed fled from Russia to bring the message to the rest of the world that something unthinkable, the nightmare of ruling classes everywhere, had happened: Communism had triumphed.

EXPORTING THE REVOLUTION

It took some time before any clear idea could be formed abroad about what had happened in Russia, or the Soviet Union as it soon became known. 'No one knows what is coming out of the Russian cauldron', declared the British War Minister, **Winston Churchill**, 'but it will almost certainly be something full of evil, full of menace.' The western leaders had only a hazy notion of what a Marxist revolution meant; and at first there seemed every likelihood that the new Bolshevik regime would fizzle out or be overthrown by counter-revolutionaries. Bolshevism itself was deplored. Lenin's intemperate language, his call for world revolution and his declared aim of 'smashing' the old order had an alarming Jacobin ring to it. Worse still, from the viewpoint of Russia's wartime allies, Britain and France, was the news that in March 1918 Soviet and German negotiators meeting at Brest-Litovsk had agreed to end the war on the eastern front, and to sign a peace treaty that gave Germany large swathes of territory in eastern Europe. The Soviet regime denounced the war and repudiated its debts to the west, including some 26 million francs owed to French investors. Soviet agents and propaganda began to seep out into war-torn Europe. For Europe's ruling classes the Bolshevik revolution presented a horrifying example. The vast Russian state had been seized in a few days by the most extreme wing of the working-class movement with barely a struggle. Could the same thing happen to them?

There was plenty of evidence of social unrest in wartime Europe to give such fears a real grounding. After four years of war there were obvious signs of strain on the home fronts. The onset of inflation, food shortages, declining health and rising accident rates at work produced growing demoralization and anger among the home populations. During 1917 and 1918 a strike wave spread across the continent, often led by the more radical elements of the workers' movement, in defiance of the official trade-union leaders. In Britain in 1918 there were 1,165 strikes involving more than 1 million workers; in Germany in the spring of 1917 a series of mass strikes against economic hardship alerted the regime to a serious crisis in the domestic war effort. In 1918, strikes in Germany assumed a more political character, with demands for democracy and protests against the annexationist peace of Brest-Litovsk. Mutinies broke out in the German navy, and among French forces on the western front. Even peasants and white-collar workers in Germany, who had previously been staunch supporters of the monarchist regime, turned against the war that subjected them to economic hardship, and the increasing coercion of the state. Declining living standards and widespread hunger contrasted sharply with the high profits made by business people out of the war. Much of the class resentment evident by 1918 was spurred on by the belief that the sacrifices of war were unevenly distributed between rich and poor.

It is small wonder that Bolshevik leaders came to believe that revolution would not be confined only to Russia [**Doc. 4**]. All the ingredients for a fundamental crisis of world capitalism appeared to be in place. Harsh military

Churchill, Winston (1874–1965): English politician, soldier and writer. He held high office before 1914 as a Liberal minister, saw service on the Western Front in 1916, before becoming Minister of Munitions. In the 1920s he became a Conservative and served as Chancellor of the Exchequer from 1926 to 1929. In the 1930s he was on the political fringes until the coming of war in 1939 when he took over the Admiralty. In May 1940 he became prime minster, a post which he held until 1945, and again from 1951 to 1995.

Ebert, Friedrich (1871–1925): German trade unionist and politician, who rose to become leader of the German Social-Democratic Party in 1913 and later the first President of the Weimar Republic.

Liebknecht, Karl (1871–1919): German social democrat politician who is best known for arguing against war in August 1914. He founded the radical Marxist Spartacist League in November 1914, took part in the Communist revolt at the end of the war and was murdered in January 1919 by nationalist soldiers.

Luxemburg, Rosa (1870–1919): Polish Marxist philosopher who played a prominent role in the German Social Democratic Party before 1914. She was hostile to Lenin's view of the revolutionary party and favoured reliance on the working masses. Imprisoned during the First World War, she became a leader of the German revolutionary movement in late 1918 and was murdered by nationalist soldiers in January 1919.

Spartacist League: Communist organization set up in Germany in 1918 to unite all those committed to radical revolution. Violently suppressed in 1919.

Levíné, Eugen (1883–1919): Radical socialist politician who led the Bavarian Communist uprising in 1919 and was assassinated that same year.

discipline and police action kept the lid on popular protest, but when the war ended abruptly in November 1918, following a German request for an armistice, protest proved unstoppable. Germany itself was the first to give way. The old order crumbled following the abdication of the Emperor, William II, on 9 November. A government consisting of social democrats (SPD) and more radical independent socialists (USPD) was set up under the moderate social democrat, **Friedrich Ebert**. But in January a breakaway group of socialists led by **Karl Liebknecht** and **Rosa Luxemburg**, the self-styled **Spartacist League**, launched a Marxist revolution to transform Germany into a workers' state in imitation of Bolshevik Russia. In April a Communist state was declared in Bavaria led by the Russian *émigré* **Eugene Levíné**, and a wave of strikes in sympathy swept Germany's main industrial cities. A new paper published in Leipzig, *The Red Flag*, called on German workers to seize the opportunity for revolution: 'The great day of the emancipation of the oppressed has dawned. Victory is near' (Fowkes, 1984: 31).

Elsewhere the combination of material hardship and pent-up expectations had the same effect. Austria saw the establishment of a social democrat government and the overthrow of the Habsburg monarchy. In March 1919 the Hungarian Communist **Bela Kun** declared a Bolshevik revolution in Budapest. Nothing as dramatic occurred in western Europe, among the victors, but even here there was widespread social agitation. In Italy the socialist movement, much influenced by events in Russia, moved to the offensive, encouraging strikes in the cities and among the poor rural workforce. In France and Britain the strike movement persisted amidst calls for more radical policies of nationalization and welfare provision. Even the moderate British Labour Party, which was anything but Marxist, adopted in 1919 the famous Clause IV calling for state ownership of the commanding heights of the industrial economy. In Spain, which remained neutral during the war, socialist and anarchist agitation reached boiling point between 1918 and 1920, in what became known as the Three Red Years, the *Trienio Bolshevista*. No state was immune from social unrest and class conflict or from the lingering shadow of revolution spreading out from the Soviet Union.

In practice, the Bolshevik threat to Europe failed to materialize. Much of the social unrest was a product of war-weariness and economic despair, and ebbed away with the return of peace. The radicalization of Europe's working classes proved to be a temporary phenomenon, associated more with 'bread and butter' issues of hours, pay and food than with wider issues of political and social transformation. The Communist uprisings in Germany were bloodily suppressed in January, and again in April 1919. On 15 January the two Spartacist leaders, Liebknecht and Luxemburg, were murdered by German soldiers. The Munich regime was destroyed within three weeks and Levíné and many of his associates shot. Before his execution he declared, prophetically: 'We communists are all dead men on leave!' In Hungary the Bela Kun government was overturned after four months, when returning Hungarian soldiers under the former Habsburg Admiral **Nicholas Horthy**, with the help of Romanian forces, crushed all working-class resistance in the cities. Even in Russia itself the Bolshevik revolution was put under siege. In 1918 the western Allies sent expeditionary forces to northern Russia to help counter-revolutionary groups fighting against the Bolsheviks. In Siberia, liberated prisoners of war and Japanese troops fought the Red Army along the Trans-Siberian railway. In southern Russia the so-called Whites formed a rallying point against the second revolution. Led by General Denikin and Admiral Koltchak, they launched a military assault on the new state with the support of Russia's erstwhile allies. Bolshevism was saved only by the decision of the Allies to end intervention and concentrate on solving their own social crises, and because of the divisions (and poor resources) of the White armies who opposed it. Nevertheless, the civil war almost destroyed the revolution, and left a legacy of massive economic dislocation and social suffering which compelled the Bolshevik leadership to abandon the attempt to impose Communism all at once, let alone try to spread the revolution elsewhere. When Soviet forces, making a final effort to seize back the lands lost at Brest-Litovsk, were defeated by the Polish army before Warsaw in 1920, the Soviet Union was forced to accept its isolation. The pursuit of world revolution was put on ice, while Soviet leaders concentrated on building what came to be called 'socialism in one country'.

Kun, Bela (1886–1937): Hungarian Communist who led the Hungarian revolutionary government in the summer of 1919 until its overthrow by force in July. He lived in exile in the Soviet Union where he was accused of spying and executed in 1937.

Horthy, Nicholas (1868–1957): An admiral in the Austro-Hungarian navy during the First World War, he led Hungarian and Romanian forces in the summer of 1919 in a counter-revolutionary civil war against Hungarian Communism. He declared himself Regent in 1919 in place of the exiled Habsburgs, and ruled Hungary until 1944 when he was deposed by German intervention.

THE FAILURE OF REVOLUTION

Why did the revolutionary tide ebb away? In the first place the issue of social revolution divided the working-class movement itself. Even in Russia there was sharp division between the moderate socialists, the Mensheviks, and the Bolsheviks. The moderates argued for a slow pace of change, working through parliamentary democracy in cooperation with liberals and more enlightened bourgeois forces. Radical socialists were a minority everywhere, as they had been in the socialist movement before the war. The bulk of socialists had more modest aims for social improvement and economic reform. The established socialist parties and their trade-union allies also perceived radicals as a political threat to their position as spokesmen for the working-class movement. In Germany, the moderate social democrats were horrified by the prospect of violent revolutionary upheaval. 'I hate revolution like sin', declared Ebert, the first Chancellor of the new republic. Some social democrats were even willing to accept the survival of the monarchy in a constitutional form.

Although there were significant pockets of working-class revolutionism – in the Ruhr area, in the cities of northern Italy, among the landless labourers of Spain and Italy – the overwhelming majority of the working class was much more cautious about change, even openly hostile to their radical colleagues. In Germany the social democrat Chancellor, Friedrich Ebert, reached a historic agreement with the army chief, General Wilhelm Groener, in November 1918 to suppress violent revolution by force. In Italy and France the socialist movement split in two in 1920, one part forming new Communist parties, linked together in Lenin's Third International, the Comintern, while the other part retained a moderate social democratic complexion. The workers themselves soon tired of protest. Support for the French trade-union movement, the Confederation Générale du Travail (CGT), dropped from 2 million to 60,000 in 1920; the British trade unions lost 2.5 million members between 1920 and 1922 (Geary, 1991).

In the second place, the threat of radical overthrow provoked an immediate reaction from conservative forces anxious to prevent revolution and achieve post-war stabilization. The social structure of the other major states of Europe was quite different from that of Russia: the bourgeoisie was much larger and more prosperous; the working class was less disadvantaged and more organized; the peasantry was already in control of much of the land. The forces anxious to retain the status quo possessed much more social power and political experience than their counterparts in Russia. Nonetheless, conservative Europe responded in the first instance with timely reforms designed to avert the further spread of revolutionary agitation. The vote was extended almost everywhere to include most adult males and, in some cases, females too. The 8-hour day, a matter of contention between capital and labour since the 1890s, was conceded in Germany in November 1918, in Italy in February 1919 and in France in April 1919. Welfare legislation was promised in Germany and Austria. Labour was invited to participate in wage-negotiating machinery. In Germany another historic pact was signed in November 1918, this time between Hugo Stinnes, spokesman for German heavy industry, and Carl Legien, head of the German trade-union movement, in which the two sides agreed to shelve their differences while they got on with the task of economic revival and demobilization. For Europe's embattled bourgeoisie it made more sense to collaborate with labour rather than confront it.

Efforts were also made to make the transition from war to peace as painless as possible. British and German workers drafted into the forces were offered their old jobs back, and the army of women who had entered industry during the war years was dismissed. In Germany, the government faced widespread economic chaos at the close of hostilities, and chose to spend its way out of the crisis, using large deficits to fund schemes for new employment and to help expand production. In Italy, veterans returning from the front were promised parcels of land, like the Roman citizen-soldiers of old. Everywhere active efforts were made to find a mix of policies that would buy labour acquiescence and heal some of the worst economic consequences of war. The strategy for stabilization did not work in all cases – Italy is a good example – but on balance the policy of prudent conciliation worked well enough, abetted as it was by the natural caution of many of the working-class communities at whom these strategies were directed. The first elections held in Germany after the war were a triumph for the moderate centre and left, which won an overwhelming 76 per cent of the vote.

The final factor was the most significant in the light of the subsequent political history of the inter-war years. The Bolshevik threat provoked a violent, popular counter-revolution which worked alongside, and not always in harmony with, the bourgeois efforts at stabilization. Violence was evident from the start, as demobilized soldiers returned home, often carrying their weapons with them. Some joined the revolutionary movement, but a great many others, resentful at what they saw as a betrayal of their sacrifice and the loss of thousands of their comrades, formed informal armies or vigilante groups in order to take revenge on left-wing activists. In Germany these home-made armies, the Free Corps (*Freikorps*), were used by the authorities to restore order and destroy the Communist threat. In the Ruhr, a full-scale civil war raged for some months in the summer of 1919 as socialist militia and Free Corps fought pitched battles for control of the industrial cities. The government turned a blind eye to the atrocities that accompanied the Free Corps movement; they were banned only in 1924 when they were no longer needed, but in the interim they terrorized working-class populations and accelerated the drift away from radical politics. In Italy very much the same thing happened. Veteran groups, armed and paid for by landlords and business people, attacked left-wing demonstrations, burned down socialist offices, and threw strikers out of factories. The most famous of these groups, the *Fasci di combattimento*, set up by an ex-socialist turned nationalist, **Benito Mussolini**, quickly won a reputation for its fiery, brutal, anti-Marxism and tub-thumping patriotism. Its success as an instrument of violent counter-revolution brought large numbers of frightened property-owners and rootless nationalists into the movement, which by 1921 became large enough to form a political party, the **Italian Fascist Party** ('Fascist' from *fasces*, the bundle of rods and axes carried by the lictors – who executed the law – in ancient Rome). A year later, in October 1922, Mussolini was rewarded for his campaign of reactionary violence with the post of prime minister. In Germany, in November 1923, one of a number of small nationalist, anti-Marxist, groups which had sprung up all over the country after the war, the National Socialist German Workers' Party, attempted to seize power in Bavaria by an armed

Freikorps: Name given to the irregular units of returning soldiers in Germany in 1919 who acted as an anti-Communist militia to suppress political radicalism.

Mussolini, Benito (1883–1945): Radical socialist politician from the Romagna who became a nationalist during the First World War, fought at the front and returned to found the Italian Fascist movement. In October 1922 he was appointed prime minister, established a single-party dictatorship by 1926 and led Italy into wars in Ethiopia (1935), Spain (1936–39), and against the Western powers (1940–43). He was overthrown by a military coup in 1943, and killed by Italian partisans at the end of the war in 1945.

Italian Fascist Party: Founded in 1921, the Fascist Party became the only permitted party in 1926. The party's Grand Council played an important part in the politics of the regime until its collapse in 1943.

Hitler, Adolf (1889–1945): Austrian-born politician who came to Germany in 1913, served in a Bavarian regiment in the First World War and joined the tiny German Workers' Party in 1919. The party became the National Socialist Party two years later with Hitler at its head. He attempted a coup in 1923 and was imprisoned. He took control of the party again in 1926, and seven years later was appointed German Chancellor. He became dictator of Germany and embarked on a programme of rearmament, territorial expansion and anti-Semitism. He attacked Poland in 1939 and launched world war. In 1941 he initiated what became the Holocaust and in April 1945 committed suicide in the ruins of Berlin.

coup d'état. The group's leader, **Adolf Hitler**, declared a national revolution to overthrow the republic, but by 1923 the wave of violence had subsided and most ordinary Germans wanted an end to radical politics. The police dispersed the conspirators as they marched through Munich. Hitler was arrested and gaoled for five years but served only a few months.

By 1923 the threat of revolutionary Marxism was much reduced. A combination of conciliation and coercion weakened European radicalism and exposed deep fissures within the working-class movement which were to weaken it as an effective political force throughout the inter-war years. The revolutionary period left a profound legacy. It promoted fierce hatreds, an ideological passion that Europe had not seen since the religious wars three centuries before [**Doc. 5**]. Conservative Europeans could never rid themselves of the fear that one day, sooner or later, Bolshevism would tunnel its way under the fortress walls and take the capitalist system by surprise. They reacted to the revolutionary danger like the Inquisition to heresy. Anti-Marxism was strong enough to bring Fascism to power in Italy in 1922; fear of the left brought a military dictatorship in Spain in 1923, and when that fell in 1931 Spanish society was polarized by deep social and political antagonisms which resulted in a sanguinary civil war, and the eventual victory of the counter-revolutionary right. In Germany anti-Communism reached mass proportions during the economic slump of 1929–32, and brought millions of Germans flooding into the National Socialist Party, which was renewed in 1925 after Hitler's release. When Hitler came to power in January 1933 the fear of Communist reaction was used as the excuse to tear up civil rights and democracy and to embark on a vicious campaign of killing, maiming and enforced exile against the German left, both Communist and social democrat [**Doc. 6**].

Communism was persecuted wherever it appeared outside the Soviet Union, in China, in India, in the Middle East, in Europe. The success of Lenin's revolution, against all the odds, was in a sense the undoing of the left. Although the Soviet experiment was the rallying point for all those disillusioned with capitalist society, with colonialism, with religion, with militarism and war, it also prompted a rallying of conservative forces which focused all their accumulated dread of social upheaval and political disorder on the task of limiting the spread of Communism at all costs. The radical left was forced to adopt a more modest profile in order to survive at all; and the Soviet Union was placed in quarantine by the rest of the international community.

Revolution and counter-revolution ushered in an age of violent, crusading politics, very different from the pre-1914 political world of bourgeois liberalism or royal autocracy. The British philosopher Bertrand Russell defined these conflicts as 'creed wars'. The conflicts of the post-war years laid the foundation for the later confrontation of the Cold War. Indeed, the strength

of feeling directed against the Soviet Union after 1945 can only be understood fully in the light of the deep well of distrust and fear already present in
the inter-war years in response to 1917. This sense of social unease, of living
on borrowed time, was at the heart of the inter-war crisis. Like the French
Revolution a century or so earlier, the Russian Revolution was a permanent
reminder that the existing order was not necessarily here to stay [**Doc. 7**].

3

A Crisis of Modernization

THE CHALLENGE OF MODERNITY

When historians describe that whole network of changes that transformed Europe and the wider world from predominantly agrarian or small-town communities, governed by ancient religions and a customary tradition-bound culture, to a largely urban, industrial, secular society, they use the term 'modernization'. It is not an entirely satisfactory term, for the processes involved are in reality more complex and uneven than this; the old can, and does, exist side by side with the new. More than this, the word 'modernization' implies a kind of necessary progression, an implicit assumption that modernity is to be preferred to tradition, rationalism to religion, industry to farming.

It was precisely this implication that produced in the early years of the twentieth century a powerful, often popular, hostility to the imperious march of the modern age. Modernization was not always regarded as liberating or enhancing; it was all too often experienced as an alienating loss of traditional skills and outlook, or as unavoidable damage to religious and cultural practices with a long pedigree. For many small communities, modernization undermined all the fixed points of their world – the structure of family and kin, the world of established status, economic well-being, complex systems of belief and social behaviour. Above all, modernity seemed ultimately destructive in its remorseless pursuit of a material, rational world, and its promotion of the anonymous, spiritually bankrupt environment of city and factory. This is just how it struck the young Adolf Hitler when he moved from the village near Linz, where he was born, to the bustling, self-consciously modern cities of Vienna, then Munich:

> Nothing is anchored any more, nothing is rooted in our spiritual life any more. Everything is superficial, flees past us. Restlessness and haste mark the thinking of our people. The whole of life is being torn completely apart.
>
> (Nolte, 1969)

For all this, modernization continued unabated during the inter-war years. In 1900 roughly two-thirds of Europe's inhabitants were peasants; in 1939, only one-third. Although industry grew unevenly after 1918, the trend was ever upward. Industrial production in Europe doubled between 1913 and 1929, fuelled by growing consumer demand for cars, bicycles, gramophones and a host of other modern inventions. There were barely half a million cars in Europe in 1914; by 1938 there were more than 7 million. In the United States the figures were even more remarkable: 1.9 million in 1913, 29 million in 1938. Modern industry spread out to parts of the world previously untouched, in eastern Europe, in the Soviet Union, the Balkans, Turkey, Spain and so on. Migration continued from the village to the city, from farm to factory. Within the cities the white-collar workforce expanded too, in response to the increasing role of the state in people's lives, and the growth of a whole range of new services in finance, the media and welfare. Governments generally regarded economic and social modernization as desirable in itself. Industrial growth brought gains in wealth, increased military strength and reduced areas of backwardness. In the post-war years there was a widespread conviction that modernity produced *better* societies. Confidence grew in the transforming power of education and of planning. There developed a craze for 'rationalization' to maximize efficiency, the technocrats' dream that planning and the machine would produce order from social chaos, a stable economy in place of the unpredictable swings of an unregulated, **laissez-faire** commerce [**Doc. 8**].

This vogue for what the French called *planisme* showed itself in all kinds of ways. Town planners assumed that it was possible to design and build new communities on rational, socially useful lines. In the Ruhr industrial region in Germany a Settlement Association was founded in 1919 to promote the construction of model villages where coal workers could be happily housed and social peace restored. In Britain, the 'garden suburb movement' led to experiments in establishing new towns on the outskirts of London – Letchworth, Welwyn Garden City – where the victims of urban squalor and overcrowding could be rehoused in clean, leafy surroundings. Then there was family planning. The rational control of family size was thought to produce healthier populations, by avoiding the debilitating effects of poverty and disease associated with large families. The British pioneer of family planning, Marie Stopes, set up her first clinic in London in 1921. Its purpose was linked closely to the prevailing ideas about eugenics and racial hygiene, that populations could in some sense be controlled scientifically to replace demographic chaos with biological order [**Doc. 9**]. The ideal of the scientifically engineered society was famously parodied in Aldous Huxley's classic *Brave New World*, published in 1932, which described a nightmarish future of test-tube babies and state-run cloning.

Laissez-faire: Literally 'to leave alone', the term was used to describe an economy in which the self-regulation of the market replaced state control or regulation of economic activity.

Planisme: Term used in France to describe the idea that every aspect of modern life, but particularly the economy and environment, was capable of rational planning.

Finally, there was the planned workplace. During the 1920s, Henry Ford, the American motor-car producer, publicized the view that factories designed on modern mass-production lines, with the activities of their workforce controlled by time-and-motion studies, should replace the sprawling, inefficient, ill-planned workshops of the early industrial revolution. Men would work to the pace of the machine, in clean, well-lit halls. Technology in the service of man would end centuries of drudgery and misplaced effort. 'Things are better today than they were yesterday', wrote a confident Henry Ford in 1931. 'They can be made better tomorrow than they are today. It is not necessary to be either an optimist or a pessimist. It is enough to move forward' (Ford, 1931: 292). These ideals were taken up with enthusiasm in the Soviet Union, where **Fordist** methods were regarded as a short cut to economic modernization. Lenin was a great admirer of Ford, and American engineers were invited to help develop the large-scale, integrated factories that became characteristic of Soviet industry in the era of the **Five-Year Plans**. At Magnitogorsk in the Ural mountains a utopian 'socialist city' was planned in the late 1920s which would combine the most modern production methods with neat communal apartment blocks and wide spaces of parkland for the model proletarians who would inhabit it. One town planner drew up a 'graph for life' which broke down the working day minute by minute, from reveille at 6.00 in the morning to 'prepare to retire – ten minutes' at 10.00 in the evening (Stites, 1989).

Some of this has come to pass since 1945. Planned social improvement and economic growth have brought obvious benefits. But in the inter-war years they touched only a relatively small fraction of the population outside the prosperous and industrially developed regions of western and central Europe. Even here modernization was often experienced as poorly paid, monotonous manual labour in squalid, overcrowded cities with low levels of amenity and poorly developed community life. But the chief losers everywhere were the social classes of the traditional world displaced by industry and city: the peasantry, the old-fashioned **artisan**, and the old elite of gentry and educated bourgeois. From the onset of large-scale industrialization and urbanization in the nineteenth century these social groups were in retreat. Their traditional social structures and economic interests were bypassed or destroyed by modernization. Their customary way of life was challenged by the spread of state intervention and the capitalist market-place. The survival of religious belief and popular religious expression was undermined by the growth of a secular, civil society, dominated by officials often hostile to traditional values, and the emergence of a large urban working class indifferent to religion altogether. The older communities were increasingly marginalized. They had little political voice. To the liberal and socialist alike they were socially conservative, reactionary communities, destined to give way to progress.

Fordism: A term derived from the efforts of the American car manufacturer Henry Ford to create large, efficient and modern factories and the rational exploitation of labour through mass-production methods.

Five-Year Plans: A series of economic plans drawn up in the Soviet Union from 1928 onwards to provide targets for industrial and agricultural development. There were three plans in the 1930s and 1940s before the coming of war.

Artisan: Skilled worker, usually independent, producing specialised hand-crafted goods.

In the years after the Great War, the peasantry were particularly affected by these changes. The war itself shook up rural society, taking large numbers of villagers and transporting them to distant fighting fronts, while an army of officials descended on the farms, seizing horses and oxen for the army, requisitioning foodstuffs, imposing new taxes and controls. During the 1920s and 1930s, small farmers faced severe economic pressures. The slowing rate of population growth and the arrival of cheap overseas imports in Europe forced food prices down. Before 1914 eastern Europe provided 50 per cent of the wheat supplies to the industrialized western European states. But, by 1929, 94 per cent of their imported wheat came from the United States. During the slump of 1929–32, primary produce was regularly sold at less than the cost of production. In Germany, farm incomes declined by over 50 per cent during this four-year period; in France, peasant income fell by 60 per cent between 1929 and 1935. While prices fell, the costs of farming rose. Peasants faced higher taxes to help pay for higher government expend-iture after the war; in some cases they had to accept the 8-hour day and insurance payments for their wage labourers, which increased costs without any improvement in productivity. High costs and falling prices made it difficult for farmers to generate a surplus to invest in improvements, and they became trapped in a cycle of low investment and low income. In some cases traditional medieval strip-farming survived well into the twentieth century, making it difficult to introduce modern farming methods. Subsistence farming was still widespread. In Poland, two-thirds of farms were less than 12 acres, providing barely enough soil to feed the families that tilled them.

The traditional response of the peasantry to such hardship was to supple-ment their income by domestic manufacture of textiles or craft goods, or by the processing of their crops. But this avenue was closed off between the wars by the rise of cheap, mass-produced manufactures, sold more vigorously in rural areas, and by the development of food-processing in larger, well-equipped industrial enterprises. The village became more and more an adjunct of the urban economy. To add to their woes, farmers found themselves sub-ject to more coercive intervention from the state, which they resented and occasionally resisted. The state compelled farmers to control crop pests and animal diseases; the state introduced marketing schemes to rationalize the pro-duction and sale of agricultural produce; the state put pressure on farmers to consolidate their parcels of land into larger units. In Italy, they were compelled to grow more wheat to fulfil Mussolini's 'Battle for Grain', when what they wanted to produce were the more lucrative cash crops, olives, tomatoes and fruit. In the Soviet Union, peasants were given compulsory quotas of grain from each village to feed the city populations, at prices fixed by the state at well below the market rate. In Poland, the state broke up the surviving medieval agriculture, forcing the consolidation of a million farms from the old strip-farming methods, and turning 70 per cent of common land over to private use.

To make matters worse the pressures of the state and of modern commerce undermined the traditional character of rural life. Many villages before 1914 could supply most of their own requirements – not only of foodstuffs, but of a whole range of services, from cobbler, to master-builder, to undertaker. But rural poverty and the lure of the city drew many skilled workers away from the village, while competition from urban pedlars and city-based services reduced the economic prospects for village tradespeople. In the French village of Morette in the Dauphiné, a thriving craft community made up of thirteen different trades in the nineteenth century declined by the time of the Great War to just one mason and one carpenter, both of whom worked outside the village. In the German village of Oberschopfheim, in Baden, four of the village's five remaining traders left during the 1920s. These villagers supplemented their income by growing tobacco and making cigars, but such activity was undermined by falling demand and increased taxes on smoking (Rinderle and Norling, 1993). The quality and variety of village life declined markedly over the early years of the century, and the countryside became impoverished in every sense. Rural poverty was a fact of life. In Germany village income was only one-sixth of the average earnings of a skilled factory operative. The result was high levels of indebtedness, large tax arrears and the threat of repossession. The peasant's ability to cope with these pressures was slight. Although the local priest, particularly in Catholic areas, had an important part in keeping communities together, the Church was no longer the force in national politics it had once been. In Fascist Italy, or Nazi Germany or Republican Spain even the Church found itself in embattled retreat.

The same crises were evident even in states, like the Soviet Union, with a predominantly peasant population. During the 1920s, following the damaging civil war, many urban Russians fled back to the countryside, threatening to de-modernize the Soviet Union. The number of farms increased steadily in the 1920s as land was parcelled out in traditional ways to the families that made up the communal village, or *obschina*. The temporary collapse of central authority after 1917, and the Bolsheviks' desperate need for grain to feed the cities and the army, permitted the peasantry to reinforce their traditional way of life largely unmolested. The traditional village assembly organized the communal and economic life of the village. Popular religion revived, a blend of **Orthodox Christianity**, magic and superstition adapted to the modern age. The Communist Party made almost no inroads into the vast rural hinterland. By 1928 only 0.7 per cent of the peasantry were party members. This was a central issue for Soviet Communism, for not only did this situation compromise the Communists' political power, but it also ran counter to the whole idea that Communism would modernize economy and society.

Orthodox Christianity: Following the division of the Catholic Church in the eleventh century into Western Catholicism and Eastern Orthodoxy, the Orthodox Church survived in the Balkans and Russia, divided in its turn between Greek and Russian Orthodoxy.

Lenin always maintained that the only way to build a workers' state was to have workers. Instead, there was a vast sea of peasants who were regarded by the intellectuals who ran the party as a permanent barrier to revolutionary development, and a potential source of a new, popular, rural capitalism.

Lenin hoped that the peasantry could be persuaded to adopt more 'socialist' forms of organization, and he set up state-run collective farms as a model for them to emulate. He had great faith in the transforming power of technology: 'Give us only 100,000 tractors!' The experiments failed. By 1927 only 1.7 per cent of farms followed the Leninist model. The traditional commune survived, and the village, with its own local government and its own artisans and traders, became more self-contained, and the villagers more reluctant to sell their produce to the big cities. 'The happiness of the village', ran a report from a peasant committee, 'consists in not having any officials about trying to see that their orders are carried out' (Lewin, 1985).

By 1928 the Communist leadership was determined to do something about the countryside. At the instigation of the General Secretary of the Party, **Josef Stalin**, the peasants were compelled to **collectivize** – to set up co-operative, large-scale farms (*kolkhozi*) – and to give up private farming and trading. Communist officials, backed by the army, went from village to village cajoling, persuading, forcing the peasants to abandon practices that were centuries old in a matter of months. By 1932 almost all the Soviet land area was collectivized and the peasants forced to become rural wage labourers for the collective farm. The village craft associations, the *artel*, were broken up, and their members sent to work in factories. At the same time the state launched a violent, country-wide campaign against religion, urged on by the Communist-backed Union of the Godless. Churches were destroyed or converted to secular functions. Icons and church treasures were seized by the state. Priests were exiled or imprisoned. By the 1937 census, 43 per cent of the population claimed to be non-believers. Popular religion was forced underground, where it retained a tenacious grip until it re-emerged into the light in the late 1980s. The social structure of the Soviet Union was transformed. The urban population rose from 16 per cent to 33 per cent of the whole, and the number of workers increased from 11 million to 33 million. It was estimated that 80 per cent of the new urban population came from the villages. In the space of only a few years the Soviet peasantry experienced a 'modernization' that had taken the rest of Europe the best part of a century [Doc. 10].

The other traditional social group most affected by modernization was the urban small-business class, the artisans, or craft shopkeepers. The small producer, once organized in guilds until they were suppressed in the nineteenth century, was still the typical business in much of Europe at the start of the century. In Germany there were 1.5 million small craft shops in the 1920s,

Stalin (Joseph Dzhugashvili) (1879–1953): Georgian Marxist who joined the Russian Social Democratic Party, followed Lenin when the party split in 1904 and became Commissar for Nationalities when the Bolshevik government was set up in November 1917. In 1922 he was appointed General Secretary of the party and used this position to help him establish a personal dictatorship in the Soviet Union from the 1930s to the 1950s. He was prime minister from 1941 until his death in 1953, and commissar for defence from 1941 to 1946.

Collectivization: The policy adopted the Soviet regime in 1928 to force the Russian peasantry to abandon private farming and create large co-operative farms on which they would work as paid employees of the 'collective'.

employing 4 million people. In France there were 4 million small businesses in 1906, each employing only one or two people. The craft shops supported a traditional system of apprenticeship, and were governed by rules controlling entry to the various trades and the acquisition of the coveted title 'master'. The war affected small businesses in a number of ways. War industry favoured large firms at the expense of small ones (in Germany some 33 per cent of small enterprises were shut down, and 50 per cent of the workers conscripted), many young men who worked in trades regarded as luxuries were drafted to the front, and the shortages of raw materials and the closure of markets massively disrupted small-scale production. In the 1920s a flood of mass-produced goods from the United States, and the mechanization of a range of activities previously done by hand, eroded the economic position of small business yet further. The trend to concentration of industry was accelerated by the war, and continued in the 1920s. In the car industry small enterprises with a predominantly craft workforce were squeezed out. In Britain the number of car manufacturers fell from 89 in 1920 to 33 in 1938, when 90 per cent of the market was dominated by six firms. In Germany the number of car companies fell from 86 in 1924 to 16 by 1930, and most of the market was taken by the big firms – Ford, Opel, Auto-Union and Daimler-Benz – which had adopted large-scale, mechanized production. Master artisans found themselves compelled by circumstances to abandon an independent existence and work in factories for wages. By 1926, 230,000 artisans in Germany had made the transition.

In traditional craft sectors the situation was no better. In Germany the successful pre-war export sectors – toys, musical instruments, luxury glassware, which were produced in countless small workshops in southern and western Germany – were faced with a much less favourable market in the 1920s. Cheap mass-produced pianos from the United States, or low-priced mechanical toys from Japan, pushed the more expensive, high-quality German products out of the market. The mechanization of the glass industry in a matter of a few years reduced the proportion of hand-blown glass from over 90 per cent to a mere 4 per cent, with the result that in a number of Saxon towns almost the whole adult population became unemployed. In the 1920s these economic pressures were compounded with state efforts to loosen the grip of the old trades on recruitment and training, by removing from master artisans the sole right to train apprentices. The state also insisted that small businesses observe the new rules on the 8-hour day and employer responsibility for insurance and welfare payments. Many artisans were forced to sack their apprenticed workers rather than pay crippling costs. By 1926, 93 per cent of craft enterprises employed fewer than three people; family members made up the loss, working long hours for a shrinking income. The slump after

1929 produced disaster. Aggregate artisan income in Germany fell by almost half between 1929 and 1932. By the end of the slump many were close to starvation.

The German example is the best documented; but the processes at work there were common right across Europe. No doubt in a period of rising prosperity and full employment many of the adjustments called for by modernization could have been coped with. Indeed, after 1945 the transformation of small-scale business was completed with much less friction and hardship, at least in western Europe. But in the inter-war years the decline of small-scale agriculture and handicrafts took place against a background of economic stagnation, reduced trade and high levels of unemployment, and in the face of governments whose main priority was to expand industry and meet the demands of the urban workforce for cheap food and jobs.

The crisis facing the village and the craft shop was taken up by conservative critics of modernization and urban-industrial predominance. Many of them were drawn from the ranks of *déclassé* Europeans – gentry forced to sell up their estates, officials and soldiers whose careers were ruined by the collapse of the old order in 1918, intellectuals hostile to the pushy commercial classes and what they saw as the drift to vulgar materialism and mass culture. They shared the view that humanity was too much hostage to Mammon and the machine age. Anti-modernists praised the peasant and the artisan as the embodiment of old values and deplored the declining spirituality of the age and the loss of religious faith.

The intellectual revolt against modernity represented a profound rejection of the technocratic dream of machine-led progress. Where Henry Ford exuded confidence that a mechanized society run on scientific lines was a desirable and necessary consequence of modernity, his critics took the view that it was dehumanizing and socially destructive [**Doc. 11**]. They blamed modern, large-scale industry for creating the social divisions which produced the revolutionary crisis at the end of the war. Mechanization was blamed for eroding the bond between master and worker, and turning everyone into a slave of the conveyor belt and the stopwatch. Mechanization destroyed the traditional skills of the artisan, and with it the dignity and value of labour itself. It threatened to create a world of gigantic factories and soulless workers in place of the diversity and harmony of older social relations in the workshop or the village. It was the nightmare world captured in Fritz Lang's classic masterpiece of the silent screen, *Metropolis*. Charlie Chaplin ridiculed it in *Modern Times*. The 'scientific manager', who rationalized work practices and speeded up the pace of production, might satisfy the shareholders, but he was also demonized as the agent of a remorseless technological dictatorship.

THE CONSERVATIVE REVOLT

The baleful influence of modernization after 1918 on peasant, artisan and the traditional middle classes provoked a widespread response. While there was never a concerted anti-modernist revolt across Europe, the conservative masses reacted to the crisis they faced with growing anger and desperation. In the Soviet Union the effort to modernize agriculture and village life provoked what was, in effect, a second civil war throughout rural Russia. The government recorded 1,000 incidents of rural violence in 1928; in 1930 the number reached 13,794. That year more than 2 million peasants took part in riots and demonstrations. The peasantry resisted the violent attempts to force them into collective farms by destroying their crops and livestock. The number of cattle fell from 70 million in 1928 to 38 million in 1933, the number of pigs was reduced from 26 million to 12 million, sheep and goats from 146 million to 50 million. Many peasants were forced into collectives at the point of a gun, and millions were denounced as rural capitalists (**kulaks**) by the Communists, and either killed or exiled to labour camps in the remoter areas of the Soviet Union.

Kulak: Name applied to alleged rich peasants in the Soviet Union in the 1920s. Those identified as kulaks were often sent to labour camps during the period of *collectivization*.

The conflict with the peasantry produced a food crisis that led to the deaths of millions more; famine in the Ukraine, where peasant resistance in defence of their religion and economic independence was most marked, was deliberately exacerbated by Stalin to crush the anti-Soviet movement. Peasants and rural craftspeople were herded into factories where they performed poorly, trying to grapple with complex machinery and keep regular hours. The result was further terror, a wave of denunciations, accusations of sabotage and a growing population of camp prisoners, which reached 1.3 million by 1936. In the end even Stalin could see that the cost of imposing modernization from above threatened to be self-defeating. In 1935 the regime ordained that villagers could keep a cottage garden for themselves, and a few animals. Within a few years the value of the produce from these allotments, which constituted only 3.9 per cent of the land area, almost equalled the value of everything produced on the collective farms. But this was the government's only concession. The violent reaction of the bulk of the Soviet population to Stalin's plans was crushed only at the cost of a terrible toll in lives and livelihood (Shearer, 2004; Viola, 1996).

Elsewhere the conservative masses were more successful. In much of central and western Europe there emerged a wave of populism, of small-town and village political protest in defence of the interests and values of small-property owners and traditional workers. The protest was directed against the city, against socialism, against big business and international finance. It would be tempting to explain this reaction simply in terms of the rise of fascism, but it would be misleading to do so. In the first place, much of this reaction was based around popular Catholicism which developed as a major political force in Poland, in Spain, in Italy, in southern Germany and Austria. The revival of the Church was closely associated with the threat of socialism and radical anti-clericalism. The Papacy lent weight to this movement in its condemnation of atheist Communism and its hostility to western liberalism.

In Italy the crisis of the immediate post-war years in the countryside, sparked off by militant left-wing labour unions, provoked a mass Catholic movement – the Popolari – which won the second largest share of the popular vote in 1919. In southern Germany disillusionment with the Weimar Republic was siphoned into the Catholic **Centre Party** or the Bavarian People's Party (BVP), which between them retained a larger share of the vote in the region than Hitler's National Socialists. Catholic militancy was forcefully expressed in Spain. In 1932 the Republican government, dominated by liberals and anti-clericals, separated church and state, and began a programme to undermine clerical influence and modernize Spanish politics and society. The result was the formation of the first mass parties of the right in Spain, mostly Catholic, which reflected the anxieties and hostility of the property-owning classes, big and small, in the face of radical reform. The various parties united under a single umbrella movement, the Confederación Española de Derechas Autónomas (CEDA), which supported the nationalist revolution launched in July 1936 by **General Francisco Franco**. The resulting **civil war** between the forces of right and left was marked by a horrifying degree of violence; perhaps as many as 1 million Spaniards died in the conflict and the Francoist terror that followed his victory in March 1939. The outcome was a triumph for tradition. Spain's Catholic masses fought for a system of authoritarian rule, for Church and for property (Malefakis, 1970; Preston, 1984).

In the second place, much of the backlash came before fascism developed as a mass political movement. In Germany a whole array of small associations and parties emerged in the 1920s to prosecute the interests of the peasantry and small-townspeople. Their success was limited, although by 1928 they held together some 68 seats in the **Reichstag**, when the National Socialists had only 12. The efforts to organize the conservative mass politically led to sporadic outbursts of violence. In the late 1920s, angry peasants burned tax records and mobbed town halls; they tried forcibly to resist evictions. Officials were assaulted and abused. None of this quite amounted to a peasants' revolt, but it indicated a level of bitterness and disillusionment that did have significant political implications. Most of the populist movements, in Germany and elsewhere, were not attracted to the idea of restoring the old world of pre-1914, which was seen to have been dominated by the interests of the large landowners and their rich bourgeois allies in the cities. Instead, the protest reflected a widespread, though not very coherent, desire for a

Centre Party: Name of the main Catholic political party in Germany, founded in 1870, dissolved under Hitler in 1933.

Franco, Francisco (1892 –1976): A career soldier from the region of Galicia, Franco fought in Spain's Moroccan wars in the 1920s and rose to be army chief-of-staff by 1935 under the new Republican regime. Fearing an imminent Communist coup, Franco led a military coup in July 1936 that resulted in a bloody three-year civil war. In March 1939 he became dictator of all Spain and established a brutal regime of repression which lasted until his death in 1976.

Spanish Civil War: Conflict between rebel nationalist forces led by General Franco and the armed forces and irregular socialist and anarchist militia in support of the Second Spanish Republic. The nationalist revolt began in July 1936 and ended with Franco's victory in March 1939.

Reichstag: German parliament, established with the founding of the German Empire in 1871.

society that gave a genuine hearing to the socially conservative masses generally ignored before the war, a society that preserved the nation, created social harmony and protected small-scale property.

Much of this confused yearning for a new order built on traditional values was expressed in the end by European fascism. Fascism was a radical, even revolutionary, movement of the right that promised to contain the worst threats posed by modernity – class conflict and 'bolshevization', and the rise of unrestricted big business and international finance. Though fascism traded on a reactionary view of the family, of the role of women, of the virtues of the simple rural life, it was not a restorationist movement, keen to return to the days of emperors and aristocrats. Fascism looked forward to the creation of a new order of class collaboration, of authoritarian, single-party rule and an invigorated, morally revived nationalism. It appealed to the 'losers' from modernization with its promise of economic and social protection and its violent crusade against Marxism. But fascism was not itself anti-modern, as many of its more conservative supporters found to their cost. Indeed, fascist leaders supposed that they offered a modern alternative, a 'Third Way', as it was called, between old-fashioned liberal capitalism on the one hand and revolutionary Marxism on the other.

It is now generally accepted that fascist movements won social support from across a wide spectrum of the population. Although this view is in a literal sense true, it disguises the fact that a much larger proportion of their support came from the peasantry and rural workforce, or from small-business people and artisans, or from the disgruntled conservative intelligentsia. In Germany it has been estimated that something like half of Hitler's 13 million votes in 1932 were secured in Germany's villages. In Italy Fascism was in direct competition with the Catholic Church, but it won support from significant numbers of landowners, large and small, and from the economically embattled petty bourgeoisie. In Romania and Hungary native fascism drew much of its support from angry and alienated peasants, who blamed the city banks and merchants for the economic plight of the countryside. In France the populist demagogue, **Henri Dorgères**, a butcher's son from the Nord region, had 35,000 peasant followers in 1935 who marched in distinctive green shirts beneath the emblem of crossed pitchfork and sickle and the slogan 'Believe, Obey, Fight' (Paxton, 1997).

For fascists everywhere the conservative revolt provided them with an obvious source of mass support. In Germany, Hitler's National Socialists started out with the aim of winning the industrial working classes away from Marxism. The manifest failure of this effort by 1928 turned them towards the peasantry and the small-town bourgeoisie, where there was plenty of evidence of political demoralization and economic despair. In 1930 the National Socialist Party launched a nationwide campaign in the villages,

Dorgères, Henri (1897–1985): Radical right-wing politician who championed the cause of the French peasantry in the 1930s along quasi-fascist lines. A keen supporter of the Vichy regime, he was arrested and imprisoned in 1944.

masterminded by **Walther Darré**, a fervent believer in the racial and social value of peasant stock. Within six months he covered the countryside with a network of party cells; local peasant organizations were penetrated by party sympathizers; the small peasant parties were absorbed into the National Socialist movement. Propaganda was tailored to what peasants wanted to hear – that the city bankers, greedy socialist workers, and Jewish merchants and money-lenders were responsible for the declining fortunes of the old rural world [**Doc. 12**]. In response, the countryside (except for the Catholic strongholds of the south and south-west) returned huge majorities for National Socialist candidates in the crucial elections of 1932 that paved the way for Hitler's eventual appointment as Chancellor in January 1933 (Childers, 1986).

Among active party members the peasantry remained under-represented. The same could not be said of small-business people and artisans, who provided not only votes but active party members too. In the Netherlands the native National Socialist Movement (Nationaal Socialistische Beweging) drew one-third of its membership from this social group, and a further 5 per cent from Dutch farmers. The Austrian Nazi Party in the period 1933–38 recruited around one-third of its membership from small independent businesses and artisan trades, and 10 per cent from farmers. A study of Nazi Party membership in a number of German localities in 1931 has shown a very high proportion of small merchants, artisans and farmers: 42 per cent in Gassen, 60 per cent in Schloppe, 58 per cent in Märkisch-Friedland, 61 per cent in Eltersdorf, and so on. In Germany as a whole these groups provided 45 per cent of the Nazi deputies in the Reichstag and the provincial parliaments in 1933, with a further 23 per cent drawn from academics and bureaucrats. Only 8 per cent came from the ranks of the unskilled workers. Where the Nazis did win working-class support, it tended to come from more marginal and less well-organized groups of workers, from rural labourers and artisans. There seems little doubt that the conservative social groups most affected by the rise of modern industry, and the social revolution it brought in its wake, provided the backbone of support for European fascism. Without it Hitler would almost certainly not have come to power in Germany (Mühlberger, 1987).

The crisis of modernity exposed deep resentments. It encouraged the search for scapegoats who could somehow or other be held accountable for what were, in effect, the consequences of broad social and economic forces. A great deal of the blame was laid at the door of godless proletarians, who became the hapless victims of both militant Catholicism and fascism. In Stalinist Russia the regime was able to divert the full fury of the countryside by creating various bogeymen – the rich peasant, the bourgeois spy, the saboteur or hooligan – who were blamed for every mistake and murdered or

Darré, Walther (1895–1953): National Socialist politician appointed by Hitler to lead the campaign to convert the German peasantry to the movement in 1931 and subsequently appointed leader of the Reich Food Estate in 1933 set up to coordinate all aspects of German agriculture. He was arrested in 1945 and sent to prison in 1949.

exiled if they were caught, although the vast majority were innocent of any crime. In the rest of Europe the diversion of resentment all too often took the form of racial persecution.

The most notorious example was German anti-Semitism. German racists blamed 'the Jew' for all the evils of the modern world. Whether it was Jewish capitalism on Wall Street or Jewish Bolshevism in Moscow, the end result was the same for the propagandists: the undermining of the race and the community through anarchic modern culture, parasitic capitalism and 'biological decomposition'. The Jew was taken as the symbol of modernity at its most degenerate. This crude racial stereotyping found an echo among the economically declining artisan/shopkeeper or the poor farmer, hostage to the banks and mortgage-holders in the city. Even before the National Socialists came to power the German government placed restrictions on new department stores and retail chains, which were popularly identified as a Jewish threat. Local Nazis led the way in campaigning for their closure [**Doc. 13**]. In May 1933 Hitler's government passed a decree protecting small retail businesses and restricting the products and services the big stores could offer (in the same year the French government prohibited the opening of any more of the cheap Uniprix stores, for the same reason). In September 1935 came the so-called **Nuremberg Laws** which turned German Jews into second-class citizens, depriving them of most basic rights. For the next four years the regime waged a remorseless programme of 'Aryanization', taking over Jewish businesses and selling them to Germans of pure '**Aryan**' racial stock. The irony was that most Jewish businesses were small in scale, craft or retail shops in those very sectors threatened by modern commercial development. When Austria was absorbed into the German Reich in March 1938, Viennese National Socialists began at once to close down the small Jewish shops, whose premises and customers were taken over by German retailers [**Doc. 14**]. By 1939 half of Germany's Jews had fled; the rest led impoverished, threatened existences, the victims of vindictive discrimination (Burleigh and Wippermann, 1991).

Nazi racism was not confined only to Jews. Gypsies – the Sinta and Roma – were also singled out. Most, the regime claimed, were of mixed blood and the so-called 'half-breed' Gypsies were targeted as an example of the dangers of race-mixing. In rural areas they were associated with crimes such as pilfering or poaching, and the hostility of farmers helped to legitimize their persecution. Nor was anti-Semitism an exclusively German phenomenon. The Jew became everyone's scapegoat. In Poland the government in the 1930s practised an official anti-Semitism that was every bit as damaging as its German counterpart. Jews were deprived of civil rights, and their property and businesses gradually expropriated until by 1938 over one-third lived on grudging welfare hand-outs from the Polish state. Thousands emigrated,

Nuremberg Laws: A series of laws passed in a special Reichstag session at the National Socialist party rally in Nuremberg in September 1935. The laws prohibited marriage or sexual relations between Jews and Germans, and conferred German citizenship only on those of so-called German blood, excluding German Jews.

Aryan: Term originally applied to languages derived from an Indian root, but later taken to mean a particular race with a distinctive physical appearance and cultural level. The word was applied under National Socialism to distinguish Nordic Europeans from Jews and Slavs.

even to Germany. A great many Polish Jews were peasants or small shop-keepers who were deeply resented by non-Jewish farmers and retailers. In the 1920s there developed a movement to establish 'Christian' shops in villages and small towns where Jewish trade flourished; 'Christian' stalls were set up at fairs and markets, and Jewish stalls attacked and boycotted. The wave of dispossessions in the 1930s benefited non-Jewish shopkeepers and farmers who coveted Jewish wealth to compensate for their own economic decline. This crude anti-Semitism was dressed up by racist intellectuals as part of a world-historical struggle between old national cultures and the corrosive modernism of Judaeo-Bolshevism, but it masked the roots of popular anti-Semitism motivated by economic anxiety, material greed or even religious conflict. Jews became the victims of a perverted anti-modernism, which salved the bruised egos of a nationalist intelligentsia made insecure by modern culture and society, and diverted the popular conservative revolt against imagined enemies of the race.

4

The 'End of Civilization'

DECLINE OF THE WEST

The impact of both the First World War and the accelerated pace of modernization provoked a widespread sense in Europe thaht the ideals of 'western civilization', which had been taken for granted in the years before 1914, faced a critical, perhaps even fatal, turning point. Even before the war, philosophers, artists and scientists had begun to challenge existing moral prejudices, cultural values and material certainties. Friedrich Nietzsche famously declared that 'God is Dead' and challenged his readers to transcend the narrow confines of Victorian morality. The French writers Henri Bergson and Georges Sorel explored the power of the irrational and impulsive and rejected the desiccated rationalism of the liberal age. A generation of radical artists and writers hailed the right to artistic self-expression and spawned an extraordinary flowering of self-consciously modernist culture.

For many educated Europeans, ideas like these were regarded as evidence of a growing decadence. For much of the nineteenth century it had been assumed that western civilization was a permanent and progressive one, slowly spreading worldwide with the march of empire, until it became a world civilization. The First World War represented a terrible disillusionment. When the German philosopher Oswald Spengler published the first volume of his *Decline of the West* in 1918 he found an audience already predisposed to assume that western civilization was in crisis. Spengler's argument, though historically complex, could be reduced in the popular mind to a single strand: all civilizations were doomed to perish, and all the signs indicated that western civilization was in the final throes of a decadent decline. 'I am a thorough and decided pessimist', Spengler later wrote. 'I see no progress, no goal, no path for humanity.' His book sold 100,000 copies in Germany alone; it was widely translated, selling 40,000 copies in the United States (Hughes, 1952: 87).

The idea that permanent progress was an illusion matched the post-war mood. The British novelist H.G. Wells warned his readers in 1921 that

another war would produce 'absolute social disaster'. The German missionary Albert Schweitzer echoed Spengler when he told an Oxford audience in
1922 that the modern age instead of heading towards limitless progress was
facing spiritual suicide [**Doc. 15**]. The avant-garde artists and novelists
revelled in the pessimism and nihilism generated by four years of war and in
many cases embraced and expressed the idea of civilization in crisis. They
drew a contrast between what they regarded as the meaninglessness and
superficiality of the old order and the vibrant, subversive, violent, often
sexually-charged art of the new age. 'It's time for bullets/to pepper the
museums' walls/hundred-throat guns to shoot the old junk', wrote the Russian
expressionist poet Vladimir Mayakovsky.

The idea that the western world was in decay exhilarated those who criti-
cized its class structure, its liberal politics or its convention-bound culture,
but for the rest it created a permanent sense of unease throughout the inter-
war years, later defined by the historian Fritz Stern as a mood of 'cultural
despair'. The sense of morbid decline could be detected in the prevailing
views of capitalism as in some sense terminally diseased and of mankind
incapable of preventing the return to a Dark Age which the death of western
civilization would provoke. In an essay written in 1940, the French writer
and philosopher Simone Weil argued that barbarism, not progress, was in
fact the 'permanent and universal characteristic' of humans throughout
history (Rees, 1962: 143).

SCIENCE AND CIVILIZATION

During the nineteenth century, confidence in progress was bound up with
the apparently limitless benefits to be generated by modern science and technology. The cult of 'scientism' from the 1870s onwards fuelled belief that the
major social and political problems of the modern age could also be solved
in some way through the application of scientific knowledge and scientific
method. The prevailing framework was still Newtonian – a natural world
that was balanced, comprehensible and permanent, an analogue of the ideal
liberal society.

This scientific world-view was undermined in the early twentieth century
as comprehensively as the challenge to conventional morality or culture.
Albert Einstein's theory of relativity, first announced in 1905, was just one of
the many breakthroughs in physics that demonstrated clearly that the
universe was behaving like 'an exploding grenade' and, as a consequence,
that its life was finite. The development in physics of the ideas of entropy and
chaos theory showed that the mechanistic science derived from Newton was
no longer tenable. The splitting of the atom, achieved by a team in Cambridge in 1932 under the New Zealand scientist Ernest Rutherford, not only

confounded earlier notions about the nature of matter, but also promised a science of uncertain, perhaps menacing novelty. 'It is characteristic', wrote the young Arthur Koestler in 1932, 'that the signs of the coming new technological age should appear in these times of social and political confusion, of a chaotic malaise' (Koestler, 1954: 205). One of the leading physicists of his generation, the German Max Planck, the pioneer of quantum theory, also recognized in an essay written in 1930 that the new science no longer provided material certainty but instead matched the existing 'moment of crisis' in 'our material and spiritual civilisation', just as old-fashioned science had matched the pre-1914 sense of equilibrium (Caudwell, 1949: xvii).

The science that had the most immediate impact was biology. Well before 1914 the relationship between improved understanding of evolution and heredity, and issues of social policy and national development was well established. In 1892 the German writer Max Nordau published a thesis on *Degeneration* that quickly became the primary text for the argument that unless efforts were made to protect the national gene pool, modern populations would be swamped by a rising class of effete, lunatic or feeble-minded individuals. One answer to the problem, which became widely popularized in the early twentieth century, lay in what another German scientist defined in the 1890s as 'racial hygiene': broadly speaking the object of modern social policy should be to maximize the reproduction of biologically useful elements of the population and to segregate or eliminate those elements whose biological effects were likely to be deleterious. Although historians have rightly pointed out that there arose major arguments among biologists about the actual effects of heredity compared with the effects produced by a poor or deprived environment, the idea of the race in peril was planted in the European mind by popular science and remained a key element of the sense of impending crisis in the inter-war years.

At its most extreme the idea of racial crisis focused on the alleged threat posed to the white races as the bearers of modern civilization by the unhindered growth of the non-white peoples [**Doc. 16**]. Books with lurid titles (*The Rising Tide of Colour, Le destin des races blanches* and many others besides) proliferated in the 1920s and 1930s. They were designed to alert the west to the dangers of declining or degenerate population and to encourage a renewed wave of demographic growth. In Mussolini's Italy a 'Battle for Births' was launched, with mixed success, while laws were passed in 1937 against miscegenation (or marriages of mixed race) in the Italian Empire in East Africa. Pro-natalist policies were encouraged in a great many European countries in the early twentieth century. In France a National Alliance for the Increase of the French Population dated from 1896, and in the 1920s new tax laws encouraged large families by generous credits and penalized the childless. In 1939 a new Family Code discouraged abortion and birth control and under the authoritarian wartime Vichy regime, abortion became in 1942 a capital offence (as it did in Hitler's wartime Germany a year later). In Germany the fertile mother was a central motif in the propaganda of the regime and Marriage Loans were introduced in 1933 to encourage earlier marriage and larger families. Abortionists faced stiff penalties if their clients were healthy ethnic Germans. In Britain fears for the future size of the race prompted a number of government commissions in the inter-war years. Alarming extrapolations derived from statistics on the prevailing rate of fertility suggested that in only a century Britain's population would have fallen to just 5 million.

However, the primary menace revealed by progress in the biological sciences was the knowledge that lurking in every human population were the recessive genes that gave rise to physical and mental disability. It was also believed that habitual criminals and alcoholics were the victims of inherited traits. This suggested that increased population on its own was not necessarily the answer to the perils of the race. **Eugenics** became interwoven with issues of population size, since all over Europe and the United States eugenists argued that the fitter, more capable citizen should be encouraged to breed more, while the less fit should be discouraged, either by state intervention or vigorous propaganda, from breeding at all. In the 1920s the eugenic movement became progressively more alarmist. In France statistics showed that the number of so-called degenerates was increasing at an exponential rate, from 10,000 to more than 121,000 in the course of a century. The number of 'idiots' and 'cretins', so it was argued, had more than doubled between 1876 and 1930 (Decugis, 1936). Although these figures scarcely constituted real cause for dismay, since they largely reflected increased asylum and hospital provision, scientists argued that here was a genetic time bomb whose explosion would mean that 'the white race will certainly lose its rank in the world' and descend 'into anarchy.'

> **Eugenics:** First developed as a science in the 1880s, eugenics was the study of scientific improvement of the human race through a combination of genetic manipulation and social reform.

The association of many conditions and afflictions with hereditary defect led to a chorus of demands for a 'negative' eugenics. The solution adopted in most states involved forcible segregation in institutions of one kind or another, but there was also strong medical and scientific pressure in favour of sterilization as the only secure means to prevent the contamination of the gene pool and avert the coming biological crisis. In Sweden compulsory sterilization was adopted in 1934, and only outlawed officially in 1975 after 62,888 people had been sterilized. In the United States a majority of states passed sterilization laws which permitted the authorities to make infertile a range of people with physical and mental disabilities, as well as recidivist criminals and rapists. The most comprehensive sterilization law was drafted in Germany in 1932 and finally placed on the statute book by Hitler's government in January 1934. The Law for the Prevention of Offspring with

Hereditary Diseases listed a wide range of allegedly hereditary conditions, including congenital deafness and blindness, all of which qualified the unfortunate victim for an investigation by a Hereditary Health Court [Doc. 17]. Some 90 per cent of all cases referred, an estimated 360,000 people, were compulsorily sterilized. Around 70,000 Germans with physical and mental disabilities, many of whom had already been sterilized, were murdered between 1939 and 1941 as the programme to cleanse the social body became more radical and uncompromising. A report produced by German race scientists suggested that 1.6 million others carried potentially dangerous hereditary characteristics, but the war ended in 1945 before the remaining victims could be identified and dealt with (Proctor, 1988; Weindling, 1989).

The German case was only the most extreme example of the anxieties generated by modern science provoking violent medical intervention. In Britain the Eugenics Society campaigned vigorously for a voluntary sterilization scheme but when it was placed before Parliament in 1931 it was rejected, largely on the ground that genetic science had not yet demonstrated conclusively that defect was inherited. Nonetheless in Britain and France, where sterilization was also rejected, the idea that inherited disabilities and general 'feeble-mindedness' (a catch-all description for all kinds of allegedly deviant or delinquent behaviour) would threaten the race was presented as an issue so serious that, in the words of Leonard Darwin, one of the sons of the theorist of evolution, it would in time 'destroy the very foundation of our civilization'.

WOMEN, SEX AND MORAL DECLINE

Much of the biological crisis was blamed on women who were natural victims of a science largely populated and driven by men. Although the inter-war years saw further advance in the efforts to emancipate women both socially and politically, the emancipated woman represented for many men and for male-dominated institutions yet further evidence of the decadent and morally bankrupt age in which they lived. During the 1930s these many male anxieties coalesced to produce a decade in which women found the gains they thought they had made eroded or stifled.

The emancipated woman posed a number of distinct threats. At work men were challenged by female claims to greater equality of treatment and pay, and demands for professions to be opened to female participation. The response was often ambiguous even when it seemed generous. In the Soviet Union special statutory leave was introduced for women during their menstrual cycle, as long as they could extract a medical certificate validating their condition. The effect was to provide male workers with grounds to limit the kind of work women could do and to avoid promoting women into managerial or supervisory positions (Ilič, 1999). During the prolonged economic slump in the rest of Europe, women were regarded as selfishly denying the man the opportunity to work. In Germany during the early years of the dictatorship, great efforts were made to give priority to male re-employment, although the rapid economic recovery soon made it necessary to keep women in work, almost exclusively in low-paid, low-status employment. The main complaint against the newly independent working woman was the fear widely propagated that the liberated wife would have too few children. Low or declining fertility, observable in almost all European countries, was blamed on the selfishness of the modern woman who chose late marriage, birth control or even celibacy as a way to limit the remorseless cycle of unrestricted births. In Britain during the 1930s the child-poor family was seen as a result of female consumerism, choosing a more indulgent life above patriotic duty or, as one critic put it, preferring 'Baby Austins to babies'.

The backlash against female liberation was almost universal in Europe. In Italy Pope Pius XI published an encyclical in December 1930 'On Christian Marriage' which, apart from condemning birth control and abortion, emphasized the 'primacy of the husband' and 'the ready subjection of the wife'. The whole movement for female emancipation was condemned as 'false liberty and unnatural equality' (Ipsen, 1996; Wilson, 2004). In Stalin's Soviet Union, which had pioneered improved conditions for women in the 1920s, including the legalization of abortion in November 1920, the backlash of the 1930s was driven by similar moral imperatives. The sexual liberation of the 1920s, with its anarchic exaltation of free love, was condemned under Stalin as bourgeois depravity. Good Communists were expected to sublimate their animal appetites in strenuous labour for the party. The ideal of a communist family based on conjugal responsibility and commitment was encouraged by the decision to permit the production of wedding rings again in 1934 (which had been banned from the 1920s) and the introduction of a more solemn civil marriage ceremony. At the same time new legislation was introduced in 1936 to make divorce more difficult and to penalize the runaway husband and father with the threat of a heavy fine or imprisonment. Abortion was re-criminalized in 1936. In Germany the divorce laws were reconstituted in 1938 to make divorce easier in cases where the woman could be shown to have deliberately refused her patriotic duty of bearing children for the Fatherland (Stibbe, 2003).

The emphasis on family values and the sanctity or social utility of marriage was an explicit effort to preserve what one historian has called 'the frail social body' from contamination by behaviour regarded as licentious, deviant or degenerate (Dean, 2000). The inter-war years marked the high point of the public effort to contain venereal disease and combat or control prostitution. Sexual delinquency was regarded as a largely female characteristic, driven by weaknesses of personality or inherited predisposition [**Doc. 18**]. The woman as seductress and the fear of social chaos and moral degeneration that sexual profligacy suggested became standard tropes in much inter-war culture. In Germany the art of the leading expressionists – Max Beckmann, Otto Dix, Georg Grosz, Max Ernst – featured women as prostitutes and seducers but also displayed their punishment in oppressive pictures of female murder and mutilation. Anxieties about masculinity fuelled some of this rejection of the sexually promiscuous or voracious woman, but it was also the product of a real concern with what was called 'social hygiene'. The social body, it was argued, was poisoned by unchecked sexual deviancy. Lurid accounts of the hidden effects of venereal diseases were linked with images of woman as both licentious and menacing to the race. Prostitutes could end up in concentration camps during the Third Reich as anti-social or 'asocial' personalities. In the Soviet Union prostitutes were given re-education sessions in special homes, but here, too, by the 1930s the regime became less tolerant, rounding up prostitutes and sending them to camps as 'socially dangerous'. The same charges of degeneracy and moral decline were directed at homosexuality. In the Soviet Union it was criminalized in 1936, although it had already carried a harsh social stigma. In Germany homosexuality among men was illegal under the 1871 criminal code, but only under Hitler were homosexuals subjected to routine discrimination and violence. An estimated 50,000 were prosecuted, of whom an estimated 5,000 died from mistreatment in prison and the concentration camps.

For some of those who linked the alleged moral decline of the modern world with the crisis of civilization, the example of the fall of ancient Rome was commonly mobilized. The casual and unsubstantiated view that the fall of Rome was a result of decadence was easily translated to the modern world. The fact that decadence was attributed to sexual licence, sexual deviancy and an exaggerated influence of the feminine merely echoed the concerns of the modern age that the pleasures of the flesh would undermine the commitment to the moral standards deemed to be necessary to sustain western civilization.

PSYCHOANALYSIS AND THE MODERN MALAISE

An exaggerated interest in sex was readily blamed on the newest of the popular sciences, psychoanalysis. Founded before the First World War, and associated chiefly with the theories of the Austrian doctor **Sigmund Freud**,

Freud, Sigmund (1856–1939): A Viennese doctor who became the founding father of modern psychoanalysis. He is best remembered for his pioneering books *Interpretation of Dreams* (1900) and *The Ego and the Id* (1923). He argued that most psychological disorders were related to problems of early sexuality, which were suppressed in the unconscious portion of the mind but later manifested themselves in neurotic behaviour. When Germany occupied Austria in 1938, Freud, who was Jewish, emigrated to London.

psychoanalysis started from the assumption that serious manifestations of mental illness could be explained by careful analysis of the unconscious mind. Freud suggested that the primary influences were to do with the experiences of early childhood and that most of them were anal or sexual in character, particularly the 'Oedipus complex' which became Freud's most famous discovery – that boys instinctively loved their mothers and hated their fathers. Freud gave to modern psychotherapy a whole range of critical concepts, from the idea that the mind tried to place some kind of order on the otherwise uncontrolled urges of the instincts by processes of regulation and repression to the view that every manifestation of abnormal, obsessive or violent behaviour could be explained by a series of 'complexes' bound up with a hidden but powerful sense of guilt.

Freud's work soon spawned a whole number of psychoanalytical schools. The principal purpose of psychoanalysis was to give therapeutic relief to those who suffered from mental illness; but the central claim – that every individual was in reality a divided self, a rational being in everyday life, but a seething mass of uncontrollable and invisible psychological urges beneath the surface – became another scientific metaphor for the inter-war years, acting, like heredity, to undermine confidence in the essentially rational and ordered nature of civilized progress. The wider implications of psychoanalysis were rejected in the Soviet Union because it suggested that man was prey to forces entirely independent of the rational, external personality which the Communist system was trying to construct. The science was banned from 1934 as mere bourgeois idealism. In Germany, where the science made rapid progress after the war, psychoanalysis was also rejected by the Hitler regime because a great many of its leading protagonists were Jewish. Elsewhere it had a mixed reception. The enlightened view was to accept that European society did indeed encourage widespread repression of sexual instincts, with often damaging effects; for the sceptic, psychoanalysis was yet another example of a decadent culture unhealthily obsessed with sex (Farrell, 1996).

The development of social psychology from the late nineteenth century also contributed to challenging or undermining conventional views about society and politics. Social psychologists developed the idea that the masses respond to many social stimuli as a whole, instinctively and irrationally. Gustave Le Bon's *The Psychology of the Crowd* (1896) and Wilfred Trotter's *The Instincts of the Herd in Peace and War* (1916) became classic statements of the idea that mob violence, political protest, even war could be explained by collective psychological behaviour. This suggested that modern politics and social development were likely to be prey to mere instinct and appetite. The Spanish philosopher Ortega y Gasset published in 1930 one of the most widely read books of the decade that followed, *The Revolt of the Masses*, in which he deplored the way in which modern society was gradually being overtaken by the crude impulses of the mass. Critics of Bolshevism and of fascism pointed to the apparent realization of these bleak prognoses in the violent prejudices and irrational enthusiasms which the new political movements released. In the inter-war years, fear of the triumph of irrationalism, itself explicable in apparently scientific terms, undermined an overarching belief in the civilizing power of Reason, whose intellectual roots lay far back in the period of European Enlightenment [Doc. 19].

Psychologists played their own part in encouraging the belief that the discoveries of their science in some sense were reflected in the current world crisis. In the last twenty years of his career Freud's work began to engage more with the wider world of politics and social development as if society as a whole could be psychoanalysed. In *Civilisation and its Discontents*, published in 1930, Freud suggested that the anxieties of the modern age reflected the growing inability of the collective 'ego' to keep at bay the instincts that lay below the social surface. The more civilized Europe became, the stronger the acts of repression needed to keep it so. Above all, Freud suggested that the instincts that drove a troubled child to acts of wanton destruction were also socially embedded, capable of control in adult life but also capable of uncontrollable recurrence in acts of war or revolutionary violence. **Carl Jung**, the Swiss psychologist who broke with Freud over his emphasis on sexuality, published a year later 'The spiritual problem of modern man' in which he also suggested that the current malaise in Europe was a product of collective anxiety, a 'profound uncertainty', whose root causes were psychological rather than material [Doc. 20]. The discovery that modern man has a great unconscious capacity for evil, manifested in the horrors of the First World War, left Europeans, Jung claimed, 'shocked and disillusioned'. Jung believed that the psychological anguish of the modern age helped to explain the sense of crisis: 'The upheaval of our world and the upheaval in consciousness is one and the same' (Jung, 1936: 231).

Jung, Carl (1875–1961): Swiss psychologist who at first supported Freud's discoveries but broke with him over what he saw as excessive emphasis on sexuality. Jung is best remembered for the idea that people are divided into extrovert or introvert personalities. He accepted the idea of the unconscious, but suggested that it was a product of a collective entity shaped by the whole experience of early human development.

WAR AND CIVILIZATION

The fashion for scientific explanation of social phenomena was applied in particular to the question of war. In 1932 the League of Nations Committee on Intellectual Cooperation invited Albert Einstein to take part in an exchange of letters with an individual of his choice on the question 'Why War?' He selected Freud, and the letters between them on the subject were published in 1933. Einstein confessed that as a scientist he had no explanation for it, but he assumed that the reason had to be psychological in character. Freud replied at length that the reasons for war were almost certainly psychological and lay, in his opinion, in the constant struggle between the life and death instincts in man which he had identified in his work. It was useless, he claimed, to try to get rid of man's 'aggressive inclinations'. The only hope, though a Utopian one in his view, was that the process of civilization itself would gradually internalize the aggressive impulses, but they could only be repressed, not removed (Pick, 1993).

During the 1930s the psychological explanations for war derived from Freud's idea about a primary instinct for aggression were elaborated and extended in competition with other scientific approaches. Before 1914, evolutionary biologists had suggested a model of development in which the struggle for survival was intrinsic to human populations as it was in the natural world. Although many biologists and anthropologists rejected this view as a product of vulgar science, the idea continued to circulate in the inter-war years that war was explicable by forces in nature that could not be accommodated by conventional politics or pacifist propaganda. This social–biological perspective underlay much of Hitler's world-view. He believed that war was a necessary part of the human condition because it was the only way in which a superior race, like a superior species in nature, could secure the resources and space necessary for its survival and evolutionary development.

All the attempts to explain war in scientific terms led to the same conclusion. War was regarded as unavoidable whatever the nature of modern humans or modern civilization. This was a profoundly pessimistic conclusion because a common assumption in the inter-war years was the relationship between the next war, if it came, and the end of civilization. European pacifism was a widespread phenomenon in the inter-war years, but the pacifist discourse relied not only on a shared belief in the essential rationality and peaceableness of civilized humans, but on a belief that the next war would be uniquely destructive and indiscriminate in its effects [**Doc. 21**]. Fear of war and its consequences was bound up with a popular belief that Europe had reached a disturbing turning point in world history. Such a view was validated by the apparent capacity of modern science to unearth the troubling and powerful forces at work in human populations which together made violence more likely. The effect of the many discourses prompted by scientific discovery was characteristically ambiguous. While science in all its many guises promised a more prosperous, ordered and protected society, it also revealed to the western world visions of social degeneration, unbridled instinct, unavoidable aggression and a material world in constant flux.

5

The 'Great Crash': Capitalism in Crisis

THE CAUSES OF THE CRASH

At ten o'clock on the morning of 29 October 1929 the gong sounded in the New York Stock Exchange on Wall Street for the start of business. What followed was an unseemly, desperate scramble to sell stocks and shares at any price. One thing was clear above the din of shouting traders: the American boom of the 1920s had crashed in flames. At the end of the day 16 million shares had changed hands at knock-down prices. When the Dow-Jones Index stopped its downward fall in July 1933, $74 billion had been wiped off share values, and shares stood at only 15 per cent of the level on that day in 1929 when the crisis began.

The Great Crash, as it became known, spelled financial ruin for thousands of American investors, big and small. But its effects were felt far beyond America. The crisis on Wall Street was a heart attack for the world economy from which it never fully recovered before 1939. The stock-market crash itself had immediate, American causes. For two or three years before 1929 a sustained boom in American industry fuelled a speculative orgy of share issues and share-buying. So high was confidence in the future of the American economy that speculators bought up options for products and output years into the future. Capital was plentiful, and companies cashed in by issuing shares when there was no real market to support the extra production. Trading was not exactly illegal, but it was wildly over-optimistic and imprudent. Ordinary investors became obsessed with the promise of windfall profits. But when the first signs appeared that the boom might be faltering, the psychological effect was devastating. The speculative bubble burst and the American economy went into decline.

The Wall Street Crash was only a small part of the explanation for that decline; it was as much a symptom as a cause. The factors that produced the crash, and explain its prolonged severity, must be traced back to the Great War. Up to 1914 the world had experienced thirty years of almost uninterrupted growth in industrial output and world trade. The international market relied on a good deal of cooperation between the major producers in maintaining a relatively open world market and establishing a stable exchange rate between currencies based on an agreed **Gold Standard**. Goods and labour moved with relative ease across frontiers [**Doc. 22**]. At the core of this international system was the economy of Britain, whose great financial strength, trading experience and far-flung imperial interests gave it a keen interest in the continued stability of world markets, and the economic means to achieve it. Britain played a role in the world economy similar to that played by the United States in the boom years after 1945.

The Great War undermined much of this structure. It dislocated world trade profoundly. While Europe was fighting the war, other economies, notably Japan and the United States, took over Europe's export markets. States outside Europe, starved of European goods and funds, began to embark on their own industrialization at the expense of their old suppliers. When the war was over there was a tendency to over-production once European industry recovered, which produced a slump in prices and a rush to set up tariff barriers to protect struggling home industries. Even Britain, the foremost champion of free trade before the war, placed duties on the import of cars and other manufactures to blunt strong American competition. As a result the growth rate of world trade failed to reach the exuberant levels of pre-1914, and the export performance of the two largest traders in 1914, Britain and Germany, stagnated. The comparatively poor performance of the British economy throughout the 1920s made it difficult for Britain to play the central role it had carried before the war. The sharp decline in Britain's major export industries adversely affected the ability of other countries to sell to Britain in return. The reduction in British overseas earnings starved the world economy of an important source of funds (see **Table 5.1**, for the comparative economic performance of the major states).

The second problem was financial. The war destroyed the stable Gold Standard system. The warring states in Europe abandoned gold as they were forced to finance their war efforts with massive loans and state deficits, or heavy borrowing from abroad. High state debts and a shrinking quantity of goods and food produced high levels of inflation. By 1919 the mark stood at only one-fifth of its pre-war value, the franc only one-third. The war effort in Russia finally produced runaway inflation during 1917 and the complete collapse of the currency. After the war, state finances were distorted by the costs of demobilization and the servicing of huge domestic debts and war loans. Before 1914 substantial quantities of British and French capital exported abroad oiled the wheels of world industry and commerce; in the 1920s the reduction of this source, a consequence of the financial impact of the war, acted as a brake on the expansion of the world economy. The other net

Gold Standard: A system of fixed currencies pegged to the value of gold. First used in Britain in 1821 it was adopted by most major states before 1914. Like the Euro, a common standard helped to ease international trade and currency exchange.

Table 5.1 Selected statistics on economic performance in the 1920s

	% growth of economy (1924–29)	% growth of exports (1921–29)	% growth of industrial output (1920–29)
Austria	18.7	63.1	51.6 (1923–29)
Belgium	22.2	359.0*	88.5
Czechoslovakia	33.9	−28.2	67.7 (1921–29)
France	18.8	86.4	101.6
Germany	10.2 (1925–29)	45.2 (1925–29)	16.1 (1925–29)
Italy	10.8	26.9	52.5
Norway	27.8	−39.7	28.3
Spain	18.8	106.1	58.7
Sweden	29.8	−20.5	50.0
UK	12.4	3.7 (1921–29)	25.6
USA	14.7	30.7 (1921–29)	89.6 (1921–29)

Column 1 expressed in constant prices; column 2 in current values. Economic growth is measured here in terms of growth of GNP except for the USA (National Income) and Norway and Sweden (Gross Domestic Product).
* This high figure reflects the slow recovery of Belgian trade after the destruction caused by the Great War.

Hyperinflation: The point at which a currency becomes valueless because of an absolute loss of confidence in its purchasing power. Experienced in the USSR in 1919–20, Germany in 1922–23, Austria and Hungary in 1923–24.

exporter of capital before 1914, Germany, was plunged into a downward financial spin in the early 1920s which culminated in 1923 in **hyperinflation** and the collapse of the mark. In a country with a strong saving ethic and a long tradition of financial orthodoxy, the sight of people pushing wheelbarrows to the shops filled with worthless banknotes was a profound shock [Doc. 23]. Though the mark was re-stabilized in 1924, millions of Germans lost their savings, and the German economy was forced to rely heavily on loans from abroad, placing it at the mercy of world financial markets.

The collapse of the German currency dragged down the other currencies of eastern and central Europe too. Hyperinflation in Austria, Hungary, Poland and Czechoslovakia was partly a reflection of the expense and difficulty of setting up new states and new economic systems from scratch after 1918 (which tempted governments to print money regardless) and partly a reflection of a real scarcity of goods. Though these currencies were also stabilized in the mid-1920s, Europe was left with a financial system that was fundamentally unsound. Currencies could not be pegged to a single, stable standard, agreed between all states. Some states returned to the Gold Standard (Britain in 1925, France a year later), others retained depreciated currencies, and still others practised controls over trade and currency transactions that distorted the operation of the Standard. Investors remained shy of investing in case inflation once again wiped out their assets, and speculators shifted assets quickly from one country to another at the first hint of trouble. Agriculture and small business were left chronically short of capital and interest rates remained high (Eichengreen, 1992; Feldman, 1994).

The only source of possible salvation was the United States, whose economy was less affected by the war. America poured $6,400 billion into the world economy between 1924 and 1929, much of it going to Germany and eastern Europe. But many of these loans were short term, subject to immediate recall in times of crisis. American investors had had their fingers burned with war loans which their wartime allies were slow to repay, and with loans to central Europe which became worthless during the inflations of the early 1920s. Though they continued to be generous with funds, foreign economies were hostage to the continued prosperity of the American people and their confidence in overseas stability. What the United States was neither equipped for, nor willing to perform, was the role of world economic leader which Britain was no longer in a strong enough position to play. Unlike Britain, the United States was more self-sufficient in food and raw materials. As a result America needed to import much less than Britain, and was less dependent on exports to pay for overseas resources. Where British pre-war prosperity was based on large imports and exports, which directly benefited the world economy, American prosperity was largely domestic in origin and benefited the world economy much less.

Of course there was economic growth in the 1920s, although it was brittle and prone to crisis, first in 1920–21, again in 1926. It was also marked by a very uneven pattern of development. Some sectors boomed while others languished; states experienced short bursts of growth, punctuated by periods of stagnation or decline. It was possible to make quick millions out of cars, radio or cinema, but the old industrial sectors – coal, steel, textiles, shipbuilding – grew sluggishly, if at all, after the wartime boom. Once the period of post-war inflation and scarcity was past, the prices of foodstuffs and raw materials fell sharply. Agriculture and primary production acted as a drag on the whole economy. This price decline was felt most keenly in the poorer parts of Europe which relied heavily on exporting food and materials, and in the less developed areas of the world outside Europe and America. The ability of these areas to absorb industrial goods from the developed world was much reduced, which contributed to higher than usual levels of unemployment in the major European export industries. The result for a great many people in the 1920s was long-term poverty and falling income. Wide areas of deprivation existed side by side with booming new industries. Even in the United States, there were obvious contrasts between the old steel towns of the east and the decaying farmlands of the central plains, and the bustling car factories of Detroit.

All of these factors suppressed business confidence and consumer demand, squeezing profits and discouraging investment. By the late 1920s, there was already evidence of an impending recession as the price fall continued and

Table 5.2 Selected statistics on economic performance in the slump

	% change in exports* (1929–33)	% change in industrial prod. (1929–33)	% change in steel output (1929–33)
Austria	−64.6	−37.2	−64.3
Belgium	−55.2	−33.9	−33.5
Czechoslovakia	−71.1	−39.4	−66.5
France	−63.1	−19.5	−30.3
Germany	−53.7	−34.0	−53.1
Italy	−59.4	−8.9	−16.5
Netherlands	−60.2	−9.2	−
Poland	−65.9	−31.5	−35.9
Spain	−68.1	−16.0	−49.5
Sweden	−39.5	−9.1	−9.2
UK	−49.5	−3.8	−27.0
USA	−69.5	−36.0	−58.9

* Exports are expressed in current values. Because of the sharp price fall over the slump, the volume of trade contracted less than the value. The volume of world trade declined 25.4% between 1929 and 1933, but by 60.9% in terms of value.

unemployment grew. In Germany the downturn began in 1928, and by the spring of 1929, six months before the Wall Street Crash, there were already more than 2 million unemployed. The crash on the American stock market had the effect of triggering a worldwide business panic, which turned a modest recession into a catastrophic slump, the worst economic crisis of the century. The panic seized bankers and investors everywhere. There was a scramble to call back loans and to cut credit. Americans who had cautiously loaned money abroad in the 1920s clamoured for repayment from governments and businesses which had locked the loans up in long-term projects. Lender and borrower both faced bankruptcy. The world financial system ground to a shuddering halt, and with it collapsed world trade and output. So catastrophic was the crisis for economies that were already in difficulty that the decline in business activity did not last for one or two years, as in most business cycles, but continued without a break for four years. For some economies – France or Spain, for example – the fall lasted even longer, down to the end of the decade. (See **Table 5.2**, for statistics on the slump.)

THE EFFECTS OF THE RECESSION

The consequences of the economic slump were uniformly disastrous. The immediate effect was psychological, a collapse of confidence in the capitalist system itself. Marxists had been predicting for years that capitalism was doomed; anti-modernists bemoaned the irrational, anarchic character of free-market economics. Here was the proof of the pudding: economic progress itself had generated the forces for its own downfall. Some critics could take a prim satisfaction that the 'Roaring Twenties', the world of bright-young-things, cocktail parties, brash music and short skirts, had finally burnt themselves out. There was always an edge of decadence to the economic life of the 1920s, personified by men like the French car manufacturer **André Citroën**, whose glossy champagne lifestyle shocked Paris until his firm went spectacularly bust in 1934. Citroën killed himself. The harsh reality of the slump ended the frothy consumer boom and the frenzy of extravagant speculation that fuelled it. The shock was immense. The social disaster that followed turned many intellectuals towards Communism or fascism in the belief that any system must be better than one so apparently planless and destructive.

The material consequences were just as bleak. The rush to recall loans created a credit drought. Businesses and farms could not get the money they needed to continue production. Governments of all complexions cut expenditure in line with the conventional wisdom that during a recession it was prudent to cut costs and balance the books. Profit levels fell sharply and investment dried up. Desperate efforts were made to sell goods at any price in the face of shrinking demand. The consequence was an accelerated price fall. Agricultural prices fell by over a half between 1928 and 1932, industrial prices by more than a third. Food rotted in warehouses for want of customers; in Brazil, the coffee crop was burnt to keep up coffee prices; Canadian farmers destroyed their wheat, or sold it for locomotive fuel, rather than sell it for next to nothing. The result of a situation where no one wanted to buy or invest was a precipitate decline in industrial output which threatened to drag down the banking system and expose governments to financial disaster. In Austria the failure of its major industrial client forced the influential Creditanstalt bank to close its doors in May 1931. The knock-on effect in Germany took the state to the edge of bankruptcy in the early summer and forced the public rescue of the entire banking system. In September 1931, anxious speculators began a run on the pound sterling which was only ended when Britain abandoned the Gold Standard for good, and with it any pretence of maintaining a stable international currency system. The crisis then moved to the United States where, between August 1931 and January 1932, 1,860 banks failed as depositors hurriedly removed their threatened accounts. A year later the entire American banking system collapsed, forcing an actual 'bank holiday' on 6 March 1933, and prompting emergency legislation to halt the decline in creditor confidence (James, 1986; Kindleberger, 1973).

The crisis in the world's financial markets reverberated in the spheres of production and trade. Industrial output declined to levels not seen since the

Citroën, André (1878–1934): Prominent French car manufacturer who helped to pioneer mass motoring in the 1920s. He was well known for his flamboyant lifestyle and advertising gimmicks. In 1934 he produced the first front-wheel drive car.

1890s. Steel output in Germany fell from 16.2 million tons in 1928 to 5.7 million in 1932. Industrial production as a whole fell by 40 per cent in four years. In France steel output in 1938 was still only two-thirds of what it had been a decade before. With so much idle industrial capacity and a fall in consumer demand, trade was stifled. World trade fell by two-thirds between 1929 and 1932, and never recovered for the rest of the decade. Its value in 1938 was still 60 per cent below the 1929 figure, although because of falling prices the volume fell less dramatically.

The instinct of governments was to protect their own industry against imports by imposing tariffs. In 1930 the Hawley–Smoot Tariff (named after the two American congressmen who proposed it) was made law in the United States. It placed severe limitations on imports at exactly the time that other states were desperate to sell to the richer American market to pay off their dollar debts. In 1929 America imported $4.3 billion worth of goods; in 1932 only $1.3 billion. The American tariff sparked off a round of competitive **protectionism**. Germany and France both subjected trade to direct control, imposing import quotas on foreign goods, and entering direct barter agreements with trading partners. In November 1931, Britain imposed duties of 50 per cent on a range of twenty-three different classes of imported goods. The British Empire Conference at **Ottawa** in July/August 1932 established a system known as **Imperial Preference** in which Britain and its empire partners agreed to exchange industrial and agricultural goods on favourable terms, and at the expense of non-empire producers. The rush to tariff protection and beggar-my-neighbour policies was understandable as a reaction to the seriousness of the economic situation, but its effect was to reduce any prospect of reviving the international economy through collaboration. The major states sought ways to save their own economic skins first; the world market became fragmented and distorted.

The human consequences were worst of all. Most older Europeans had experienced some degree of economic crisis in their lifetime, but there was nothing to compare with the severity and length of the inter-war slump. It is difficult to comprehend the sheer scale of the impact on communities that had just begun to find their feet again after the disruptions of war and the post-war crisis. The most conspicuous indicator was unemployment. No country was immune (see **Table 5.3**). In the United States unemployment affected one in four of the labour force at its peak, in 1933. In Germany there were more than 8 million unemployed at the end of 1932, out of a workforce of 20 million. Two out of every five Germans were out of work, a figure that says a great deal about the political crisis raging in Germany in the same year.

The raw data on unemployment, however, tell only part of the story. Many of the unemployed remained without work for three or four years, creating whole communities of men and women resigned, through joblessness, to a

Protectionism: Policy of erecting tariff walls to protect domestic industry from foreign competition.

Ottawa Conference: Conference of the major British Emprie states in Canada in July/August 1932 to agree on a system of so-called **Imperial Preference** under whose terms Britain agreed to take raw materials and food from Empire states who in return bought industrial goods from Britain.

Table 5.3 Unemployment in the slump*

	1928 (thousands)	1932 (thousands)	1935 (thousands)
Germany	1,400	5,775	2,151
Austria	182	378	349
Belgium	5	71	66
Czechoslovakia	39	554	686
Denmark	50	100	76
France	16	301	464
Italy	324	1,006	964 (1934)
Netherlands	22	271	385
Poland	126	256	382
UK	1,217	2,745	2,036
USA	1,982	11,586	12,830

* Registered unemployment only, average for the year. The actual number of unemployed was considerably higher than what these official figures suggest. In Germany, by January 1933 there were almost 9 million fewer people in work than in 1929.

life of destitution and dull, empty routine. Secondly, unemployment was indiscriminate, affecting all sectors of the economy, including white-collar and professional groups. In Germany 800,000 of the unemployed derived from these two sectors, including a good many of Germany's young graduates. Thirdly, many of the unemployed came from younger-age groups which arrived in the labour market after 1929 with little prospect of a job. A quarter of the German unemployed in 1932 were under 25. Finally, the figures disguise the very large number of workers who were forced on to short-time working. Two-thirds of those still working in Germany in 1932 worked less than a full week (Stachura, 1986).

The direct result of unemployment was desperate poverty. Even in the few states with a welfare system, the very scale of the problem soon exhausted the welfare budget. The collapse of business activity cut government revenue from taxation, making it almost impossible to fund an adequate level of relief. In many countries there was little more than charity to fall back on. European and American cities saw an explosion of small, unofficial relief programmes, giving jobless workers a hot meal, or food for their families. But these schemes were mere palliatives. For a great many the slump was a period of terrible poverty; diet and health both declined, and the birth-rate fell. There developed a movement of city-dwellers back to friends or relatives in the countryside, who could provide the prospect of some food, although rural areas were by no means immune to hardship, even hunger. Working communities fell back on their own resources, those in work helping those without. For many families the woman became the main breadwinner. In Germany employers preferred to keep on female workers because they were cheaper. Average wages for women in the German metal industry were only 59 per cent of male wages. Every city had its groups of men huddled on street corners, the stream of aimless unemployed drifting from one encounter to another [Doc. 24]. The incidence of crimes against property went up as destitute families supplemented their meagre resources with what they could steal or poach.

THE SEARCH FOR RECOVERY

A crisis of such proportions had serious political implications. The Communist parties increased support in response to what seemed to be a terminal crisis of capitalism. There was less overt revolutionary activity than there had been between 1917 and 1923, but there was plenty of evidence of social unrest and political desperation. In Britain and France cross-party National Governments were arranged to fight the common enemy of economic crisis. Even in Germany the government appointed in January 1933 with Hitler at its head was a government of 'National Concentration', bringing all the forces of the right and centre together to combat the recession. Ruling groups everywhere feared that the slump would revive the spectre of 1917. Even in the United States there was open talk of political crisis, with 17 million Americans on public relief in 1932. According to one Republican senator, America that year was 'closer to revolution than we have ever been in our lives'. In France, the government was brought down by violent, popular demonstrations in February 1934 in central Paris, the first time this had happened in the history of the Third Republic. In Spain, popular uprisings in the mining area of Asturias in 1934, and of desperate rural workers in Andalusia in December 1933, were bloodily suppressed. The social fabric everywhere was stretched taut by economic misery.

It has often been argued since the 1930s that governments should have done much more, and sooner, to combat the effects of the crisis. But there were important factors inhibiting a more vigorous response. In the first place, it took some time before governments were fully aware that the crisis was of unusual severity. The popular expectation was a repeat of previous business cycles, one- or two-year slump, and then a slow revival. Only by 1931 was it clear that the recession was still deepening and that extraordinary measures were called for, but by then the scale of the crisis threatened to swamp any counter-cyclical strategy. Governments were also anxious to avoid economic experiments and to stick with orthodox remedies. With the memory of inflation fresh in their minds, and the more recent evidence of speculative irresponsibility in the United States, politicians tried to avoid anything that threatened the stability of the currency or balanced budgets. The call for government public works funded with deficits was resisted as a radical threat to financial security and business confidence, and was answered only at the end of the recession when all other expedients had failed. Instead, most governments followed the textbook, and cut state expenditure and employment. In France the state pursued a narrow monetarist strategy right through to 1936, reducing the income of civil servants and state workers, and cutting the money spent on defence and welfare. In Germany in 1932 a round of compulsory cuts was imposed on public salaries, on rents and on pensions. Finally, many of those who advocated more radical economic policies came from the political extremes, right and left, and were distrusted not only by governments but also by the moderate trade-union leadership. Those who still had jobs wanted to keep what they had, and they worried lest economic experiments might make things worse and bring the entire system crashing down.

For all these reasons the impact of the state on the recession was limited. Only by 1932, with unemployment still rising and no prospect of reversing the crisis, was there a general recognition that more needed to be done. There was a pronounced move away from the conventional view that under capitalism markets are self-regulating. In its place came a chorus of voices calling for an international political solution [**Doc. 25**]. This meant, in effect, a reversal of the drift towards protectionism and economic isolation, and an increase in collaboration between the major economies to solve their common problems through planning and regulation. This was easier said than done. There was some cooperation forced by circumstances. The major powers agreed to a moratorium on debt payments in 1931, and at Lausanne in July 1932 it was agreed to let Germany postpone reparations payments until its economy was in better shape. But beyond that the goodwill was lacking. Each state took the view that the chief priority was its own economic revival and social stability, and none was willing to take the first decisive steps away from economic nationalism in case the others failed to follow.

The lack of any firm leadership in the world economy created a vicious circle. Initiatives taken by one state to help its own economy were generally damaging to the interests of other states, which prompted retaliation in kind and a further reduction in prospects for economic cooperation. American tariffs in 1930 provoked French, British and German protectionism; British devaluation of the pound in 1931 (designed to make British goods more competitive abroad) was followed by competitive devaluation from the United States in 1933. Measures to help farmers in Germany penalized the food exporters in Denmark and the Netherlands; and so on. The gulf that existed between the crisis-ridden nations was publicly displayed when, at Britain's rather grudging instigation, a World Economic Conference was called in London in June 1933. It assembled in the Natural History Museum in Kensington, where, amidst the dinosaurs and butterflies, delegates debated the merits of tariff reduction, debt rescheduling and currency stabilization. There was little genuine common ground. When Roosevelt let it be known that he would not allow the United States to be party to any fixed currency system, the conference broke up after only three weeks. Even before Roosevelt's intervention it was clear that no programme could be devised binding on all parties, which could reconcile national differences and widely divergent economic interests. From 1933 to the outbreak of war in 1939, economic nationalism remained in the saddle (Clavin, 1991).

Each of the major states pursued its own recovery programme. They shared a number of common features. In the first place came an increase in direct state intervention and planning, even in countries with a strong liberal, anti-government tradition. In the United States, **President Franklin Roosevelt**, elected in 1932 on his promise to reverse the recession, introduced into Congress a package of economic and welfare measures which became known collectively as the **New Deal**. New legislation was introduced to stabilize the American banking system and capital market in order to avoid another speculative bubble. Agriculture was given special state assistance through subsidized price increases, marketing agreements and state regulation of rural credit. Industry was boosted by a huge programme of public works authorized under the National Industrial Recovery Act (1933) and operated by the Public Works Administration. By the end of the decade over $10 billion had been expended, including funds for the construction of 122,000 public buildings, 664,000 miles of new road, 77,000 bridges and 285 airports. Finally, legislation was introduced to improve labour conditions and to fix minimum wages with the aim of pushing out what Roosevelt called 'the frontiers of social progress' (Badger, 1989).

In Britain nothing quite as spectacular as the New Deal was introduced, but the government from 1931 onwards accepted the responsibility for stimulating credit, developing public works, supporting and regulating agriculture, and interfering in industries such as steel or cotton, which were badly in need of rationalization. In Germany, on the other hand, the almost complete collapse of the private economy by 1932 necessitated more radical steps. A limited public works programme was started in 1932, but when Hitler came to power in 1933, the state undertook a more thorough programme of reform and recovery. The banking and financial system was brought under close state supervision; agriculture was reorganized in the so-called **Reich Food Estate**, which permitted higher food prices and encouraged greater rural investment and the rationalization of farming methods. Taxes and debt repayments for farmers were reduced. State schemes for public works were initiated, targeted initially at infrastructure investment (roads, bridges, public buildings, canals); large funds were secretly made available

Roosevelt, Franklin Delano (1882–1945): A prominent Democrat politician who served under Woodrow Wilson as Assistant Secretary for the Navy in the First World War. After struggling against polio in the 1920s, he became first Governor of New York State in 1928 and four years later was elected US President. He held the office for an unprecedented four terms, and played an important role in holding together the wartime Grand Alliance with Britain and the USSR.

New Deal: General term to describe the package of reform measures introduced by American president Franklin Roosevelt in 1933/4 to cope with the impact of the economic recession.

Reich Food Estate: National organization for agriculture and food production set up in Germany in 1933 under Walther Darré.

for rearmament and the industries vital for war. Direct subsidies and tax concessions were granted for housebuilding and house repair, and for the motor car and furniture industries. Prices and wages were pegged by law to avoid inflation, and the government ran modest deficits which were designed to be repaid out of future tax income. In the years 1933 to 1936 public investment in Germany totalled 21 billion marks, almost half of all investment. In 1936 the government took a further step towards a state-managed economy with the introduction of a **Four-Year Plan** in October, the purpose of which was to prepare the German economy and armed forces for war. The call for military goods and industrial capacity for future warfare resulted in state regulation, even state ownership of industry, in order to divert economic activity away from consumer goods and exports. By the time of the war, the German state owned more than 500 companies. In Italy, the state-backed **Institute for Industrial Reconstruction** controlled 80 per cent of naval shipbuilding, 77 per cent of the iron and steel industry and 50 per cent of armaments production (James, 1986; Overy, 1994).

The second feature was the worldwide adoption of trade protection and currency control. In order to safeguard the fragile recovery after 1932 most states set up high tariff walls to keep out foreign products. The flow of capital abroad was limited or outlawed, and the strength of the currency and the balance of payments carefully monitored and regulated by the state. The 1934 **Johnson Act** in the United States prohibited the export of capital to any state that had defaulted on its war debts or commercial obligations, leaving Finland as the only honest broker still entitled to American loans. The flow of investment from London into the world economy was reduced to a trickle. Instead, investors put money into their own economies, while governments set up closed trading blocs to protect markets at the expense of other traders. Britain and France traded more with their empires, the United States with Latin America. Germany and Japan sought to construct new economic blocs in eastern Europe and in east Asia, partly through economic pressure, partly through the threat or use of force. This trend to 'bloc-building' and trade discrimination gave short-term advantages at the expense of reviving a healthy, fast-growing world market.

The third feature was closely linked with controls over output and trade. A number of states in the 1930s adopted an economic strategy of '**autarky**', or self-sufficiency. Autarky became a fashionable panacea following the shattering of international economic collaboration during the slump. It appealed particularly to fascist states anxious to champion an economic alternative to what they regarded as a defunct system of open, liberal trade. But it was a strategy not confined only to Italy and Germany. It reflected a natural response to a world market whose imperfections made it difficult to obtain access to the materials or equipment which would, under normal

Four-Year Plan: Name given to the planning organization created for Hermann Goering in Germany in October 1936 to prepare the armed forces and the economy for war. It was the second four-year plan following the plan for re-employment and recovery launched in 1933.

Institute for Industrial Reconstruction: Organization set up in Italy in 1933 to direct investment and resources into key areas of production.

Johnson Act: Legislation introduced in the United States in 1934 prohibiting the export of American capital to any state that still owed war debts or commerical debts. Only Finland was exempt from the ban.

Autarky: Term used in the 1930s to describe a policy of economic self-sufficiency at the expense of international trade.

circumstances, have been imported. In France, the state ordered petrol to be diluted with domestically produced alcohol because of problems in obtaining oil from abroad. In Japan, extravagant plans were drawn up for the domestic production of synthetic oil, and popular campaigns were launched to collect scrap metal, in order to reduce Japan's expensive reliance on outside sources of supply. In Italy and France, agricultural production was controlled to reduce luxuries and expand the output of basic foodstuffs, such as wheat. In Germany, the mentality of the protected siege-economy sprang from Germany's harsh experiences during the 1920s and the slump. A whole range of substitute goods was developed – synthetic oil (produced from lignite, or brown coal), synthetic rubber, synthetic textiles (which had a tendency to disintegrate after a few weeks' wear) – all of which could be produced from domestic resources. Germans were encouraged to save their household refuse – tins, paper, cloth – for recycling. Here, too, there were short-term gains for the recovery programme in reduced import bills and increased domestic investment, but at the expense of a lively export trade.

The results of all these recovery programmes were patchy, and the experimental character of many of the remedies did nothing to quell persistent fears that world capitalism was still facing a critical period of transition. Economic revival was most marked in Germany, where unemployment was reduced to almost nothing by 1939, and the peak of industrial production reached in 1929 was exceeded by a third ten years later. Britain recovered steadily over the decade, helped by cheaper import bills and cautious state intervention. But even in Germany there remained serious balance-of-payments difficulties, while in Britain unemployment remained high for the whole decade. Elsewhere achievements were more muted. In the United States there were still 9.5 million unemployed in 1939, and wide areas of rural and working-class poverty remained. The French economy was in almost permanent crisis throughout the 1930s, and revived only in 1939 due to a brief rearmament boom. The Italian economy stagnated; the smaller economies of eastern and central Europe remained financially weak, dependent on barter trade with their wealthier neighbours. Living standards, which had grown steadily in most states in the 1920s, declined, dragged down by surviving levels of unemployment and great pockets of economically deprived workers or subsistence farming. Efforts to reverse the trend through union pressure or strikes met stronger government resistance. In Germany, the Hitler government closed down trade unions on 2 May 1933 and seized their assets; in Italy, the unions were absorbed into Fascist labour corporations. Labour remained in a weak bargaining position everywhere, and business people took advantage of this to keep wages low and to defy union negotiators.

Plate 1 A picture of the German philosopher and historian Oswald Spengler, whose influential book *The Decline of the West*, published in two volumes in 1918/22 became a major reference point for Europeans anxious about the current 'crisis of civilization' in the 1920s.

Source: Mary Evans Picture Library.

Plate 2 A poster issued by the British Eugenics Society in the 1920s highlighting the alleged danger to the population if families suffering from inherited 'mental defect' were allowed to continue having offspring. Some eugenists advocated the use of the 'lethal chamber' to rid society of individuals deemed to be a genetic risk.

Source: © The Galton Institute, London, image L0030836 from the Wellcome Library, London.

Plate 3 Benito Mussolini, the leader of the Italian Fascist Party, [fourth from left] accompanies other Fascist leaders in October 1922 during the 'March on Rome' to seize power. The march was a failure, but Mussolini was appointed prime minister a few days later and turned Italy into a new form of modern dictatorship.

Plate 4 A picture postcard of Hitler promoting one of the National Socialist rallies held at Nuremberg in the 1930s. The annual gathering each autumn was an opportunity to celebrate the 'national revolution' and was a spectacle of enormous power.

Source: Photo by Bob Thomas/ Popperfoto/ Getty Images.

Plate 5 A poster by Gustav Klutsis from 1931 welcomes 'millions of workers' for the new factories being built under the Soviet First Five-Year Plan. Russia was transformed in a matter of years from a largely peasant-based economy to a major industrial power.
Source: Bridgeman Art Library.

Plate 6 The Ford Motor Company assembly line at the plant in Minnesota, USA, 1935. The modern mass-production identified with 'Fordism' drove smaller companies and old-fashioned skills out of business. The motor-car became a symbol of the new age of technical modernity.

Source: © Minnesota Historical Society/ Corbis.

Plate 7 The failure of world capitalism in 1929 produced a long period of economic crisis and high unemployment. Here a group of British workers are seen on the famous 'Jarrow March' of 1936 from the north-east of England to London, to petition parliament for jobs. The Jarrow MP, Ellen Wilkinson, leads the marchers.

Source: © Hulton-Deutsch Collection/ Corbis.

Plate 8 A poster from the Spanish General Workers' Union (UGT) calling on Spanish peasants to support radical politics in the Spanish Civil War (1936–9): 'The revolution is as necessary as the shoots on the vine.' Spain became the battleground between democracy, fascism and communism.

Source: Mary Evans Picture Library.

Plate 9 The cover of a French pamphlet from 1936 supporting a Popular Front against poverty, war and fascism. Fear of war was widespread in much of Europe where it was believed a second world war would destroy what was left of European civilization.

Source: Bridgeman Art Library.

Plate 10 Neville Chamberlain, the British prime minister, arrives at Munich on 29 September 1938 for the conference to decide the fate of Czechoslovakia. To his left is the German foreign minister, Joachim von Ribbentrop. To his far right is the SS leader Reinhard Heydrich who headed the German security police.

Source: Popperfoto/ Getty Images.

THE END OF CAPITALISM?

From the longer perspective of the twentieth century it is clear that capitalism was in a stage of transition in the 1930s, not of terminal decline. The failure to produce a self-balancing international economy in the difficult circumstances of the 1920s accelerated the trend to state intervention and managed trade. In the 1930s it was widely assumed that a new economic order was called for. 'The times of economic liberalism as such are definitely over', announced Hitler's Economics Minister, **Hjalmar Schacht**, in 1934. Fascist governments liked to think that they had a new system that was uniquely fascist, but most of what they practised could be found in the economic armoury of non-fascist states too. Fascism certainly hijacked the economy to serve its ideological ends – military expansion, racial cleansing, a 'classless' society – and fascist regimes generally coerced labour and business unscrupulously to get what they wanted, but the actual instruments of economic control over trade, investment, agriculture and banks were also utilized in the democracies. The larger degree of state regulation, of compulsory marketing arrangements, of controlled trade and managed currencies reflected a general commitment to crisis management by capitalist regimes. The drift to greater *dirigisme*, towards state direction, was a product of economic circumstances. After the slump, business was no longer in a position to set its own house in order. Regulated capitalism, what German economists called the '**managed economy**' (*die gelenkte Wirtschaft*), came to replace the passive state and business freedom.

   The general movement away from the traditions of laissez-faire economics caused deep concern among business communities. The growth of the interventionist state looked to them suspiciously like socialism by the back door. They resisted where they could the nationalization of industry, although the rescue of bankrupt firms in the recession often made this unavoidable. They disliked being told how to invest and where to sell. The example of one of Germany's leading iron and steel barons, Fritz Thyssen, is instructive. In 1933 he was one of the few German entrepreneurs to welcome the advent of Hitler with enthusiasm, in the belief that he would end class conflict. Six years later, prompted by his growing disillusionment with the foreign policy of the regime, Thyssen fled from Germany on the grounds that state control under the Nazis made life there little different from life in Soviet Russia. His industrial fortune was seized by the state, and his businesses taken under public trusteeship. Three years earlier Gustav Krupp, Germany's leading armaments producer, complained to a Swiss banking friend that capitalists in Germany 'were no better off than the natives in Timbuctoo'.

   Business reacted to the changing character of the economy in a number of ways, but in general they had little to offer in the way of a positive alternative

Schacht, Hjalmar (1877–1970): German banker who was chosen to help solve the inflation crisis in Germany in late 1923, then to head the German Central Bank until his resignation in 1929 in protest at reparation payments. In 1933 Hitler appointed him to head the Central Bank again and in 1934 he also became Economics Minister. He helped to supply the finance for German rearmament, but argued with Hitler over its extent and was forced to resign his posts. He was put on trial at Nuremberg but acquitted.

Managed economy: Term used to describe an economy that was not owned by the state but was subject to state regulation and planning to maintain economic equilibrium.

for fighting the recession. Indeed, much of what they did tended to make the economic situation worse rather than better. Many chose to set up defensive trade associations or price-fixing cartels to help resist state encroachments and to restrict output. They were shy of investing in such an unstable environment, and often resistant to new technologies or new production methods. The changed climate of the 1930s made them cautious and conservative. Some business communities reacted to state policies by sending their money abroad to safer havens. The capital flight in France provoked by the plans of the centre-left **Popular Front** government, elected in May 1936, substantially weakened efforts to revive the French economy, as capital flight had weakened Germany in 1931. In the United States business lobbies fought against Roosevelt's social programmes and minimum-wage legislation, and the programmes of state investment, and succeeded in getting a number of New Deal laws declared unconstitutional by the American Supreme Court. Officials in the New Deal agencies were branded as Communists.

Business fears now seem much exaggerated, but it is not difficult to understand how the imagined threat of social revolution after 1917, and the reality of economic disaster after 1929, created a powerful cocktail that nourished fantasies about the end of capitalism. Business felt itself to be embattled in the 1930s, surrounded by hostile, impoverished workers, enthusiastic prophets of a new economic order, and interfering bureaucrats. In practice, most states wanted to pursue the same aim as the business community to find a route back to prosperity and social peace. But in the 1930s the growth of political extremism and military confrontation made that route difficult to follow, encouraging a persistent sense of capitalist crisis, and the involuntary retreat of old-fashioned capitalism.

Popular Front: Term used in 1935 to describe a political alliance between progressive political forces to combat the threat of Fascism. Usually applied to the alliance of social democrats and Communists in France and Spain in the mid-1930s.

6

Democracy and Dictatorship

THE DECLINE OF DEMOCRACY

At the end of the First World War, when the victorious Allies remade Europe under the heady slogans of '**self-determination**' and 'international justice', the age of democracy seemed about to dawn. Here was the high tide of nineteenth-century liberalism, the belief that all states were progressing on more or less uniform lines towards popular parliamentary politics, the rule of law and civil rights. In 1920 almost all of Europe was democratic. Twenty years later, on the eve of the Second World War, most European states were dictatorships, dominated by the authoritarian rule of a single man and a single party. Democracy was in retreat in its turn, confined to Britain, France and the smaller states of northern Europe. Outside Europe only the United States and Britain's settler dominions remained democracies. This apparent decline of political progress sustained a sense of crisis throughout the inter-war years.

The course of democratic reverses must first be briefly outlined. There was no uniform path to dictatorship and no standard pattern of authoritarian rule. Dictatorship was not just a right-wing phenomenon. The first democratic casualty was the brief moment of political freedom in Russia in the transition from Tsarist rule to the 'dictatorship of the proletariat'. The Russian people exercised their democratic voice in the winter of 1917/18 in elections to the Constituent Assembly called to decide the nature of the new state. The assembly was scrapped the day it first met by the minority ruling group, the Bolsheviks, who won only 25 per cent of the seats. Although Bolshevik leaders liked to call themselves democrats, their concept of democracy was far removed from the western form, with free elections, civil rights for all, and popular accountability. Democracy in the Soviet Union was what Lenin called '**democratic centralism**', which purported to involve a careful assessment of popular views and ideas before the central authority – in this case the Central Committee of the Party – made decisions which were binding on the whole population. Inevitably, the 'centralism' prevailed over the

Self-determination: The right of all nationalities to find expression through the creation of a national state.

Democratic centralism: Concept used to describe the operation of the Bolshevik party in Russia. Decisions were taken by the central authority, but only after 'consultation' with the voice of the people. In practice the centralism always triumphed over the democratic principle.

'democracy'. Opposition groups were forcibly suppressed and elections consisted of voting for one candidate from one party. When Stalin became General Secretary of the Communist Party in 1922 the groundwork was slowly laid for a system based not on the rule of one party, but of one person. By the mid-1930s Stalin had ousted from the party any remaining opponents to his style of leadership, and imposed a brutal dictatorship in which his word was effectively law even though, in 1937, the new Soviet constitution claimed to make the Soviet Union the most democratic state in the world. In the rest of Europe the shift to authoritarian rule was a move to the political right, either to fascist or quasi-fascist regimes dominated by a popular civilian dictator, or back to more traditional conservative rule based on the military or on royalist circles. The first major state to take this path was Italy. In October 1922 the leader of the anti-democratic Italian Fascist Party, Mussolini, was appointed prime minister. The appointment did not create the dictatorship straightaway. There followed a period of four years in which the Fascists gradually increased their representation in the Italian parliament and in local government, and bullied and persecuted their political enemies. Not until 1926 did the movement feel confident enough to impose a one-party state, and then only in cooperation with the King, the Church and the army. Not until the 1930s did Mussolini, like Stalin, come to dominate his own party and exercise virtual one-man rule, until he was kicked out by the army in 1943 following Italy's military failure in the war.

Primo de Rivera, Miguel (1870–1930): Spanish general who took over power in Spain in 1923. He established a dicta-torship but alienated his army supporters and was forced out of office in 1930.

In 1923 Spain followed suit. On 13 September **General Miguel Primo de Rivera** seized power from a weak parliamentary regime elected in 1918. He appointed a National Assembly made up of his nominees, and ruled as dictator, supported by the military, the wealthy elites and sections of the working-class movement hostile to the more radical Communist and anarchist elements. In 1931 Primo was in turn overthrown and a new parliamentary republic established. But in 1936 the republic broke down in civil war, and by 1939 another general, Francisco Franco, had become Spain's supreme authority, the *caudillo*, or leader. The military also came to power in Poland. In 1926 Marshal Pilsudski, who was head of the democratically elected government, declared a *coup d'état* and established a military dictatorship run by what was called the 'Colonels' Group'. Although parliament remained in existence, opponents of the military were imprisoned and tortured, and real authority lay in the soldiers' hands. In 1935 Pilsudski died and was succeeded by Marshal Smigly-Ridz. A new constitution was drawn up allow-ing only pro-government candidates to stand at elections, and in 1937 a 'National Unity Movement' was set up, turning Poland into a virtual one-party state under military domination.

Post-war democracy survived for much longer in Germany. Not until the recession did the anti-democratic forces in German political life become a serious political threat. By 1932 popular confidence in the parliamentary regime was at a low ebb. The National Socialists, violently anti-democratic but profiting from the democratic process, became the largest party, although far short of an overall majority in parliament. Like Mussolini or Primo de Rivera, Hitler came to power in 1933 through the support of the conservative elite of generals and landowners who agreed to share power with him in a national government. During the course of 1933 the Nazis destroyed the power-sharing arrangement, against a background of violence and intimidation directed by the party at anyone, right or left, who stood in the way of the new dictatorship. In August 1934, on the death of the President elected in 1925, **Field Marshal Paul von Hindenburg**, Hitler fused the jobs of chancellor and president into one and became formally the German Führer, or Leader. The other political parties were abolished in 1933 and the German parliament was peopled with Nazi yes-men. On 30 June 1934 Hitler bloodily suppressed opponents in his own party on the so-called **Night of the Long Knives**, when **Ernst Röhm** (head of the paramilitary wing of the party, the **SA**) and many of his associates were murdered. In 1936 Heinrich Himmler, head of Hitler's personal security guard, the **SS**, assumed leadership of all the police and security forces in Germany and, with Hitler's blessing, established a vast apparatus of terror and repression. By this stage the Nazi dictatorship was firmly entrenched.

Elsewhere in Europe the fragile democratic experiments toppled one by one. The Baltic states produced single-party, anti-Communist dictatorships dominated by the army and the big landowners. In Lithuania, Antanas Smetona seized power in a coup in 1926; in Latvia, Konstantin Ulmanis established a dictatorship in May 1934; and in Estonia a coup in 1935 resulted in a new constitution the following year, which endorsed single-party rule under the so-called 'Eldest of the State', Constantin Paets. In Portugal, a republic since 1910, the weak parliamentary regime was overthrown in 1926, and in 1932 **Antonio de Salazar** became prime minister and dictator. His *Uniao Nacional* (National Union) was declared the only party, and the National Assembly was filled with government candidates. Salazar developed a state organized on 'corporatist' lines on the pattern of Fascist Italy. In Hungary the old aristocracy and the armed forces continued to dominate the state after the collapse of the Habsburg monarchy. Power was seized in 1919 by Admiral Horthy, who declared himself Regent, pending the restoration of the monarchy. Parliament was run by the government-controlled National Union Party, in alliance with small peasant and Christian parties. In the other half of the old Habsburg Empire, Austria, a democratic republic survived until 1934, when it was subverted by a right-wing alliance of political Catholicism and fascism under **Chancellor Engelbert Dollfuss**. For the next four years Austria remained an authoritarian regime until it was

Hindenburg, Paul von (1847–1934): German soldier who fought in the Franco-German War of 1870 as a young officer and became by the First World War one of a coterie of senior officers who dominated the German war effort. In 1916 he became commander-in-chief of the German armies. In 1925 he was elected President, a position which he used to encourage a revival of German nationalism. He agreed to make Hitler Chancellor in January 1933.

Night of the Long Knives: The night of 30 June 1934 when the SS at Hitler's order murdered the leaders of the paramilitary SA (including Ernst Röhm) and a number of other political opponents.

Röhm, Ernst (1887–1934): A German soldier who became prominent in radical nationalist circles in the early 1920s before joining the Hitler movement. He was made chief-of-staff of the *SA* in 1931 and murdered on 1 July 1934 on the 'Night of the Long Knives' for allegedly plotting to overthrow Hitler.

SA: The 'Sturmabteilung' were the shock troops of the NSDAP. Founded in 1922, the SA grew to be more than 2 million men by 1934. Their role was to fight the enemies of the movement. During the 1920s they murdered hundreds of political enemies.

absorbed into Hitler's Reich in March 1938 in the ***Anschluss***, or union, of the two German-speaking states.

The situation in the Balkans was the most incoherent. Conflict between popular left-wing forces, the old elites, nationalist radicals and fascists, produced a merry-go-round of regimes and political forms. In Greece, a democratic republic introduced in 1923 witnessed a long period of political instability which ended in 1935 with the restoration of the monarchy and a year later the appointment of General Metaxas as premier for life and virtual dictator. The political parties were abolished and Greece was ruled by its soldiers. In Bulgaria, the political system, which was nominally a constitutional monarchy, was dominated in the early 1920s by a radical peasant party under Alexander Stambolisky. A military coup in 1923 ushered in a period of violent crisis, which was finally resolved in favour of parliamentary democracy in 1926. But the revival of the left that this permitted was stamped out again in 1933 when the military seized power once more and suspended the constitution; then, two years later, the King himself, Tsar Boris, carried out a further coup which established a royal dictatorship. In Romania, also a constitutional monarchy, parliamentary politics were dominated in the 1920s by the People's Party, a broad centre-left movement. The emergence of mass right-wing parties reversed this situation after 1927, but it proved difficult to maintain stable parliamentary rule. Elections were manipulated and majorities engineered. In 1938 King Carol declared a royal dictatorship, and abolished all political parties except his own creature, the government of 'national concentration'. This in turn was overthrown by a pro-fascist coup led by **Marshal Ion Antonescu** in 1941.

Of the new states created out of the collapse of the old European empires only Czechoslovakia remained democratic. Even here it was difficult to make the parliamentary system work. There were sixteen political parties in the first elections, held in 1920, and there were still fourteen of these left in the elections in 1935. Of these parties, fascists and Communists polled 12 per cent, and nationalist opposition parties, representing the national minorities of Germans, Hungarians, Poles and Slovaks, took a further 31 per cent. The government relied on a solid bloc of left and centre parties recruited from native Czechs to stay in power. In Yugoslavia, democracy survived on the same fragile basis, with the large number of parties reflecting the ethnic and religious diversity of the country. The political system in the 1920s was dominated by the major Serb parties, and violent conflict between Croats and Serbs developed over the imbalance of ethnic influence. When, in November 1928, the leader of the Croat Peasant Party, Stjepan Radic, was murdered in the parliament building by a Serbian deputy, **King Alexander I**, backed by the military, declared a dictatorship. Although his successor in 1934, Prince Paul, adopted a less authoritarian style, Yugoslavian politics remained only nominally democratic, and in practice the Serbian dynasty and the Serbian army exercised control. Only in 1939, in the face of growing threats from Italy and Germany, did the regime make concessions to the smaller nationalities in order to rally the population to the defence of south Slav interests, as the Serbs had done before in 1914.

Outside Europe democracy made little progress, not least because the European imperial powers, even democratic ones like Britain and France, were unwilling to concede democracy to the overseas territories that they governed. In Turkey, the collapse of the Ottoman Empire was followed by a new military-backed dictatorship under the widely popular **Kemal Ataturk**, whose People's Party was the only political movement permitted. In China, the overthrow of the Manchu Emperor in 1911 ushered in a long period of political confusion, which ended in the 1920s with the consolidation of most of China under the dictatorship of **General Chiang Kai-shek**, who headed the only legally permitted party, the Kuomintang. In Japan, the imperial system became a parliamentary democracy in the 1920s under the new emperor, Hirohito, who came to the throne in 1926. But here, too, the effects of the slump produced a powerful nationalist reaction, and in the 1930s government was dominated by the armed forces, while democrats were intimidated and murdered in a wave of patriotic violence generated by quasi-fascist movements hostile to parliament and westernization. Throughout Asia and Latin America democracy was associated with the aspirations of the rural and urban poor, and it was either suppressed, or manipulated through popular nationalist movements which masked the reality of authoritarian rule.

Alexander 1 (of Yugoslavia) (1888–1934): Succeeded to the Yugoslavian throne in 1921, and played an important part in subverting federal democracy from 1929. He was assassinated at Marseilles in 1934.

Ataturk, Kemal (1881–1938): Turkish soldier who after the First World War played a leading part in transforming the former Ottoman Empire into the modern Turkish state. He became Turkish President in 1920 and suppressed both Communism and Islamic fundamentalism.

Chiang Kai-shek (1887–1975): Chinese army officer who rose to power in China in the 1920s and fought a long civil war against Chinese Communists and native warlords. He led Chinese resistance to Japanese invasion in the 1930s and 1940s but was defeated by Communist insurgents in 1949 and retired to the island of Taiwan which he ruled until his death.

THE APPEAL OF DICTATORSHIP

There is no simple answer to the question of why dictatorship came to supplant democracy. There were, of course, features peculiar to each country. The sheer diversity of political experience in the inter-war years has discouraged the search for more general explanations. Yet even making allowance for particular circumstances there are clearly general factors at work which help to explain the emergence and survival of the phenomenon of modern dictatorship, and the crisis of liberal democracy that resulted.

In the first place, there developed in the 1920s a strong anti-democratic movement in Europe, which united both left and right in opposition to liberal parliamentary politics. Liberal democrats, then and since, have been prey to the assumption that with the breakdown of the old monarchical order in 1918, democracy ought to have been in some sense the natural successor. This is a historical assumption that should not be taken for granted. Parliament was regarded by a great many as simply a front for the power of the upper and middle classes. Democracy was for Lenin merely a 'bourgeois sham', a system that pretended political freedom but which left power in the hands of a capitalist elite [Doc. 26]. European parliaments before 1914 had a mixed reputation. The German **Reichstag** had, in practice, very little power under the old empire, and was looked upon as an instrument for manipulating the political masses in the interests of the political ruling class. The Italian parliament was notoriously corrupt and narrowly based. The pre-war Russian parliament, the Duma, and the Habsburg assemblies, were little more than talking shops, dominated by the interests of the crown.

Liberal politics were not regarded with much favour either. Part of the intellectual appeal of fascism can be traced to the insistence of fascist writers that parliament represented stuffy, establishment politics, and wishy-washy compromises. Hitler regarded the bourgeoisie as 'contemptible' for their self-interested trimming politics and endless party squabbles. Rule by committee and discussion looked singularly inappropriate to deal with the vivid issues of social revolution and national struggle. A generation of European thinkers rejected the 'outworn epoch of liberalism' and embraced what Mussolini called 'the politics of action'. The German writer **Ernst Jünger** argued that the eruption of mass politics did not necessarily mean the triumph of liberal parliamentary politics: 'the people may also decide against democracy' (Kolnai, 1938). Throughout the inter-war years there were intellectual movements all over Europe prosecuting the idea that some kind of political '**New Order**', based on authoritarian rule, and active, decisive government should supplant parliamentarianism. It was argued that dictatorship was better equipped to represent the whole nation.

The 'New Order' ideas were by no means confined to Italy and Germany, where fascism came to power. Even in Britain and France, homelands of modern democracy, there were elements hostile to the values of parliamentary rule. In France, quasi-fascist political leagues brought down the government after a night of violent rioting on 6 February 1934 [Doc. 27]. A galaxy of small movements and associations sprang up calling on Frenchmen to transcend the narrow limitations of the republican order. In 1933 the writer Robert Aron founded the journal *L'ordre nouveau*, which was committed to exposing the drawbacks of modern capitalism and democracy, and endorsed a radical rethink about the nature of modern authority. 'New Order' intellectuals were much influenced by fashionable ideas on personality and charisma, derived from a misreading of Nietzsche's idea of the 'superman' as a political phenomenon. They argued that old-fashioned elites, based on education and wealth, were destined to give way to a new elite of powerful

Reichstag: German parliament, established with the founding of the German Empire in 1871.

Jünger, Ernst (1895–1998): German soldier in the First World War who became a leading radical nationalist writer in the 1920s. Most famous for his depiction of war in *Storm of Steel* (1921), he was hostile to Hitler and lived a long life after 1945 as a conservative philosopher and writer.

New Order: Term widely used in the 1930s to describe a politics of national rebirth. Usually used to describe the political system set up in Europe under German occupation.

characters, forged from the struggle of life, who would rise to the top through sheer will-power and force of personality. Paradoxically, they also rejected liberal individualism, and urged that the masses should follow the new style of leader in strict obedience, submerging themselves entirely in the new collectivist system and in loyalty to its extraordinary leader. This conception of the New Order became known by the term '**totalitarian**', first coined in Italy in the 1920s to describe the aspirations of the Italian Fascist Party. The original meaning of the term has been distorted through current usage to apply to any authoritarian regime. Mussolini had something rather more specific in mind. Under a totalitarian regime the whole population would be embraced by the system, which would organize both public and private life in their 'totality', and merge the interests of the individual completely with those of the state or the nation. An almost mystical bond of allegiance was supposed to bind the masses to the charismatic leader [**Doc. 28**].

Totalitarianism: Political concept first coined in the early 1920s to describe the aspirations of the Italian Fascist Party to control the totality of society. More commonly misused to describe authoritarian systems with a 'total' control over the population.

The ideas of 'New Order' or 'totalitarian state' were not unattractive to those who felt themselves to be the victims of weak parliamentary rule, or of economic crisis sustained by the failures of liberal capitalism. These failures were seen as essentially 'western' in origin, and were blamed on the self-interest of the major liberal states, Britain, France and the United States. In Germany, the Soviet Union or Japan, liberal democracy was rejected by its critics as an alien system, imposed from without to further the economic interests and cultural imperialism of westerners and internationalists. The enemies of western democracy emphasized forms of the state which they regarded as more appropriate to the conditions and cultural heritage of their society. Hostility to democracy was closely linked to the general spread of ideological politics in the inter-war years, with its sharp rejection of the idea of a single, western path of development.

The second explanation concerns the nature of the state. Many of the new states created at the end of the Great War faced very great difficulties in providing a stable alternative to the collapsed dynastic system. Even in monarchist states that survived – Italy, Portugal and Spain – the old conservative order was in full retreat by the 1920s. The traditional ruling class was much reduced as a force in national politics. The traditional institutions of state either withered away or were eliminated. The hierarchical social structure, for all the strains it was showing before 1914, had acted as a source of social stabilization and political allegiance. The new states had to fill this vacuum as best they could. They had to build new public institutions and a new state apparatus. They had to create new forms of allegiance to replace those based on dynastic loyalty and social deference. They had to establish their legitimacy in the eyes of the population.

This task of state-building was made all the more difficult because it came at a time of social unrest and revolutionary threat, and against a background of economic crisis. The post-war inflations hit the new states of eastern Europe more severely than elsewhere. Financial stability was generally seen as one of the primary responsibilities of the state. The failure to save the currency in Germany, Austria, Poland, Hungary and elsewhere was seen as a kind of moral lapse on the part of the state and highlighted its fragile and immature character. The new states also had to cope with developing a popular civic culture – respect for the rule of law, local self-government, freedom of expression and association, the popular defence of civil rights – which was commonplace in Britain or France, but was largely absent in much of the rest of Europe. In the old Tsarist Empire, or the new Balkan states, or Spain and Portugal, the concept of the 'citizen', enjoying civil rights and vigilant in their defence, was poorly developed, or absent altogether. Habits of obedience were traditionally enforced by the local elites or by the state. When these disappeared, as in Russia, or were placed under threat from the rise of mass politics, as in Spain or Italy in the early 1920s, the willingness or ability of populations to generate their own modern civil life to underpin liberal democracy was restricted to the educated classes in the cities and small sections of the moderate working-class movement. In Russia and eastern Europe much of the population, faced with the collapse of royal power, fell back on the age-old village community as a source of identity and social cohesion. In the poorer rural areas of Spain the population adopted anarchism and rejected the modern state altogether. In the cities, populations, cut off from their rural roots, were divided between allegiance to the socialist myth of New Jerusalem and an exaggerated, passionate nationalism.

The problems of modern state-building exposed a more fundamental failure of consensus. In Britain or the United States there existed, despite party political differences, a broad agreement about the character of the political system and the socio-economic structure, which was based on respect for property, the rule of law and representative democracy. But in the new democracies, where mass politics was often experienced for the first time, there existed no liberal consensus. Instead, the right to vote exposed very deep social divisions and very different conceptions about the nature of the new society. These conflicts owed a great deal to the revolutionary years at the end of the Great War. Democratic politics was seen by many of Europe's educated or propertied classes as simply a stepping stone to the rule of the proletariat or the rural poor, and they preferred, and in a great many cases got, authoritarian governments hostile to the left [**Doc. 29**]. The exception was the Soviet Union. Here, too, there was no liberal consensus, although there was popular support for some kind of democracy. The forces arguing for social order and defence of property were too small and socially isolated after 1917 to create an authoritarian government of the right, although that is what they would have liked. Instead, the weakness of the new state, the social fragmentation, the under-developed civic life, were all exploited by an authoritarian movement of the Communist left, which established a dictatorship every bit as thorough as those of the right.

The failure of consensus was also reflected in the multiplicity of weak political parties thrown up by the arrival of democracy. Rather than representing the interests of broad integrated sections of the community, the new parties tended to be single-interest parties, narrowly based, with poor finances and little experience of the practices of parliamentary politics. They bore little resemblance to the broad-based, historically rooted parties of the British and American systems – Tories and Whigs, Democrats and Republicans. The fragmentation of political allegiance in the new states owed a great deal to the claims of regional or local identity. Like the Irish in the British Parliament in the nineteenth century, regions with a strong sense of their own identity produced political parties with powerful separatist aims. The Basques and Catalans in Spain, the **Sudeten Germans** in Czechoslovakia, Hungarians in Transylvania, Ukrainians in the Soviet Union, Bavarians in Germany, were only a few of the many groups representing a clear regional interest. Localism was also evident in the voting habits of much of central and southern Europe. Small splinter parties backed by peasant or artisan groups were spawned in particular provinces or cities.

The result of this democratic decentralization was a weak parliamentary system, based on constantly shifting coalitions. This situation reduced still further the appeal of democracy and confirmed the wisdom of those who argued for centralist, dictatorial governments. In Germany in the 1920s no party ever obtained an overall majority under the system of proportional representation adopted in the Weimar constitution. Governments were formed from a bloc of either centre-left or centre-right parties. By 1928 there were fourteen separate parties in the Reichstag, not counting the tiny splinter parties. In Bulgaria there were at least nine parties; in Czechoslovakia fourteen; in Poland, eight (not counting all the small parties from the national minorities); in Portugal, twelve; in Spain under the Republic there were seven major parties, a whole range of small right-wing parties, and the anarchists, who refused to participate in elections until 1936; in Yugoslavia, ten. Under such conditions it proved very difficult to develop parliamentary governments that were strong enough on their own to make the democratic system work. Opposition was difficult to cope with too, for much of it was hostile to the very system it participated in and had little vested interest in its survival. The result, in many cases, was declining confidence in parliament as an institution, and the pursuit of political alternatives to democracy (Jones, 1988; Luebbert, 1991).

Sudeten Germans: German-speaking inhabitants of northern Bohemia, former subjects of the Habsburg Empire who formed a hostile minority in the post-1919 Czechoslovak state until they were incorporated into Germany in October 1938.

THE 'NEW ORDER' IN POLITICS

The answer to the weaknesses and divisions of democratic politics was a new style of popular politics altogether, what one historian has called 'the politics of commitment'. Mussolini's Fascists or Hitler's National Socialists, even Lenin's Bolsheviks, offered a form of political life radically distinct from the conventional democratic party. Though they were formally called a 'party', none of them was committed to a narrow parliamentary role and the task of organizing and fighting elections. Hitler preferred to call his party a 'movement' (*Bewegung*). Like Fascism or Soviet Communism, National Socialism offered something much more than paying party dues and turning out on polling day. The movement dominated the lives of its members, calling from them a strong sense of loyalty, and offering in return a clear sense of identity and belonging. Each movement was dominated in turn by a powerful, charismatic figurehead to whom the rank and file owed strict obedience. The movements were far from democratic in their organization, reproducing in their authoritarian, centralized structures the kind of wider political system that they favoured. Each movement sustained its own ideology, which was binding on its members. Whether the ideology was of proletarian dictatorship or national revival or racial regeneration, it was typically exclusive. Those who did not belong were by definition enemies – of the revolution, of the nation, of the race – and deserved persecution. This kind of mass politics played on collective prejudice, and permitted extravagant, violent revenge (Getty, 1985; Overy, 2004).

The movements also operated quite differently from the ordinary democratic party. They were organized around the exaltation of the central leader, whose word was, in effect, law. The leader as prophet or lawgiver helped to reduce conflicts within the party over aims, and acted as a rallying point in the absence of more rational grounds for association. In Germany the 'myth of the Führer', which was developed by the movement's propagandists, created the image of Hitler as a man of destiny, capable of transcending the weaknesses of the democratic world and performing miracles of national rejuvenation. In Italy, 'Mussolini is always right' was publicly proclaimed from hoardings and newspapers. Stalin was lionized by the propaganda of the 1930s as the saviour of Lenin's revolution and the source of all wisdom and salvation (Kershaw, 1987; Melograni, 1976). These images were sustained by the mass media, spread by party journals and endless party rallies and displays. The new political movements were much more *visible* than the old parliamentary parties. Their members wore distinctive uniforms and insignia. They placed great emphasis on maintaining a high public profile, and enthusing and engaging the political public. Each had its paramilitary organization, its youth wing, its women's organization. What they provided was a new set of rituals and public displays to replace the glossy royalist regimes [**Doc. 30**]. The appeal of the movements owed a great deal to these efforts to generate a new sense of allegiance, of binding together, which parliamentary politics conspicuously failed to provide. They were movements that succeeded in appealing across the divide of social class and regional loyalty.

Whatever liberals thought of the appeal to crude emotion, the authoritarian, ideologically fired movements were undoubtedly popular. As a manifestation of mass politics they differed in radical ways from liberal democracy, but they were, nonetheless, a product of genuine mass enthusiasm. Of course, even these new mass movements won only a fraction of the popular vote – the Communists achieved 29 per cent in Russia in 1918, Hitler won 37 per cent in July 1932 – but this fraction gave each a sufficient mass base to achieve and consolidate power. The dictatorships were not simply the fruit of ruling-class intrigue, but were the product of a populist revolt from below. The success of dictatorship as a political form in the inter-war years cannot be understood without acknowledging its debt to popular rejection of liberal democracy in favour of authoritarian, mass-based regimes promising social order, economic revival and a strong state. The yearning for a 'Bonapartist' solution was a symptom of the sheer difficulty of creating a workable political system at a time of acute economic crisis and social tension. Dictatorship was accepted as a form of crisis management that offered better prospects for success than limp-wristed democracy.

The new dictatorships also rested on coercion. Because in most cases they were supported by only part of the community, their survival depended to a considerable extent on their willingness and ability to reduce or neutralize the opposition. Here again there was a striking contrast with the pre-war period. The old dynastic states certainly faced opposition, but it was either contained within the (generally powerless) parliament, or subject to limited forms of police harassment and censorship. The post-war dictatorships faced the hostility of rival mass movements which rejected their rule entirely and fought bitterly against the ideological enemy. The violent character of the confrontations this produced – the Russian Civil War, the Spanish Civil War, the German and Soviet terror in the 1930s – bred further violence. Once in power, the new authorities developed the trappings of modern terror which eclipsed anything generated by the old pre-war regimes. Beside the formal banning of other parties, or the censorship practised on a wide scale in all areas of political and cultural life, or the denial of free speech and freedom of association, there developed the inhuman instruments of repression – the secret police, the torturers, the concentration camps.

One of the first acts of the new Bolshevik government in December 1917 was to set up a secret state police force. It grew into the notorious **Cheka**

Cheka: The so-called Extraordinary Commission set up by the Bolshevik revolutionary government in November 1917 to combat all political enemies of the regime. It operated as a political police force until superseded by the GPU (State Political Directorate) in 1922.

Russian Civil War: Conflict between the Bolshevik-controlled 'Red Army' and counter-revolutionary, nationalist and anarchist forces in Russia from 1918–21.

(Extraordinary Commission), responsible for executing or murdering up to 250,000 enemies of the revolution during the **Russian Civil War**. In 1922 it was renamed the GPU, or State Political Administration, but in whatever guise, the state security apparatus hunted down political opponents real or imagined, tortured, imprisoned or executed them, usually on the basis of forced confessions and manipulated evidence. In the mid-1930s Stalin turned the apparatus even against Communist Party members who were accused of a range of crimes, from spying to corruption and sabotage. Between 1930 and 1953 state security executed around 770,000 people. The nature of these allegedly political crimes was dictated from the centre. There was seldom any opportunity to appeal, and in most cases there was only a sham judicial procedure (Getty and Manning, 1993).

OVRA: Italian political police organization established in 1927 to combat the enemies of Fascism at home and abroad.

In Italy, Mussolini set up a Fascist secret police, the **OVRA**, responsible for the secret war against the opposition to Fascism. His political opponents were exiled or imprisoned in special camps. Local opponents of Fascism were routinely humiliated by beatings or a dreaded purging with castor oil. Hitler's Germany rivalled Stalin's Russia. As soon as Hitler came to power, the SA and SS paramilitary arm of the party set up small unofficial concentration camps for political opponents. Here prisoners were tortured, humiliated and sometimes murdered. In April 1933 a new Secret State Police Office was established in Berlin. Its officials, known as the **Gestapo**, or Secret State Police, were given extraordinary powers of arrest and detention. During 1933 and 1934 the party camps were closed down and state concentration camps set up under the control of **Heinrich Himmler**, who in 1936 became chief of all the German police and security organs, including the Gestapo. Political opponents of the regime had no appeal, in most cases no trial. The camp system was lethal in the extreme. Out of an estimated 1.6 million prisoners who entered the camps at some point during the dictatorship, as many as 1.1 million are thought to have perished.

Gestapo: Secret State Police set up in Prussia in April 1933 to combat resistance to the Hitler regime, and the heart of the security police organization later set up in 1936 under Heinrich Himmler. The head of the Gestapo from 1935 to 1945 was a career policeman, Heinrich Müller.

Himmler, Heinrich (1901–1945): Fanatical member of the German National Socialists in the 1920s, he was appointed head of the SS in 1929, and police chief in Bavaria when Hitler came to power. In 1936 he took over the whole police and security network and ran the concentration camps. He organized the genocide of the European Jews and committed suicide when captured in 1945.

There can be little doubt that the willingness of dictatorships to embrace the new instruments of violent control and illegal terror, and to use them against millions of their subjects, helps to explain the survival and spread of this particular form of authority. But it also contributed to a deepening sense of political crisis and moral decline. The evident readiness of the new political movements to use violence to help them achieve power and hold on to it infused inter-war politics with a spirit of vengeance and destructiveness. The tactics of the bandit and the bully were consciously adapted to the conduct of public affairs. Liberals and democrats bewailed the collapse of political morality and the rise of criminals to power on the back of crude propaganda and violent repression. The brutal reality of dictatorship, and its specious defence by a generation of excitable, disillusioned intellectuals, was flung like a gauntlet in the face of liberal progress.

It is sometimes argued that the post-war political crisis and the rise of dictatorship was part of a broader crisis of the western capitalist system, which reacted against the shock of revolutionary socialism by embracing a radical authoritarianism of the right. There are certainly strong arguments in favour of this view in the case of Germany and Italy, where economic crisis and social conflict threatened the existing order with collapse. But the argument fails to account for the survival of democracy in the three leading capitalist states, Britain, France and the United States, and for the rise of dictatorial Communism in the Soviet Union, and later in China and eastern Europe. Indeed, capitalism hardly appears to be the issue. Britain and France survived as democracies because they had parliamentary systems that went back for well over a century or more, a strong tradition of local self-government and civic responsibility, and relatively strong and adaptable state structures and social elites. Despite the rise of socialism and the severe consequences of the slump, both societies retained a sufficient commitment to liberal values and popular participation to avoid giving way to political extremism. Both also enjoyed long periods of relative prosperity, France in the 1920s, Britain in the 1930s.

The crisis of the post-1918 period owed more to the sudden collapse of the old political order and the explosion of mass politics that followed. There was little desire to restore the old systems, but no real agreement on what the new order should look like. Liberal democracy vied for the political high ground with revolutionary socialism and popular, nationalistic authoritarianism. Efforts were made to find some kind of consensus, but weak, underdeveloped state institutions, immature political parties and a strong current of anti-liberalism made it difficult to find political compromises or common points of allegiance. At the first sign of economic crisis or social conflict, the fragile new systems gave way to forces which then tried to hold the states together by force and ideological persuasion. Dictatorship was, in this sense, a product not of capitalist development, but of political modernization. It was a means to harness popular political energies where traditions of popular politics were weak or non-existent, as in Russia or China, or incapable of stabilization, as in Germany and Italy. The threat this posed to western liberalism was shown by the rapid, often imitative, spread of dictatorship inside and outside Europe. It was evident, too, in the growing international crisis of the 1930s.

7

The International Crisis

THE UNSETTLED PEACE

In mid-December 1918 the President of the United States, Woodrow Wilson, arrived at the French port of Brest on board the ship *George Washington*. He was bound for the Paris Peace Conference where the victorious powers of the Great War, Britain, France, the United States and Italy, were to sit together to produce a lasting settlement of the international order. His role, as he saw it, was to knock the heads of the European great powers together to get them to collaborate over keeping the peace. He was a messenger of good neighbourliness sent from the New World to rescue the Old.

Some of this vaunting ambition was certainly achieved. The powers agreed to establish a **League of Nations** with its headquarters in the Swiss city of Geneva, which would act as a force for conciliation between states, by bringing the collective strength of its members to bear on any aggressor. Under the Covenant of the League the signatory powers pledged themselves gradually to disarm. The Peace Settlement also set up a whole string of newly independent states in eastern and central Europe based, loosely, on the principle of national self-determination. But right from the start things went badly for the settlement. The American Senate refused to ratify the Treaty of Versailles, on which the new system rested, and abandoned the League, leaving the one power perhaps capable of enforcing conciliation out of the collective scheme entirely. Despite Wilson's efforts, the European Allies insisted on a punitive peace for Germany, Austria and Hungary. Germany was disarmed, its merchant fleet and its colonies and overseas assets forfeited, and important mineral-bearing territory in Silesia and Alsace-Lorraine lost to Poland and France. Germany was excluded from the League. Finally, the Allies insisted that Germany should pay for the physical damage resulting from the war for which it was held to be responsible. **Reparation** payments were eventually fixed at a total of 132 billion gold marks, to be paid down to the year 1988, and Germany was forced in the Treaty to confess its 'war guilt'.

League of Nations: Set up in 1919 under the terms of the international agreements at Versailles, the League was responsible not only for keeping the peace but also for international collaboration on labour conditions, refugees, drugs, intellectual collaboration and culture. It was based at Geneva in Switzerland.

Reparations: Term used to describe the payment in goods or money from the defeated states in the First World War to the Western Allies in compensation for war damage.

Disarmed and in revolutionary turmoil, there was no alternative but for Germany to accept the terms. But this left a legacy of bitterness and resentment for a whole generation of Germans who felt that their only crime had been to lose the war. No party in Germany, either right or left, was reconciled to the Treaty. In the 1920s, restricted to a tiny army of 100,000 and denied the use of modern armaments, there was nothing to be done; but revision of the settlement remained a powerful cause in German politics. Revision was not only a German aim, however. Hungary lost 75 per cent of its pre-war territory in the post-war settlement, and almost 3 million Hungarians were compelled to live under Romanian, Czech and Yugoslav rule. Bulgaria, which had fought alongside Germany in the war, lost territory to Yugoslavia and Greece, was disarmed and compelled to pay reparations. One million ethnic Bulgarians lived under foreign rule after 1919. Austria, the central province of the Habsburg Empire, became a small rump state, its imperial territories dispensed as largesse by the Allies to the new states of Poland, Czechoslovakia and Yugoslavia. A section of the German population in the South Tyrol was handed over to Italy. The victors were not entirely satisfied either. Italy complained that it was not rewarded sufficiently for participating on the Allied side, and Japan was deeply offended by the western states' refusal to include a clause on racial discrimination, of which Japan felt itself to be a victim, in the final Covenant of the League. None of this augured well for the ambition to create a stable world order out of the ruins of war. It was a treaty that almost no one liked except Britain and France, which were manifestly its principal beneficiaries but here, too, disillusionment soon set in.

Even without the United States, Britain and France were strong enough in the 1920s to enforce the Treaty and run the League. During the post-war decade they were the major world powers. Their global empires were puffed up to their fullest extent when, under mandates from the League, they absorbed the captured German colonies in Africa and the Pacific, and took control of Turkey's captured territories in the Middle East – Syria, the Lebanon, Jordan, Palestine and Iraq (see **Map 2** for the territorial settlement after the war). Although both states undertook extensive disarmament after the war, they remained the major military and naval powers. They dominated the League of Nations, which could not have functioned without their active participation. In the 1920s they were widely regarded as 'satiated' states, anxious to defend the status quo from which they so clearly profited. They were active in promoting 'liberal diplomacy', the resolution of international squabbles through compromise and discussion. They shared the illusion that the values of progressive democracies could be transferred to the international arena (Marks, 1979; Northedge, 1986).

In this spirit the democratic states worked in the 1920s to construct a secure and peaceable environment. In 1922 at Washington, the major powers

Locarno Treaty: Agreement signed in October 1925 between Britain, Germany, France, Italy and Belgium to guarantee the frontiers of western Europe drawn up in 1919.

Kellogg-Briand Pact: Agreement signed between 68 states, including Germany, to outlaw war as a means of settling disputes between them. The Pact was used at the *Nuremberg Trials* as a basis on which to accuse German leaders of crimes against peace.

in the Pacific – Britain, Japan and the United States – signed agreements limiting naval armaments and confirming the territorial integrity of the region. In 1925, at **Locarno** in Switzerland, treaties were drawn up between Britain, France, Germany, Italy and Belgium guaranteeing the frontiers in western Europe against violation. In 1926, Germany was invited to join the League. Finally, in 1928, the French foreign minister, Aristide Briand, proposed to the United States a pact between them renouncing war. The American Secretary of State, Frank Kellogg, suggested making the agreement universal, and in August 1928 the major states again met in Paris to sign what became known as the **Kellogg–Briand** Pact. Under its terms the signatories undertook to exclude war as an option in their foreign policy, except in self-defence. In all, sixty-five nations signed the declaration, including Japan, Germany, the Soviet Union and Italy. It was greeted by the public as a major landmark in the construction of a peaceful world order. It amounted, in the words of the American sponsors of the Pact, to 'the outlawry of war'.

The persistence of internationalist idealism in the 1920s masked important weaknesses in the international order. In the first place, there was a certain moral ambiguity about the British and French position. While they preached the virtues of self-determination and democracy, they strenuously denied granting either to the subject peoples of their empires. Although liberal enough at home, both states could be thoroughly illiberal in the colonies when they were dealing with nationalist forces hostile to European imperialism. When Britain adhered to the Kellogg–Briand Pact, it was only on the condition that it could still resort to force in its own empire. When the League of Nations tried to outlaw aerial bombing in 1931, Britain refused to abandon it as an instrument of colonial control. These double standards did not go unnoticed. The moral authority of the League suffered from what was perceived to be the hypocrisy and self-serving of the 'satiated' powers. This situation made it difficult for Britain and France to resist the claims of other states in the 1930s that wanted to build an empire, or to ignore the strident demands for self-determination from the national minorities created by the Peace Settlement.

In the second place, the League was weakened as a system of collective security by the absence or exclusion of most of the major powers. The two largest states, with enormous military and economic potential, the United States and the Soviet Union, stood on the sideline. Their absence gave Britain and France an exaggerated importance in world affairs, out of proportion to the real distribution of international power. American public opinion was firmly **isolationist** in the inter-war years. After 1919 there was a widespread feeling that America had been tricked into intervening in the Great War to save the skins of the western Allies, while the American taxpayer footed the bill. The punitive Peace Settlement disillusioned even sympathetic Americans. Britain and France were widely regarded as selfish imperialist states

Isolationism: Name give to that strand of American opinion hostile to foreign commitments and unwilling to endorse the League of Nations.

incapable of a genuine internationalism. The Soviet Union was excluded from the League because of its Communist credentials. Lenin regarded it simply as an instrument to further the narrow interests of world capitalism and imperialism – the 'robbers' League', he called it. Soviet leaders were never reconciled to the loss of former Tsarist territory in eastern Europe, particularly the loss of Russian Poland, and they hoped at some point, like Germany, to revise the post-war settlement in their favour.

Finally there was defeated Germany. The most powerful European state before 1914, thanks to rapid industrial growth and military expansion, Germany was reined back in the 1920s by its enforced disarmament and the damaging economic consequences of the war. During the 1920s Germany's economy revived sufficiently to make it once again the foremost industrial power on the Continent. German nationalists were utterly unreconciled to what they regarded as the 'dictated peace' or **Diktat**, and they chafed at the bit over Germany's involuntary and frustrating powerlessness. Although Germany was admitted to the League in 1926, and German leaders generally acted with restraint in international affairs, this did little to dispel the issue for other states of how to contain within the structure of collective security a country with a strong national and militarist tradition, a powerful industrial economy, and a permanent grudge against the injustices of the Peace Settlement.

Diktat: Term used in Germany to describe the 'dictated' Peace Settlement of 1919.

The influence of Britain and France, in this sense, rested on an unreal foundation. They were faced with states which had little sympathy for an international order so obviously constructed in the interest of the major empires, at least two of which, Germany and the Soviet Union, harboured very specific ambitions to overturn the post-war territorial arrangements as soon as an opportunity presented itself. Only the military weakness and domestic distractions of the two states prevented more serious tensions. It was an unreal foundation in yet another sense. During the 1920s Britain and France assumed more global responsibilities than ever before, but throughout the period they reduced their military expenditure to a level that made it unrealistic for them seriously to defend those interests if they were threatened by war. Disarmament was popular with home populations who could see little need to pay extra taxes for military forces with nothing to do, but the result was an imbalance between international obligations and military strength which left both empires more vulnerable than they appeared on the surface.

THE WORLD CRISIS

The peaceful world order of the 1920s was a fragile plant. Yet even the most pessimistic observer in 1929 could hardly have foretold that the whole structure would be in complete disarray within five or six years, and would be plunged into another world war after ten. There were, as we have seen, severe structural faults in the system constructed after the Great War, but it nonetheless survived a troubled decade without serious incident. To explain why the world order collapsed into unmanageable crisis in the 1930s it is necessary to look elsewhere.

The first part of the explanation lies in the remarkable rise of Soviet power in the wake of Stalin's modernization drive. In 1928, the Soviet government launched the first of three Five-Year Plans to turn the Soviet Union into a major industrial and military power. Fear of the capitalist west was a strong motive. In the 1920s there were numerous war scares and rumours of war in Moscow. Soviet leaders were all too aware of the hostility of the rest of the world, and the plans for economic modernization were designed to create the means to defend the revolution against external as well as internal threats [**Doc. 31**]. Stalin deliberately placed emphasis on heavy industrial sectors (coal, steel, oil, machinery) which would make it possible to build up large armaments production. From the early 1930s Soviet industry began to turn out large quantities of weapons, which soon made the Soviet Union, on paper, the strongest military state in the world, and laid the foundation for Soviet superpower status after 1945. Between 1928 and 1936 steel production increased from 4 million tons to 16 million; machine tools increased in quantity from 2,000 to 44,000 a year over the same period; electrical output rose from 5 billion kilowatts to 32 billion. Between 1930 and 1936 the Soviet Union produced 15,853 aircraft, 18,877 tanks and 23,000 artillery pieces (Harrison, 1985). By that stage Hitler's Germany had produced only 10,600 aircraft, two-thirds of which were trainers, and possessed no modern tanks. Germany, like the western states, was faced with the transformation of the power balance in eastern Europe and Asia in a matter of a few years, and it was this, rather than fear of the west, that prompted Hitler to launch his own Four-Year Plan for military preparation in October 1936. Soviet power aroused real fears in Britain and France for the safety of their Middle Eastern and Asian empires, and particularly India. For Japan in the Far East, the rise of Soviet power threatened to undermine the Washington system in the Pacific and north-east Asia. If rearmament increased the Soviet sense of security, its effect elsewhere was the very opposite.

The second issue was in many ways more serious. The economic crisis of 1929 to 1932 did more than anything else to sour relations between the major states and to bring to an end the era of internationalist collaboration. Policies of economic selfishness revived old grievances and created new ones. Resentments that had simmered beneath the surface in the 1920s burst into the open with a fresh urgency. The social consequences of the slump pushed populations in the weaker economies towards political extremism and violent national self-assertion. The obvious failure of the liberal capitalist order to cope with economic disaster produced a backlash against liberal internationalism, just as it produced domestic hostility to weak parliamentary politics. The domestic antagonism between fascism, Communism and liberalism became internationalized. The economic crisis intensified calls not only for some kind of 'New Order' in domestic politics, but in world affairs as well.

The most important of the states arguing for a new international order were Japan, Germany and Italy. They constituted what Mussolini called the '**have-not**' or 'proletarian' states, whose fortunes differed sharply from the 'plutocratic' nations, Britain, France and the United States, the 'haves', which possessed vast territories and economic resources. Nationalists in all three 'have-not' states boiled with resentment at the social and economic damage caused by the slump, and blamed the west for allowing it to happen and then doing nothing to alleviate the suffering it caused. If this distorted the reality of the crisis, it appealed to their listeners who wanted someone to blame for the social disaster all around them.

Have-not states: Term used to describe those major powers who lacked a large empire and/or secure access to adequate supplies of food and raw materials.

The three 'have-not' states produced no concerted plan of action to challenge the world order. Indeed, for much of the 1930s Italy deeply distrusted German ambitions in Europe, while German sympathies lay traditionally with China rather than Japan. The three states reached no military agreements or formal political alliance until the German–Italian Pact of Steel, signed in May 1939. But what they shared was a common ideological rejection of the liberal order, and a growing sense of opportunity. The weakening of the world system as a result of the slump created something of a power vacuum. The democratic states responded to the crisis by drawing in their horns and concentrating on healing the domestic wounds inflicted by economic decline. They cut back further on military expenditure. Industrial collapse and financial weakness made them less formidable opponents. Britain and France were in a weaker position to defend the status quo in the early 1930s than at any point since 1919, and it was precisely at this juncture that the revisionist states made their move.

In Japan domestic politics were profoundly affected by the crisis of the world economy. During the 1920s Japanese statesmen were willing to work within the western international system as long as they were treated as equals. But during the slump Japanese goods were the victim of discrimination, Japanese emigration was restricted by immigration laws drawn up on racial lines, and Japan was denied access to markets and sources of raw materials on equal terms. Japanese nationalists reacted to Japan's economic isolation with calls for a crusade against the west and a new order in Asia. Leading circles in the Japanese military called for Japanese conquests to provide Japan with secure areas for colonization and economic exploitation, and an empire to match those of Britain and France [**Doc. 32**]. For Japan the natural area of expansion was northern China. For years the coal mines and iron deposits of Manchuria had been operated by Japanese companies, and the government

Kwantung Army: The name given to the portion of the Japanese army stationed in northern China, which staged a coup and seized Manchuria in 1931.

kept forces there – the so-called **Kwantung army** – to protect Japan's economic interests. Deteriorating relations with the Chinese warlords who dominated northern China and the growing threat of Soviet forces on the northern border placed those interests in peril. At the instigation of leaders of the Kwantung army Japanese forces seized the whole of Manchuria in September 1931. The Tokyo government acquiesced in the coup. A puppet state called Manchukuo was established, ruled by the last of the Chinese Manchu emperors, Pu Yi, but in reality controlled from Japan as part of the empire.

Although China appealed to the League powers to confront Japan's aggression, little was done for fear of antagonizing Japan still further and threatening western trade and colonial interests. But the seizure of Manchuria marked a decisive break with the collective security system of the 1920s. It demonstrated the weakness of the League when faced with a violent fait accompli. The Manchurian crisis showed that no state could expect to be protected by the League if it were attacked. This lesson was not lost on Mussolini. In Italy the slump became the occasion for a shift in Italian foreign policy, away from grudging cooperation with the west. Italian nationalists, like their Japanese counterparts, argued for a new order in world affairs that would permit Italy to dominate its main regions of interest, the Mediterranean and northern Africa, and to demonstrate clearly Fascism's independence of the western system. They planned to achieve this by enlarging Italy's small colonial inheritance – Libya, Somalia, Eritrea – into a second Roman Empire. For Mussolini the time had come to apply the values of Fascism itself to the international arena. In 1932 he told his biographer, Emil Ludwig, that he would become a new Julius Caesar, 'the greatest man that ever lived'.

In 1932 he began planning for the conquest of Ethiopia, the only independent state (bar Liberia) remaining in Africa after the scramble for colonies in the late nineteenth century. Italian links with the area went back to the nineteenth century although imperial ambitions had been thwarted in 1896 when Ethiopian forces won the Battle of Adowa. Italian trade and investment were prominent in the region. Italy sponsored Ethiopia's application to join the League in 1923. The Italian government regarded the area as part of their sphere of interest, and when Mussolini cast round for some means of demonstrating the new course in Fascist foreign policy, the seizure of Ethiopia seemed the logical course. Experts argued that the country was rich in mineral resources, perhaps even oil. Mussolini did not think that the western powers would intervene to save 'an African country, universally stamped as unworthy of taking its place among civilized peoples'. In October 1935 Italian forces invaded, confident of a brief war of conquest. The war turned out to be anything but straightforward, and victory was only secured the following spring after the use of poison gas and indiscriminate bombing. The Ethiopian Emperor, **Haile Selassie**, appealed to the League, which imposed

Haile, Selassie (1892–1975): Emperor of Ethiopa (Abysinnia) who succeeded to the throne in 1930. He was overthrown by Italian forces in 1936, fled to London and returned as emperor in 1941 when Italy was expelled in turn by British Empire forces. He was forced from the throne a second time in 1974.

half-hearted economic sanctions, but did nothing to prevent the Italian seizure of Ethiopia. The crisis alienated Italy from the western states and discredited the League mortally.

The economic recession in Germany certainly contributed a great deal to the revival of militant nationalism and the rise of Hitler. Germans across the political spectrum resented the price Germany paid for its post-war fragility, and were quick to blame reparations or the loss of German colonies for their predicament. National Socialism capitalized on these resentments, but it did not cause them. Whether Hitler had come to power in 1933 or not, it is unlikely that any German government would have tolerated for much longer the restrictions imposed by Versailles. Even before 1933 secret rearmament was in progress; reparation payments were suspended in 1931. Aristocratic and military circles in Germany eagerly awaited the opportunity to revive German military power on a par with that of its neighbours, and to argue from strength for a revision of the territorial arrangements imposed in 1919. The difference that Hitler made was critical for the collapse of international stability later in the 1930s. For Hitler had a vision of Germany as a superpower, morally renewed, economically powerful, militarily revived, whose destiny was to carve out a vast Eurasian empire to provide what he called *Lebensraum* or 'living space'. Hitler believed much of the racist, geopolitical literature circulating in German nationalist circles, which suggested that to become a world power Germany must conquer areas to colonize for its surplus population, and to ensure a healthy, thriving race [**Doc. 33**]. He viewed world history as a constant struggle between races and cultures, and he saw warfare as the 'ultimate weapon' in a people's contest for survival. War, for Hitler, was inevitable, like the survival of the fittest in nature. For Germany, war was revenge for what the rest of the world had done to it in 1919.

With views like this, a Hitler-led Germany was perceived as a profound threat to the existing order. Hitler regarded the liberal states as a declining force in world history, whose decadent grip on their crumbling empires matched the decadence of liberal, parliamentary systems in general. From the outset of his regime in 1933 he embarked on the path of treaty revision, with the longer aim of subverting and transforming the world order in Germany's favour. He saw his ultimate enemies not in the weak bourgeois democracies, which he came to despise, but in the Soviet Union, home to the bitterest opponents of European fascism, and in the Jews, whose alleged efforts to dominate the world paradoxically through both Marxism and international capitalism were used to justify anti-Semitic persecution in Germany, and during the war a programme of systematic annihilation.

Hitler's initial step was to begin Germany's rearmament, first of all in secret, then from 1935 in public defiance of the Versailles Treaty. In 1935 the Saar region returned to Germany after a plebiscite gave overwhelming

Lebensraum: Term commonly used in Germany in the 1920s to describe that amount of territory thought to be necessary to allow a nation to feed and provision itself to a reasonable standard. 'Living space' became the excuse for programmes of territorial expansion.

support to reunion. In March 1936 Hitler ordered German troops to reoccupy the Rhineland, which had been demilitarized at French insistence in 1919, and confirmed in the Locarno Treaties. Coming as this did at the height of the Ethiopian crisis, the western states were wary of running additional risks, and did nothing. In March 1938 Hitler absorbed Austria, the land of his birth, without resistance, into a Greater Germany. By that stage there was almost nothing left of the settlement that had been imposed on Germany to prevent it from ever again becoming a threat to the peace of Europe.

The final factor that undermined the collective security system was the attitude of Britain and France, the only two states with any real interest in sustaining it. Neither of them was willing to stem the tide. This was not a result of simple loss of will, as is often argued, but rather the product of a number of domestic and international pressures which made it difficult to respond with greater vigour, however sensible such a course might appear to be, with hindsight. The first constraint was the sheer range and diversity of issues which the two states were forced to confront in a relatively short space of time: the rise of Soviet power, the threat in Asia, Italian pressure in Africa and the Mediterranean, the revival of an extreme form of German nationalism. Both states recognized that their military resources could never hope to contain all these threats simultaneously. Yet to confront only one of them might well open the way for other states to exploit the opportunity offered by British or French distraction. The attempt to solve issues by negotiation or compromise, to find a peaceable way of containing threats, a policy usually described as 'appeasement', was a recognition of realities. It also reflected the value both states placed in the 1930s on conducting international affairs in the spirit of the League rather than in a mood of violent antagonism. Other powers, however, saw their attitude as an admission of weakness. In 1936, after the German reoccupation of the Rhineland, Hitler commented: 'Britain will yet regret her softness. It will cost her her Empire.' A Japanese writer observed that same year: 'England is on the downgrade; Japan is on the upgrade' (Mommsen and Kettenacker, 1983; Overy and Wheatcroft, 1989).

The attitude of Britain and France was also conditioned by domestic circumstances. The economic slump encouraged politicians in both countries to concentrate their efforts on solving the economic crisis and averting serious social unrest. The economic situation reduced the financial and industrial strength of both states at a critical juncture in world affairs. As late as 1938 France still produced only 60 per cent of the steel it had produced a decade earlier. There was not much domestic enthusiasm for an active foreign policy, let alone the prospect of armed conflict. Public opinion was important for democratic governments. The prevailing mood at home was 'never again', no more war. There were large pacifist movements among both populations. In Britain in 1935 a **Peace Pledge Union** was formed which

Peace Pledge Union: Anti-war organization founded in 1934 by the British clergyman Richard Sheppard, which became the largest of its kind in the 1930s.

organized a popular ballot that secured 9 million votes repudiating war. When the Popular Front was elected in France in May 1936, 1 million people marched through Paris celebrating peace. When the National Government tried to introduce higher expenditure on armaments in Britain in 1936, the Labour leader, **Clement Attlee**, led a fierce attack on a policy that was 'leading his country back to the blood-stained tragedy of 1914'. Politicians who argued for a firmer line, or who, like **Neville Chamberlain**, the Chancellor of the Exchequer, urged higher military spending, were branded as warmongers.

Very much the same mood was evident in the United States. During the 1930s popular pacifism became an important force in domestic politics. In 1934, at the instigation of the senator for North Dakota, **Gerald Nye**, Congress set up a Munitions Inquiry to examine the link between the manufacture of arms and the incidence of foreign wars with a view to limiting the trade in weapons. From the public's viewpoint the Inquiry exposed all kinds of malpractices by the armaments industry, and in 1935 President Roosevelt found himself under strong pressure to declare formal neutrality in any future conflict between foreign states. In August 1935 a provisional **Neutrality Act** was passed in the Senate by 79 votes to 2. Two years later a full Act came into force, effectively insulating the United States from any involvement in other people's wars. Hostility to war in all three major democracies was an important element in restraining active attempts to maintain the League order. American neutrality was a clear public statement that the largest and most economically powerful democracy would remain committed to isolation and disarmament, leaving Britain and France even more vulnerable, particularly in the Pacific and Far East where they had assumed that the United States would play a more forward role (Dallek, 1979).

Britain and France also faced serious problems in their colonial empires. The export of nationalist and socialist ideas from Europe to the empire created significant pressure for democratic reform or even independence. This made it even more difficult to confront the external threat to empire posed by the revisionist states. In the French Empire there was dangerous unrest in Indo-China (present-day Vietnam), where in 1931 nationalists and Communists staged armed insurrections. The Communist leader, **Ho Chi Minh**, learned his politics in Paris where he arrived in 1917, forging oriental art by day and attending radical socialist meetings in the evenings. The insurrections were suppressed by force, but 10,000 Vietnamese were kept in prison. In the Middle East and North Africa, France faced a broad nationalist revolt, spurred on by the general revival of Islam in Syria, Tunisia and Algeria, which had to be met by armed conflict or repression. There was hardly a year in the 1930s when French troops were not engaged somewhere in the empire (Betts, 1990).

Attlee, Clement (1883–1967): Labour politician who led the party after it split in 1931 when Ramsay Macdonald set up a National Government. He joined Churchill's war cabinet in 1940 and became prime minister in July 1945. He presided over the introduction of the NHS and the widespread nationalization of British industries. Defeated in the 1951 election, he retired in 1955.

Chamberlain, Neville (1873–1940): Conservative politician from a prominent Birmingham political family. He was a successful minister in the 1920s, Chancellor of the Exchequer in 1934 (when he oversaw the programme of British rearmament), and from June 1937 prime minister. He is seen as the architect of the policy of 'appeasement', but declared war on Hitler in September 1939. He resigned in May 1940.

Nye, Gerald (1892–1971): American Republican senator from Illinois who campaigned in the 1930s against armaments manufacture and promoted American *isolationism*.

Neutrality Acts: A series of legislative acts passed in the United States between 1935 and 1937, when a permanent state of neutrality was secured. Under the terms of the 1937 Act the United States could not ship arms or give financial assistance to the combatant powers.

Ho Chi Minh (1890–1969): Vietnamese nationalist politician who led the struggle against French rule in Vietnam in the 1930s and established the Communist state of North Vietnam in 1954. He became a symbol of popular defiance of imperialism in the youth revolt of 1968.

The British faced the same kind of problems in Egypt, which was granted virtual independence in 1936 after a long period of violent agitation. Iraq was granted independence in 1927, and Palestine was host, then as now, to a bitter civil conflict between Arabs and Jewish settlers, with British soldiers stuck uncomfortably in the middle. Catholic Ireland won independence in 1922, leaving Britain to rule Ulster. In India, which British statesmen regarded as the lynchpin of the whole imperial structure, the nationalist Congress movement threatened the very survival of British rule. Repeated concessions, which culminated in the India Act of 1935, granting a considerable degree of local autonomy, produced an uneasy compromise. Last, but not least, the white settler dominions, Canada, New Zealand, Australia and South Africa, won independent status in 1926, and in 1931, under the Statute of Westminster, the right to declare war on their own behalf. By the mid-1930s Britain could no longer rely on their uncritical support, and Canada and South Africa made it known that in any European conflict they would remain neutral. During the inter-war years the British and French empires reached their fullest territorial extent just as they began the slow process of internal dissolution. The military effort required to maintain their fragile security was a powerful argument against running the risk of general war (Porter, 1975).

For all these reasons, the active military defence of the status quo was politically unattractive (and it is important to remember that only military action could have dislodged Japan from Manchuria, or Italy from Ethiopia, or Germany from the Rhineland). It was also hard for western statesmen to grasp the full extent of the crisis that confronted them. A great gulf separated the leaders of parliamentary regimes – drawn for the most part from a conventional upper-middle-class background, with many of the advantages of social privilege and education – from the new generation of populist dictators from a more plebeian background, who had fought their way, often quite literally, to the top. British and French leaders assumed that the noisy nationalism they were faced with was just a front to keep the masses happy, and that dictators too were governed in the conduct of foreign affairs by sober calculation and willingness to compromise, as they were. It seemed inconceivable that any leader would willingly risk a repeat of the horrors of 1914–18, and not until the late 1930s did the British and French governments come to realize that the revisionist states really did consider war, or the threat of war, as an acceptable option in foreign policy. Chamberlain, who became British prime minister in June 1937, treated Hitler and Mussolini, according to an unkind critic, 'like the Lord Mayors of Liverpool and Manchester'. After meeting Hitler in 1938 Chamberlain himself confessed his incomprehension: 'What I found so difficult – apart from his fits of temper, and his habit of wandering off the subject – was the fact that he was so irrational' (*Decade*, 1941). The inability of liberal statesmen to grasp the nature of the forces unleashed by modern nationalism and ideological conflict left them poorly equipped to cope with the threat to the world order when it finally materialized [**Doc. 34**].

THE SLIDE TO WAR

By the mid-1930s the system of collective security, and the treaties of Versailles (1919), Washington (1922) and Locarno (1925) on which it rested, was in ruins. The League ceased to be taken seriously as an organization, and the great powers bypassed it in the conduct of their foreign policy. Japan left the League in 1932, Germany in 1933, Italy in 1937. The entry of the Soviet Union to the League in 1934 at French instigation made little difference, for both the western states continued to harbour strong doubts about Soviet goodwill throughout the 1930s. When the Soviet Union invaded Finland in December 1939 it was expelled from the League.

Unlike the period before 1914, when the international order was characterized by large alliance blocs, there existed no firm military alliances between the major powers in the 1930s, although there remained an identity of interest between Britain and France on the one hand, and the revisionist states on the other. The result was a fragmentation of the power structure as states pursued their own path, largely in isolation. The agreed rules for the conduct of international affairs broke down, and were not replaced. Something like a Hobbesian state of nature was imposed on the international order, where all states competed with one another for their own security, and as a result none could find it: a 'war of all against all'.

The result of insecurity was a renewed scramble for military protection. Rearmament was not just a response to German revival, but was also prompted by the tensions generated by Soviet military strength, and by Japanese and Italian imperialism. Britain began to rearm in 1934, and accelerated the programme with a £1,500 million commitment over four years to strengthen the navy and imperial defences, and, above all to build up a large air force. France embarked on a similar four-year programme in 1936, most of which went on the modernization of the army, a large tactical air force and the completion of a long defensive fortification on its eastern frontier, the **Maginot Line**. Hitler authorized a substantial increase in the size of the military the same year. He aimed to match Soviet achievements, and German efforts were concentrated on building up a large air force to support land operations, spearheaded by mobile tank armies. Japan and Italy launched large armaments programmes in 1938, though the high costs of the wars in Ethiopia and China, and the weak raw material resources of both states,

Maginot Line: A series of defensive fortifications along France's eastern border, begun at the inspiration of the Defence Minister, André Maginot, in 1929, and still incomplete ten years later.

severely reduced what could be achieved. By the late 1930s the world bristled with arms. In 1935 the great powers produced between them some 10,000 aircraft, mostly biplanes; in 1939 they produced almost 42,000, most of them modern monoplanes. Military expenditure increased more than six-fold between 1934 and 1939 in Britain, Germany and Japan, in the Soviet Union eight-fold, and in France ten-fold. Though rearmament did not directly cause the war in 1939, the huge military build-up in a matter of a few years created a climate of uncertainty and crisis, which reduced the very security that greater military force was supposed to bring.

Here, then, were all the ingredients for international crisis: on the one hand, Britain and France nursing their ailing order in the face of domestic pressures for peace, imperial disturbances, and an array of what Chamberlain called 'poor adventurers', hungry for the succession. On the other hand, there were powerful new states – Germany, the Soviet Union and Japan – which could no longer be contained satisfactorily in the old system, and whose leaders sensed the possibility of profitable change. None of them had specific plans for a general war, although Hitler indicated to his generals and party colleagues that he expected a great reckoning between the powers in the mid-1940s, when Germany would be militarily ready. But both Hitler and Mussolini saw war as unavoidable in the long run. 'War', Hitler wrote in 1929, in his unpublished sequel to *Mein Kampf*, 'is the ultimate weapon with which a people fights for its daily bread' (Hitler, 1961: 32). 'The war between the plutocratic and therefore selfishly conservative nations and the densely populated and poor nations is inevitable', wrote Mussolini to his fellow dictator in May 1939.

For populations that contemplated the bleak prospect of war for the second time in a generation, there was frightening evidence that the next war would be worse than the last. In 1914 the generals counted on a war of two or three months, won or lost in a few great infantry battles. Instead, the war became a struggle of attrition, testing the physical endurance of the whole population, the strength of the economy, and the ingenuity of scientists. In the 1920s this kind of warfare was defined as '**total war**'. The revolution in warfare produced by aircraft, tanks, machine-guns and poison gas, relied on the mobilization of the home front to produce the weapons of industrialized warfare. The experience of the Great War, when thousands of civilians died from bombing and shelling, or from the effects of economic blockade on the food supply, blurred permanently the distinction between soldier and civilian. It was widely expected that if war should ever break out again it would be a war waged between whole populations, with no holds barred.

The concept of total war revived the French revolutionary idea of the 'nation in arms', and legitimized the use of weapons against civilians, if by so

Total war: Term usually associated with the German general Erich Ludendorff, who in 1919 described the First World War as a 'total war' because it had demanded the total commitment of the economic, social and moral resources of the nation. The term was also understood to describe a war in which civilians as well as soldiers were part of the war effort and a legitimate target of attack.

doing it was possible to win the struggle for survival. The prospect of national war-to-the-death explains why there was so much popular hostility to rearmament when international tension returned in the 1930s, and the evident dread of war even among the strongly nationalist populations. The greatest terror of them all was the threat of bombing. In 1921 an Italian general, **Giulio Douhet**, wrote a bestseller on air warfare, *The Command of the Air*, in which he argued that to win the next war states must prepare large bomber forces to carry out a 'knock-out blow' against the enemy's economy and the morale of the people. The idea that aircraft could bring a country to defeat in a matter of hours or days by the merciless bombardment of defence-less civilians took root in the popular imagination. In the 1930s most European governments authorized a programme of civil-defence prepara-tions, issuing gas masks to the whole population and building air-raid shelters in vulnerable urban areas. Ordinary people saw themselves as tar-gets. They were terrified of bombing in much the same way as people have dreaded nuclear war since 1945 (Bialer, 1980).

After the Japanese air forces bombed Chinese civilians, and German and Italian aviators attacked open towns in the Spanish Civil War (most famously the Basque city of Guernica, which became a symbol for the horrors of modern warfare), it was widely assumed that in any war between the great powers bombing would be used indiscriminately and brutally to exact a rapid victory. So strong was this popular fear that it acted as a serious brake on British and French reaction to German aggression, and was one of the major reasons why Chamberlain was so reluctant to push Hitler too far when Germany demanded the return of the German-speaking areas of Czechoslovakia in 1938 [**Doc. 35**].

The threat of war in the late 1930s could have been averted only if the revisionist states had accepted the need for self-restraint, or if the two status quo powers had abandoned the attempt to defend the old order and accepted their relative decline as a force in world politics, as they later did in the Suez crisis of 1956. Neither of these things happened. Italy and Japan, both indi-vidually weaker than Britain and France, acted cautiously, but certainly did not reverse the course of expansion. In November 1937 Japan began a more general war with China. By January 1938 Japanese troops had seized the Chinese capital at Nanking, and by the end of the year most of northern and eastern China was in Japanese hands. In Italy, prominent nationalists called on Mussolini to extend Italian interests in the Mediterranean, and demanded the 'return' from France of Corsica, Savoy and Tunisia and from Britain the island of Malta, all of which were regarded as part of a historic Italy. Anxious to be seen to do something, Mussolini ordered his forces to occupy Albania, across the Adriatic Sea, which, like Ethiopia, had long been a region of strong Italian influence.

Douhet, Giulio (1869–1930): Italian general who pioneered the strat-egy of modern air power. His book *The Command of the Air* (1921) became a classic statement of the capacity of aircraft to act independently of the army and navy by pursuing the defeat of the enemy nation by bombing.

The key issue was Germany. Up to the *Anschluss* with Austria in March 1938, Hitler had taken back what many in the western states regarded as reasonable, even justified, given the harsh terms of the Versailles Treaty. But from the summer of 1938 onwards Hitler began to encroach on the sovereign interests of non-German states. His next target was Czechoslovakia, where 3 million Germans from the former Habsburg Empire lived in the frontier areas of the Sudetenland. In May he ordered his armed forces to plan the conquest and seizure of the area for the autumn. During the late summer Britain and France put pressure on the Czech government to make concessions to avoid a war, but both states made it clear to Hitler that if he invaded Czechoslovakia and ignored the negotiations they would be forced to fight. The final settlement of the issue at the Munich Conference in September 1938 granted Germany the Sudeten territories, in return for promises not to attack the rest of the Czech state, and to keep the peace in future. The crisis was the closest Europe had come to war since 1918, and the settlement was widely welcomed at the time. War was avoided only because neither side was strong enough to get exactly what it wanted. Hitler's forces were not sufficiently prepared for a general war, and there was strong evidence of popular hostility to war. Hitler bowed to reality with an ill grace. The western states failed to restrain German ambitions entirely, but were not willing to risk a war to do so with their rearmament at an immature stage, and their populations deeply divided over the issue.

From Munich onwards a collision course was almost unavoidable. In the months following the conference Hitler stepped up the pace of military preparation and increased German pressure on the states of eastern Europe to become part of a German power bloc. Hitler assumed that Britain and France had given him a green light at Munich to extend his sphere of influence in the east, and he regarded them both as too militarily enfeebled and politically decadent to develop the means or the will to obstruct him. In March 1939 his forces occupied the rest of Czechoslovakia, and took back the city of Memel from Lithuania. Economic agreements with Romania and Yugoslavia brought both states further into the German orbit. After Polish leaders, against Hitler's expectations, refused in March 1939 to negotiate the return to Germany of the Baltic port of Danzig, which had been made a Free City under the League of Nations in 1919, Hitler planned to launch a punitive war against Poland in August 1939. He insisted to his generals and colleagues that this would be a short, localized war, and consistently argued throughout the summer that Britain and France would not seriously obstruct him. To avoid Soviet involvement in an area where there were strong Soviet interests, Hitler concluded a non-aggression pact with Stalin on 23 August, with a secret protocol dividing Poland between them, and granting the Soviet Union a sphere of influence in the Baltic states. The pact was a marriage of convenience between ideological enemies. Hitler felt that Britain and France, faced with the combined weight of Germany and the Soviet Union, would have to accept the reality of a new European balance of power, while Stalin gained from the pact the opportunity to revise the post-war settlement by seizing back the lands of the old Tsarist Empire without German or western resistance.

Throughout 1939 Hitler entirely misread western intentions. After Munich, Britain and France rallied at last to the armed defence of the status quo. Both states speeded up military preparations, until by the summer their combined aircraft and tank production exceeded Germany's. There developed a popular nationalist revival which turned public opinion in both states strongly against Germany and in favour of firmer action. In the summer of 1939, early opinion polls found that 87 per cent of those polled in Britain and 76 per cent in France expressed a firm commitment to fight if Germany invaded Poland and seized Danzig. Hitlerism was now widely regarded as a profound threat to the survival of western values and interests, and Poland was chosen as an issue not for its own sake, but to demonstrate to Hitler the west's determination to defend those interests when threatened. Their empires rallied to the cause too. Canada abandoned neutrality; Australia and New Zealand pledged support; colonial armies were raised in French North Africa, India and Indo-China. Even neutral America began to give encouragement to the western cause, although Roosevelt was too wary of isolationist opinion to commit the United States to a more active foreign or military policy.

For all these reasons western statesmen were willing to confront Hitler if it came to a showdown in 1939. Neither Britain nor France viewed the prospect of war with enthusiasm. They hoped that Hitler would be deterred by the sight of western firmness, and that there would be a peaceful outcome on terms acceptable to them. But both states pledged their support to fight for each other and for Poland if Hitler tried to solve the Polish question by force. Both states reckoned that the cost of not fighting, which would amount to the loss of international prestige and European security, even of western civilization itself, was greater than the cost of fighting. Right up to the declaration of war on 3 September, which followed the German invasion of Poland on the morning of 1 September, it was hoped that Hitler would see sense and back down, conceding a moral and diplomatic victory to the democracies. Right up to the end Hitler clung tenaciously to his conviction that 'France and Britain will not take action'. What was supposed to be a local war to complete the destruction of the hated Versailles order in eastern Europe was turned, by the powerful destabilizing sense of crisis generated by German ambition, into a second Great War.

The coming of war in 1939 terminated the 'inter-war crisis' and fulfilled the worst of forebodings. For many it gave a sense of release. 'It feels good to

Goebbels, Joseph (1897–1945): An enthusiastic and radical National Socialist in the 1920s, Goebbels rose to be first party propaganda chief, then Minister for Propaganda and Popular Enlightenment in Hitler's regime. In 1944 he was made Plenipotentiary for Total War, but following German military failure he committed suicide in Hitler's bunker in Berlin in May 1945.

be in battle', wrote Hitler's propaganda minister, **Joseph Goebbels**, in his diary on the evening of Germany's invasion of Poland, 'everything around us is calm, the dice are cast.' The American ambassador in Paris watched the soldiers leaving for the front. 'The men left in silence. There were no bands, no songs . . . There was no hysterical weeping of mothers, sisters, and children.' Instead, he found 'self-control and quiet courage' which had about it a 'dream quality'. The war promised to resolve all those confused elements of the inter-war crisis, the ideological confrontation, the ill-functioning economies, the social distress, the world out of balance. Fascism, Communism and democracy faced the critical test of war. The long malaise was over. On New Year's Eve 1939 the poet David Gascoyne sat and wrote an epitaph for the old world:

> And so! the long black pullman is at last departing, now,
> After those undermining years of angry waiting . . .
> Years like a prison-wall, frustrating though unsound,
> On which the brush of History, with quick, neurotic strokes
> Its latest and most awe-inspiring fresco soon outparad:
> Spenglerian lowering of the Western skies, red lakes
> Of civil bloodshed, free flags flagrantly torn down
> By order of macabre puppet orators, the blind
> Leading blindfolded followers into the Devil's den . . .
>
> And so, Good-bye, grim Thirties.

Part 3

ASSESSMENT

.

8

The Challenge of Progress

'Crisis' is an overworked word. It is used to describe anything from a brief personal setback – 'I've had a crisis at work' – to the very brink of nuclear war – 'the Cuban Missile Crisis'. This makes it difficult for the historian to distinguish a period that might properly be defined as one of crisis from the ordinary ups and downs of the historical process. Two things allow us to view the years between the two world wars as a crisis in a significant sense. The first is the sheer range and scale of the upheavals and conflicts that define the period. The second is the very keen sense that contemporaries themselves had that they were living through an age of chaotic, dangerous transition and the development of a morbid culture that reflected these anxieties. Not for nothing did Winston Churchill christen his study of the era of the Great War, published between 1923 and 1927, *The World Crisis*.

There was nothing neat about the chronology of the crisis. It did not start in 1919 and end in 1939. The wars at either end of the period are inseparable from our understanding of the crisis, the first as cause, the second as terrible consequence. Even before 1914 the effects of industrialization and mass politics were evident in sharper social conflicts and a shaky balance of power; science and medicine were dissolving the material certainties of the nineteenth century. The war itself was a powerful transformer, wrecking the old international and political order, pulling down the pillars of economic stability, and opening the gate to social revolution. The revolutionary chaos encouraged by wartime hardship cast a shadow across the whole inter-war period. The triumph of Communism in Russia threw all political conflicts into sharper relief, and reduced prospects for social compromise and evolutionary democracy. It helped to generate a strong counter-revolutionary movement which mobilized the socially conservative masses in defence of Church, property and order. Fear of revolutionary crisis and the weakness of parliamentary systems pushed these groups to the political extremes in Italy, in Germany, in Spain and in a dozen other places. Dictatorship came to be preferred to democracy, repression replaced compromise.

These conflicts might well have been softened if the post-war economy had picked up the pre-war trajectory of high growth rates and rising prosperity. But the war created all kind of frictions and distortion in the world economy. Industrial modernization continued, but its fruits were very unevenly distributed, and large communities of villagers and craft workers were left stranded, their livelihood in decline and their traditional values challenged by glossy consumerism and an interfering state. Modernity was full of promise before 1914; now it seemed a curse. To make matters worse, the modern economy itself failed cataclysmically after 1929, throwing large numbers of industrial workers and white-collar employees into unemployment and poverty. In the 1930s confidence in the survival of liberal capitalism melted away. The economic crisis prompted a search for some alternative system, derived either from Stalinist planned economy or fascist ideas of state-led **corporativism**.

Corporatavism: The concept of corporate organization of industrial workers and employers. Adopted in Mussolini's Italy in the late 1920s and copied by fascist movements everywhere as an alternative model to class conflict.

The collapse of the world economy had important implications for the international order. The attempt to construct out of the ruins of war a New Order based on collaboration and mutual respect between nations broke down during the slump. Countries looked to their own interests first. Economic deprivation encouraged domestic nationalism, which prompted growing tensions in foreign policy. As a result of the slump, states searched for a new world order based on closed economic blocs and imperial spheres of influence. As Hitler crudely put it in 1939, it was impossible to do this 'without breaking in to other countries or attacking other people's possessions'. Japanese expansion in China, Italy's invasion of Ethiopia and German penetration of eastern Europe were all examples of a violent economic imperialism, designed to tear aside the established liberal order, dominated by Britain and France, and replace it with a New Order of militaristic, racial empire. In the wings stood the Soviet Union, heavily armed and keen to revise at some point a world system that kept it isolated and under threat from German or Japanese aggression. During the 1930s the domestic conflicts between democrats, radical nationalists and Communists were projected onto a world stage, dissolving the old balance of power and throwing world politics into the melting pot.

Orwell, George (1903–1949): British author and journalist who fought in the Spanish Civil War in the International Brigades. His disillusionment with Communism produced the classic satire *Animal Farm* (1945) and the futuristic *1984* (1949), best remembered for the idea that 'Big Brother' is always watching you.

All these crises – of the social order, of the modern economy, of the international system, of the threats revealed by modern science – prompted a real moral crisis. By the 1930s the optimistic expectations of the post-war years about the restoration of social peace and international justice had given way to a widespread sense of profound unease, an anxious recognition that the world was at a critical juncture [**Doc. 36**]. The 1930s had more than their share of doom-laden writing, from Freud's *Civilization and its Discontents* published in 1930 to **George Orwell's** *Coming up for Air*, published in 1939, just before the outbreak of war, a novel crafted to convey the sense of a moral dead end, of modern societies overshadowed by a spiritually bankrupt modernity and the threat of war. 'Millions of others like me', declared Orwell's narrator, 'have got a feeling that the world's gone wrong. They can feel things collapsed and cracking under their feet.'

There were naturally some in the 1930s who revelled in crisis. For Communists it promised the terminal eclipse of capitalism and imperialism and the dawn of what the British socialists **Sidney and Beatrice Webb** called 'a New Civilization'. For intellectuals of the radical right the crisis offered an opportunity to transcend what they regarded as the flabby, worn-out values of bourgeois society and establishment culture, and to liberate the human spirit from rationalism and materialism. In their place they promised the violence of nature, the necessity of struggle and pain, a new barbarism, actions without conscience, a whole litany of irrational impulses which exemplified what Freud called 'the primal man in each of us'. The urge to tear up civilization, to revel in destruction and brutality, was not just an intellectual pose – as the Second World War and the Holocaust showed – but a deeper reflection of a world in dissolution and decline. In 1939, on the eve of war, a French professor of philosophy, André Joussain, compared the crisis facing European civilization with the fall of the Roman Empire. He saw in the rise of Communism and Fascism the 'revenge of the barbarians' who had tried to destroy the Graeco-Roman heritage, only to be defeated by the rise of Christianity and humanism. Now Europe was confronted with a new Dark Age. Nations weakened by the decline of religious faith, the rise of mass politics and modern culture, oscillating 'between anarchy and despotism', could no longer withstand the new wave of 'barbarian invasions' (Joussain, 1939).

For conservative intellectuals like Joussain the crisis of civilization was self-evident. But most of those who experienced war, revolution, economic crisis, and war again did so in material, personal ways, not as a set of ideas. It was not for them simply a spur to spiritual anxiety, but the cause of real physical deprivation. The Russian *muzhik* experienced the transformation of the Soviet Union in terms of grain seizures, the loss of his land, forced labour or exile, fatal persecution. The artisan experienced the modern industrial age as the gradual erosion of their livelihood and independence. Millions of workers in the 1930s in Europe and America suffered years of unemployment on meagre hand-outs. The costs of the years of crisis were enormous, dwarfing anything that had happened in the century since the Napoleonic Wars. In the First World War 7 million died and 13 million were wounded. In the Russian Civil War an estimated 10 million died from the fighting, or the starvation that followed in its wake. In the Spanish Civil War an estimated 1 million lost their lives. In the Stalinist drive for modernization in the 1930s and the terror that followed around 5–6 million died. In 1932 there were 24 million unemployed across the developed world; there were still

Webb, Sidney and Beatrice (1859–1947) (1858–1943): Campaigning British socialists who helped to launch the Fabian Society in 1884 and pioneered ideas about welfare reform and effective local government. In 1935 they published a study of the Soviet Union as a new civilization which helped to persuade many western intellectuals that Stalin's Russia was progressive and enlightened.

16 million by 1938. The war between Japan and China led to the deaths of more than 11 million Chinese. The total of deaths inflicted by war, civil war and state terror between 1914 and 1945 is well in excess of 80 million people.

This horrifying catalogue of human destruction has no equal in history; not even the Thirty Years War, nor the French wars of the revolutionary period, could match the horrors of the age between 1914 and 1945. The terrible cost in lives and human misery was the product of a unique set of forces – the application of science and industry to war, the rise of mass politics fired by bitter ideological conflicts and class hatreds, the sudden collapse of the old world order in the First World War, the failure of liberal capitalism to cope with an unstable economic system, and last, but not least, the disappearance of moral certainty.

All of this begs a large question. Why did the crisis end? Why did the world not rush headlong into chaos, into this new Dark Age? The Second World War itself resolved a great deal of the crisis. When it ended, there was a perceptible psychological shift, away from a sense of frightening *fin de siècle* evident before 1939, to a belief in the possibility of hopeful reconstruction. The revelation in 1945 of the costs of the war (55 million dead, millions systematically exterminated) and the dehumanizing descent into barbarism that the war permitted, served to discredit any more talk of 'new orders' or the 'revolt against liberalism'. Violent extremism was pushed to the margins of European politics. Moral certainty was reaffirmed from the victory over Hitlerism. In 1945/6 the Allied powers placed German leaders on **trial at Nuremberg** for 'crimes against peace' and 'crimes against humanity'. The purpose of the trial was not just to impose the law of the victors on the vanquished, but also to demonstrate to world opinion a renewed belief in the universal values of peaceableness and human decency. The trials exposed the barbarous reality behind the fascist pursuit of the 'Third Way' between socialism and capitalism, and confined to the sidelines views on race and authority which had been widely fashionable in the 1930s.

Nuremberg Trials: A series of trials of senior German political and military leaders which began in November 1945 with the Trial of the Major War Criminals, but also included later trials against businessmen, officials, SS officers and concentration camp personnel.

In the second place the balance of power was re-established to match the real distribution of economic and military strength. A bipolar system was created around the two superpowers produced by the war, the Soviet Union and the United States. Germany was divided, and the new West German state integrated into the western, American-dominated bloc. The states of eastern Europe, including the eastern part of Germany, were integrated into a Soviet-led security system. The resulting confrontation between the two sides in the Cold War created, paradoxically, a long period of equilibrium. Both superpowers retained a monopoly of large nuclear arsenals and had sufficient political will and economic strength to defend the interests of their separate blocs. For the liberal west the critical factor was the willingness of the United States to abandon its inter-war policy of isolation and disarmament. Though western states have often disliked their dependence on American strength, the prospects for security and economic revival after 1945 would have been much reduced, perhaps impossible, without it. There has been no shortage of small wars since 1945, but there has been no war between the great powers.

Finally, the problems generated by industrial modernization, scientific discovery and social conflict, which appeared acute in the inter-war years, were resolved after 1945 by a remarkable economic boom which created unprecedented prosperity throughout the industrially developed world, and dragged a great many less-developed economies into the modern industrial and technical age. For artisans and peasants, social adjustment has been much easier in a prosperous environment, with widening opportunities. The greater intervention of the state, the internationalization of the large industrial corporations, and the restoration, under American pressure, of a more open world trading economy, all contributed to sustaining the boom through to the 1970s. In the Communist bloc high levels of modernization were achieved by introducing the Stalinist model of forced industrialization and the transformation of rural life, but without the terrible costs of the 1930s. The revolution in communications and mass consumption – particularly associated with the motor car, television and the telephone – helped to break down social isolation and the gulf between city and village. The aeroplane bridged the gulf between states. These changes have certainly not occurred without friction or tension, but sustained economic growth and a more equitable distribution of its fruits eased the transition, and reduced fears of social revolution or agitation for territorial empire in the developed world. Democracy became firmly entrenched in western Europe and confidence in liberal values revived. After 1945 there developed the comfortable assumption that all states were at last moving, inexorably, towards representative democracy and liberal capitalism.

In an article which first appeared in 1989, an American State Department official, **Francis Fukuyama**, suggested that the rise of democracy and the spread of industry had produced a common pattern of development, a convergence between states which would put an end to the prospect of any serious crisis. This amounted to what he called 'the end of history'. Like the early nineteenth-century German philosopher Georg Hegel, on whose views he strongly relied, Fukuyama predicted the arrival of an age of world harmony and peace, the triumph of a rational world order. The publication of these views provoked widespread criticism, not least because it took place at a time when there was every evidence that the exact opposite was happening, that the long period of relative political stability and economic progress was drawing to a close.

It is tempting at this point to ask whether that conjuncture of factors which generated the crisis between the wars could be repeated. There are

Fukuyama, Francis (1952–): American State Department official who became famous in 1989 when he published *The End of History* in which he claimed that liberal capitalism had triumphed worldwide and that there was no necessity for further historical development. He has since written other books on the state of the world which have modified his original claims.

some disturbing parallels. Again, forces beyond the control of individuals or governments have created serious social and economic pressures. Population growth has slowed throughout the developed world, but global population has exploded, from 2.7 billion in 1950 to 5.3 billion in 1990. The spread of industrialization has exhausted natural resources and created prolonged damage to the environment. Outside Europe and America modernization has benefited only a relatively small part of the population and has created poverty and social displacement on a vast scale, as it did in Europe between the wars. Economic growth has slowed down significantly since the 1970s, and the recession of the early 1990s, accompanied by the economic stagnation of large regions (Russia in particular), had echoes of the 1920s and 1930s.

Finally, the distribution of international power has altered dramatically since the 1970s. In 1988 Paul Kennedy published a study of the rise and fall of the great powers, which sought to demonstrate the close link between economic strength and international power. He argued that the inter-war years were crisis-ridden because the states trying to run the system, Britain and France, were in relative economic decline, while the states that had the economic power were outside it (Kennedy, 1988). Since the 1990s this situation has been repeated. The states with growing economic power, particularly China, have played little part in the conduct of international affairs, while the collapse of the Communist bloc in Europe after 1989 has left the United States in a position where they have assumed international responsibilities that they lack the economic strength to sustain without growing indebtedness. A barbarous civil war in former Yugoslavia in 1991–95, persistent violence in the Caucasus region, and the collapse of stability in the Middle East have all provoked a growing sense of anxiety and uncertainty in western states accustomed to forty years of growing prosperity and international security. The publication in 2006 of a book under the title *Suicide of the West* was symptomatic of those concerns (Koch and Smith, 2006).

All of this has produced a discomfiting sense of change running out of control. Like the 1920s and 1930s, change provoked fears of social and moral decay – the decline of standards of behaviour in public and private life, the failures of modern education, the rise of violent crime, the birth of an alleged 'underclass' of economically and culturally deprived communities. Liberal values were said to be under assault from a number of quarters, from neo-fascism and racism, from religious fundamentalism of all kinds, and from worldwide networks of Islamic terrorism. It is too early to predict if these really are the seeds of a new period of 'crisis' in any real sense, but what matters is the willingness of anxious westerners to believe that there is one. Progress in the modern age has all too often been regarded, rightly or wrongly, as fundamentally ambivalent and uncertain.

Part 4

DOCUMENTS

THE DISILLUSIONMENT OF WAR   **Document 1**

When I speak of disillusionment, everyone at once knows what I mean . . . True, we have told ourselves that wars can never cease so long as nations live under such widely differing conditions . . . But we permitted ourselves to have other hopes. We had expected the great ruling powers among the white nations upon whom the leadership of the human species has fallen, who were known to have cultivated world-wide interests, to whose creative powers were due our technical advances in the direction of dominating nature, as well as the artistic and scientific acquisitions of the mind – peoples such as these we had expected to succeed in discovering another way of settling misunderstandings and conflicts of interest . . . Then the war in which we had refused to believe broke out, and brought – disillusionment. Not only is it more sanguinary and more destructive than any war of other days, because of the enormously increased perfection of weapons of attack and defence; but it is at least as cruel, as embittered, as implacable as any that has preceded it. It sets at naught all those restrictions known as International Law, which in peace-time the states had bound themselves to observe; it ignores the pre-rogatives of the wounded and the medical service, the distinction between civil and military sections of the population, the claims of private property. It tramples in blind fury on all that comes in its way, as though there were to be no future and no goodwill among men after it has passed. It rends all bonds of fellowship between the contending peoples, and threatens to leave such a legacy of embitterment as will make any renewal of such bonds impossible for a long time to come.

Source: S. Freud (1915) 'Thoughts for the times on war and death', in S. Freud (1952), *Collected Papers*, vol. iv (Hogarth Press, London), pp. 289–93.

NIETZSCHE AND LIBERALISM   **Document 2**

Liberal institutions cease to be liberal as soon as they are attained: later on, there are no worse and no more thorough injurers of freedom than liberal institutions. Their effects are known well enough: they undermine the will to power; they level mountain and valley, and call that morality; they make men small, cowardly, and hedonistic – every time it is the herd animal that triumphs with them. Liberalism: in other words, herd-animalization.

These same institutions produce quite different effects while they are being fought for; then they really promote freedom in a powerful way. On closer inspection, it is war that produces these effects, the war *for* liberal institutions, which, as a war, permits illiberal instincts to continue. And war educates for freedom. For what is freedom? That one has the will to assume responsibility for oneself. That one maintains the distance that separates us. That one becomes more indifferent to difficulties, hardships, privation, even to life itself. That one is prepared to sacrifice human beings for one's cause, not excluding oneself. Freedom means that the manly instincts which delight in war and victory dominate over other instincts, for example over those of 'pleasure'. The human being who has *become free* – and how much more the *spirit* who has become free – spits on the contemptible type of well-being dreamed of by shopkeepers, Christians, cows, females, Englishmen, and other democrats. The free man is a *warrior*.

Source: F. Nietzsche (1889) *Twilight of the Idols or How one Philosophizes with a Hammer* (p. 38), reproduced in H. Kariel (ed.) (1964), *Sources in Twentieth-Century Political Thought* (Free Press, London), pp. 23–4.

Document 3   STEMMING 'RACIAL DEGENERATION'

Eugenics is indispensable for the perpetuation of the strong. A great race must propagate its best elements. However, in the most highly civilized nations reproduction is decreasing and yields inferior products. Women voluntarily deteriorate through alcohol and tobacco. They subject themselves to dangerous dietary regimens in order to obtain a conventional slenderness of their figure. Besides, they refuse to bear children. Such a defection is due to their education, to the progress of feminism, to the growth of short-sighted selfishness. It also comes from economic conditions, nervous imbalance, instability of marriage, and fear of the burden imposed upon parents by the weakness or precocious corruption of children. The women belonging to the oldest stock, whose children would, in all probability, be of good quality, and who are in a position to bring them up intelligently, are almost sterile. It is the newcomers, peasants and proletarians from primitive European countries, who beget large families . . .

   The free practice of eugenics could lead not only to the development of stronger individuals, but also of strains endowed with more endurance, intelligence and courage. These strains should constitute an aristocracy, from which great men would probably appear. Modern society must promote, by all possible means, the formation of better human stock. No financial or moral rewards should be too great for those who, through the wisdom of their marriage, would engender geniuses. There is a need today of men of larger mental and moral size. The establishment of a hereditary biological aristocracy through voluntary eugenics would be an important step toward the solution of our present problems . . .

For the first time in the history of humanity, a crumbling civilization is capable of discerning the causes of its decay. For the first time, it has at its disposal the gigantic strength of science. Will we utilize this knowledge and this power? It is our only hope of escaping the fate common to all great civilizations of the past.

Source: A. Carrel (1935) *Man, the Unknown* (London), reproduced in J. Thurber et al. (1941), *Decade 1931–1941: A Commemorative Anthology* (Hamish Hamilton, London), pp. 107–9.

TROTSKY'S 'PERMANENT REVOLUTION' **Document 4**

The great imperialist war is that frightful instrument by means of which history has disrupted the 'organic', 'evolutionary', 'peaceful' character of capitalist development. Growing out of capitalist development as a whole, imperialism acts as if to discount the difference in levels attained by the development of the respective capitalist countries. At one and the same time they were all drawn into the imperialist war, their productive foundations, their class relations were shaken simultaneously. Given this condition, the first countries to be driven out of the state of unstable capitalist equilibrium were those whose internal social energy was weakest, i.e., precisely those countries youngest in terms of capitalist development.

Precisely because of the entire preceding development, the task of initiating the revolution, as we have already seen, was not placed on an old proletariat with mighty political and trade-union organizations, with solid traditions of parliamentarianism and trade unionism, but upon the younger proletariat of a backward country. History took the line of least resistance. The revolutionary epoch burst in through the most weakly barricaded door. Those extraordinary and truly superhuman difficulties which thereupon fell on the Russian proletariat have prepared, have hastened, and have to a certain degree made easier the revolutionary work that lies still ahead for the Western European proletariat.

The revolutionary 'birthright' of the Russian proletariat is only temporary . . . The dictatorship of the Russian working class will be able to consolidate itself finally and to develop a genuine, all-sided Socialist construction only from the hour when the European working class frees us from the economic yoke and especially the military yoke of the European bourgeoisie, and having overthrown the latter, comes to our assistance with its organization and its technology. Concurrently the leading revolutionary role will pass over to the working class with the greater economic and organizational power. If today the centre of the Third International lies in Moscow then tomorrow

– of this we are profoundly convinced – this centre will shift westward: to Berlin, to Paris, to London . . . For a World Communist Congress in Berlin or Paris would signify the complete triumph of the proletarian revolution in Europe and consequently throughout the world.

Source: L. Trotsky (1919) 'Thoughts on the progress of the proletarian revolution', April 1919, in I. Deutscher (ed.) (1963), *The Age of Permanent Revolution: A Trotsky Anthology* (Dell Publishers, New York), pp. 127, 130–1.

Document 5   THE REVOLUTIONARY THREAT

It would be extremely instructive if the Bolshevik leaders could all be psycho-analyzed. Certainly many of their acts suggest peculiar mental states. The atrocities perpetrated by some of the Bolshevik Commissars, for example, are so revolting that they seem explicable only by mental aberrations like homicidal mania or the sexual perversion known as sadism.

One such scientific experiment of a group of Bolshevik leaders has been made. At the time of the Red terror in the city of Kiev, in the summer of 1919, the medical professors of Kiev university were spared on account of their usefulness to their terrorist masters. Three of these medical men were competent alienists, who were able to diagnose the Bolshevik leaders mentally in the course of their professional duties. Now their diagnosis was that nearly all the Bolshevik leaders were degenerates, of more or less unsound mind. Furthermore, most of them were alcoholics, a majority were syphilitic, while many were drug fiends. Such were the 'dictators' who for months terrorized a great city of more than 600,000 inhabitants, committed the most fiendish atrocities, and butchered many leading citizens, including scholars of international reputation.

Of course, what is true of the leaders is even truer of the followers. In Russia, as in every other social upheaval, the bulk of the fighting revolutionists consists of the most turbulent and worthless elements of the population, far outnumbering the small nucleus of genuine zealots for whom the revolution is a pure ideal . . . The Bolshevik leaders from the start deliberately inflamed the worst passions of the city rabble, while the 'pauper' elements in the villages were systematically incited against the thriftier peasants. When the Bolshevik Government became firmly established, proletarian violence was controlled and directed against its enemies.

The spirit, however, remained the same – a spirit of wild revolt, of measureless violence, of frenzied hatred of the old order in every form. All glory, honour and triumph to the revolution; to the fury of the *proletarian will*; to the whirlwind of unfettered brute action; to the madness for *doing things*!

This spirit is vividly portrayed in Alexander Blok's famous poem, *The Twelve**. Blok preaches implacable hatred of the old world; of the 'lazy bourgeois'; of all that belongs to yesterday, which fancied itself secure and has become the booty of the Red Guards.

> 'For the bourgeois woe and sorrow.
> We shall start a world-wide fire.
> And with blood that fire we'll blend.'

* Blok was one of the famous Russian expressionist poets who converted to Bolshevism in the Revolution. The Twelve are Red Guards whose heroic revolutionary deeds are compared to those of the twelve disciples of Jesus.

Source: L. Stoddard (1922) *The Revolt against Civilization: The Menace of the Under-Man* (Chapman and Hall, London), pp. 177–8. (Stoddard was an American author and journalist, who also wrote *The Rising Tide of Colour*.)

THE REVENGE OF THE RIGHT **Document 6**

From then on the slaughter of working-class politicians became systematic. The Nazis marked down the local Communist member of the Reichstag, Walter Schütz of Königsberg, as their prey. Schütz had volunteered for war service when seventeen years old, had been three times seriously wounded, and after the war became prominent in the revolutionary working-class movement in Königsberg in East Prussia. He had frequently been threatened by the National-Socialists. One of them named Koch, now SA Leader and President of the Administration of East Prussia, during a session of the Königsberg members of the Reichstag, had shouted to him:

> 'Wait till we catch you! Then we'll beat you to death!'

And so it happened. One night at the end of March 1933, Koch himself led a gang of Storm Troopers into Schütz's house. The subsequent events have been secretly reported by one of the persons who took part and who subsequently relented to the deed:

> 'Schütz was taken to a room in the old station so that his screams should not be heard. He was stripped naked. Then my companions beat him with iron rods so that after some time he collapsed unconscious. He was then douched with water. When he came to his hair was pulled out in handfuls . . . After two and a half hours of this treatment Schütz lay

prone on the floor. He was hardly a human creature, but an unrecogniz-
able mass of still breathing flesh. My companions took him and dragged
him along the whole length of the Schleusenstrasse, raining blows upon
him all the time. When they arrived at the police Headquarters they
took him on their backs and sat him on a chair in the office of Landhöfer,
an official in the Criminal Investigation department. Landhöfer later said:
"I have never seen a more dreadful sight in my life." '

Source: G. Dimitrov (1934) *The Reichstag Fire Trial: The Second Brown Book of the Hitler
Terror* (John Lane at the Bodley Head, London), Appendix by Lion Feuchtwanger,
'Murder in Hitler-Germany', p. 327.

Document 7   THE LEGACY OF 1917

This means, firstly, that the October revolution inflicted a mortal wound on
world capitalism from which the latter will never recover. It is precisely for
this reason that capitalism will never recover the 'equilibrium' and 'stability'
that it possessed before October. Capitalism may become partly stabilized, it
may rationalize production, turn over the administration of the country to
fascism, temporarily hold down the working class; but it will never recover
the 'tranquility', the 'assurance', the 'equilibrium' and the 'stability' that it
flaunted before; for the crisis of world capitalism has reached the stage of
development where the flames of revolution must inevitably break out, now
in the centres of imperialism, now in the periphery, reducing to naught the
capitalist patchwork, and daily bringing nearer the fall of capitalism . . .

   This really explains the brutal hatred which the exploiters of all countries
entertain for the Bolsheviks. History repeats itself, though on a new basis.
Just as formerly, during the period of the decline of *feudalism*, the word
'Jacobin' evoked horror and loathing among the aristocrats of all countries,
so now, in the period of the decline of *capitalism*, the word 'Bolshevik' evokes
horror and loathing among the bourgeois in all countries. And just as formerly Paris was the refuge and school for the revolutionary representatives of
the rising *bourgeoisie*, so now Moscow is the refuge and school for the revolutionary representatives of the rising *proletariat*. Hatred for the Jacobins did
not save feudalism from collapse. Can there be any doubt that hatred for the
Bolsheviks will not save capitalism from inevitable destruction?

   The era of the 'stability' of capitalism has passed away, taking with it the
legend of the indestructibility of the bourgeois order.

   The era of the collapse of capitalism *has begun*.

Source: Speech by Josef Stalin, 'The international character of the October Revolution', given to mark the tenth anniversary of the Revolution, on 6 November 1927, in J. Stalin (1947), *Problems of Leninism* (State Publishing House, Moscow).

A BRIGHT NEW TOMORROW   **Document 8**

We are convinced that to the engineer all things are possible. He can give us a pure atmosphere and noiseless streets, he can remove slums and make wholesome factories, he can wipe away degrading occupations and improve the occupations of leisure, he can make a fair country out of a blasted waste, and clean rivers out of foul ditches. All these things, and a thousand more, he can do without robbing us of a single one of the benefits and advantages which his works confer. We say this with confidence, because we witness daily all that he has achieved. But a vast amount remains to be done, a mountain of ugliness remains to be removed, and we deem it a good thing that the coming generation of engineers should grow up in the belief that it is the duty of engineers to make the countries in which they live more beautiful and more pleasant and wholly free from the taunts which artists, literary men, and philosophers may justly throw at them today.

Source: Article in the *Engineer*, reproduced in R.E. Flanders, 'The new age and the new man', in C.A. Beard (1930), *Toward Civilization* (Longmans, Green and Co., London), p. 30.

CONTRACEPTION AND RACE   **Document 9**

A modern and humane civilization *must* control conception or sink into barbaric cruelty to individuals. What our progenitors achieved crudely and clumsily, often painfully, we, aided by modern scientific knowledge, can and should achieve painlessly and precisely.

Apart from the needs of individual patients, a word should be said of the national, indeed the racial position. For want of contraceptive measures the low-grade stocks are breeding in an ever-increasing ratio in comparison to high-grade stocks, to the continuous detriment of the race. Hence the medical practitioner who has a practice among the low-grade elements, has a double duty to inculcate contraceptive knowledge, a duty to his individual patients and a duty to the State.

Source: M. Stopes (1928) *Contraception: Theory, History and Practice* (John Bale & Sons, London), pp. 9–10.

Document 10   OLD AND NEW IN A RUSSIAN VILLAGE

The fields were again humming with work. Peasants were getting ready for the winter sowing. Some of them were drawing manure in their little one-horse carts. Others, mostly women and children, were scattering this manure with their bare hands. Others again were ploughing with wood-framed ploughs that stirred up only a thin layer of earth, and still others were vainly trying to break up the lumps of soil with their toothpick harrows. These, of course, were individualist farmers, who from necessity more per-haps than from choice, were clinging to their ancient tools and their ancient methods of tillage. Across the road from their fields, was the *kolkhoz*, spread-ing majestically to the horizon. No tractors or other machines were now at work, but the mere sight of it made one think of the huge steel mechanisms, which like a conquering army were marching onward and onward, all over the Russian countryside.

Now I was likewise overcome with incredulity. This ancient countryside seemed like a legend. These *muzhiks* who fumed and railed, who wept and despaired or who thrilled and gloried, and all their new ideas and trans-formations, their dreams and conflicts, seemed too fantastic to be real. I knew these *muzhiks* so well in the old days. They were shut off from the tumult and excitement of the times. None of them ever read a newspaper or heard of foreign lands save America and perhaps Turkey. Very few of them ever saw a railway train or heard of electricity or any of the machines that had been coming to the *kolkhoz*. They trembled in the presence of officials and the landlord was to them the great master of the world. Their thoughts, their ambitions, their daily pursuits, were bounded by their village and the nearest town bazaar. Nor could they escape from their antecedents. They were born *muzhiks*, they would always remain *muzhiks* and they would die *muzhiks*. That was their destiny and they could conceive of none other. They were all but buried in these ancient marshlands.

Yet now here they were all of them, the *koolack* and the revolutionary, the *bedniak* and the *seredniak*, and above all the children with their games of war between proletarians and *bourzhuis* . . . A flood of new ideas was mercilessly beating down on them and a whole new world was rising before their very eyes. Whatever their future, the past with all its anchorages was fast break-ing down. They could never again be what they had been throughout the ages, never!

Source: M. Hindus (1931) *Red Bread: Collectivization in a Russian Village* (Jonathan Cape, London), pp. 329–32. (Hindus was a Russian emigrant to the United States, who wrote extensively on Soviet affairs. This extract concerns a visit to the village where he was born.)

————◀●▶————

'IMPERSONALIZATION' AND THE MACHINE AGE   **Document 11**

To this depersonalization of science, the discipline of the modern factory lends its compelling support. The operative is a functioning datum fitted, much as any other piece of machinery, into a mechanically controlled and regulated routine of interlocking mechanical and chemical processes. Personal contact between man and man, whether equal or superior, is either lost entirely or reduced to rest pauses, explanation of instruction sheets, or leisure hours. The goods turned out are typically standardized and uniform, and bear few if any marks of craftsmenlike skill. Workmanlike pride in the job as such is largely gone. Often the operative knows nothing of the other processes which go to make the finished product, and little concerning the source of the materials or the destination of the finished goods. Typically he has even less of a hand in control over any phase of the functioning complex which he serves. Under highly standardized production methods, he tends to become as readily displaceable as any other component part. Training, even up through some of the more skilled and directing staff, tends to be short, formal, schematized, and standard. Any individual is easily displaced; factors of personality have relatively little to do with performance, given willingness to work and the necessary adeptness . . .

Plan and order, and scientifically defensible patterns of organization and procedure are the essence of rationalization, regardless of the field of human activity which it touches. The human equation and the elements of personal judgement, individual taste, and caprice are ruled out and set aside as these changes are made. Rationalization on the human side is practically synonomous with impersonalization, and, under modern conditions, with secularization.

Source: R.A. Brady (1933) *The Rationalization Movement in German Industry: A Study in the Evolution of Economic Planning* (University of California Press, Berkeley), pp. 403–4. (Brady was Professor of Economics at the University of California.)

THE NATIONAL SOCIALIST APPEAL TO THE PEASANTRY   **Document 12**

In disregard of the biological and economic significance of the peasantry and in contradiction to the vital necessity of increasing the productivity of agriculture, the present German state has permitted the maintenance of an economically sound peasantry to be most severely threatened.

A considerable increase in agricultural production is in itself perfectly possible to achieve, but it is being prevented because the farmers, increasingly indebted, lack the necessary tools and materials, and because the incentive to increase production is lacking, for agricultural labour no longer pays well.

The reasons why agricultural labour earns insufficient return (profit) are to be found:

1. In the present tax policy, which burdens agriculture disproportionately. This happens because of party politics and because the Jewish world financial monopoly, which in actuality runs the German parliamentary democracy, seeks the destruction of German agriculture. The German people, and especially the workers, are utterly at its mercy.
2. In our competition with foreign agriculture, which produces under more favourable conditions, which is not sufficiently curbed by our tariff policy, which is hostile to agriculture.
3. In unacceptably high profits which go to the wholesale trade in agricultural products. It steps in between producer and consumer and today lies mostly in the hands of Jews.
4. In the usurious prices which the peasant has to pay for artificial fertilizers and electric power to concerns which are mostly Jewish.

High taxes can no longer be paid out of the poor returns on agricultural production. The peasant is forced to contract debts on which he has to pay usurious interest. He finds himself more and more in bondage to interest and in the end loses house and farm to the predominantly Jewish owners of loan capital.

The German peasantry is being uprooted

A sweeping improvement of the lot of the farmers and the recovery of agriculture will not occur as long as the international money magnates, with the help of the parliamentary-democratic government system, actually rule the German empire, for they want to destroy indigenous German forces.

Only in the new German state, essentially different from the old, which we are seeking to establish, will the farmers and agriculture find that consideration which they deserve as the mainstay of a true German popular state.

Source: 'Official Party statement on its attitude toward the farmers and agriculture', *Völkischer Beobachter*, 6 March 1930, reproduced in B. Miller Lane and L.J. Rupp (eds) (1978), *Nazi Ideology before 1933: A Documentation* (Manchester University Press, Manchester), pp. 119–20.

REJECTING THE DEPARTMENT STORE   **Document 13**

Attention! Gravediggers at work!

Middle-class citizens! Retailers! Craftsmen! Tradesmen!

A new blow aimed at your ruin is being prepared and carried out in Hanover! The present system enables the gigantic concern

WOOLWORTH (America)

supported by finance capital, to build a new vampire business in the centre of the city in Georgstrasse to expose you to complete ruin. This is the wish and aim of the black-red system as expressed in the following remarks of Marxist leaders.

The Marxist Engels declared in May 1890: 'If capital destroys the small artisans and retailers it does a good thing . . .'

That is the black-red system of today!

Put an end to this system and its abettors! Defend yourself, middle-class citizen! Join the mighty organisation that alone is in a position to conquer your arch enemies. Fight with us in the section for Craftsmen and Retail Traders within the great freedom movement of Adolf Hitler.

Put an end to the system!

Source: Draft Nazi pamphlet, *c.* April 1932, in J. Noakes and G. Pridham (eds) (1983), *Nazism: A Documentary Reader. 1: The Rise to Power 1919–1934* (Exeter University Press, Exeter), p. 76.

A 'JEW-FREE' VIENNA   **Document 14**

Fischböck – In Austria, Herr General Field Marshal, we already have a precise plan. There are 12,000 Jewish craft businesses and 5,000 Jewish retail stores . . . Of the 12,000 craft businesses approximately 10,000 should in the end be closed and 2,000 maintained. Of the 5,000 retail stores 1,000 should be kept going, that is aryanized, and 4,000 closed. According to this plan therefore, 3,000 to 3,500 of the total of 17,000 businesses would stay open, all the rest will be closed. This has been adjusted on the basis of enquiries about the local requirements of every single branch, has been approved by all the responsible offices, and can be given out tomorrow as long as we get the law that we asked for in September, which will empower us in a general sense, not just linked to the Jewish question, to withdraw the right to trade.

Göring – I'll publish the decree today.

Fischböck – . . . It is now of concern if it is carried through in a form only involving the remaining 3,000 businesses, which are fixed for aryaniza-tion according to the branch planning. There are firm purchasers for approximately half these businesses, whose contracts of sale have been checked up to the point that they could be approved immediately . . . For the approximately 1,500 remaining businesses negotiations are in a great many cases also far advanced. In this way we could, by the end of the year, have eliminated the whole visible world of Jewish business.

Göring – That would be splendid! I must say the proposal is wonderful. For this whole business would actually be cleared up by Christmas or the end of the year in Vienna, one of the chief Jewish cities, so to speak.

Funk – We can do it here too. I have prepared an order for this contingency, which states that from the 1st of January 1939 Jews are prohibited from engaging in retail trade, mail-order business, or an independent craft trade.

Source: 'Stenographic minutes of a discussion of the Jewish question in the Air Ministry with General Field Marshal Göring, 12 Nov. 1938', in International Military Tribunal, *Trial of the Major War Criminals*, vol. 28 (Nuremberg, 1947), pp. 524–5.

Document 15   THE SUICIDE OF CIVILIZATION

We are living to-day under the sign of the collapse of civilisation. The situ-ation has not been produced by the war; the latter is only a manifestation of it. The spiritual atmosphere has solidified into actual facts, which again react on it with disastrous results in every respect. This interaction of material and spiritual has assumed a most unhealthy character. Just below a mighty cataract we are driving along in a current full of formidable eddies, and it will need the most gigantic efforts to rescue the vessel of our fate from the dangerous side channels into which we have allowed it to drift, and bring it back into the main stream, if, indeed, we can hope to do it at all . . . It is clear now to everyone that the suicide of civilisation is in progress. What yet remains of it is no longer safe. It is still standing, indeed, because it was not exposed to the destructive pressure which overwhelmed the rest, but, like the rest, is built on rubble, and the next landslide will very likely carry it away.

Source: Albert Schweitzer (1923) *The Decay and Restoration of Civilization: Part I, the Philosophy of Civilization* (A & C Black, London), pp. 1–3. (Schweitzer was a well-known doctor and missionary from Alsace who spent much of his life working in equatorial Africa.)

RACE MIXTURE AND THE FUTURE OF CIVILIZATION   **Document 16**

Any race which is in possession of a land should take all these facts [about racial mixing] into consideration. Such a race is morally bound to give the closest attention to the effects of race-migration, not only as it affects the present generation of its citizens, but as it affects the future generations, both as regards their heredity and their environment.

It is surely of great significance that all the peoples of our own Celtic-Anglo-Saxon stock who have had the most practical experience of these problems are doing their utmost to exclude the Mongolian and the Negro races from their countries. I need only refer to recent legislation in Canada, Australia and the United States to show this. But this is much more than an Imperial problem, it affects the future of the white race itself and through it the future of civilisation.

. . . The Negro in the past has not shown any great genius for stable political institutions. The native states established a century ago in South Africa ended in collapse. The Black Republics of Hayti [sic] and Santo Domingo in the West Indies are examples of Negro rule after a considerable degree of white influence and their record is wholesale massacre. Even in Liberia, at the present day, slavery and torture are common. Thus, there is good reason to fear that if Africa is to fall back under Negro rule, it will deserve its name – the Dark Continent.

When we turn to the Mongolian races of Asia, we must recognize that, speaking practically, they are the most serious menace to the Caucasian race. Even now we are feeling severely the commercial competition of one of them [e.g. Japan] and there is nothing incredible in the idea of another invasion of Europe from the East. It has happened several times before, and evidences of these invasions remain, not only in written history, but in the Hungarians and the Lapps, who are Mongolians, and in the Alpine Sub-race which is Asiatic in origin.

We have all heard of the Yellow Peril, and a recent writer expresses his opinion of its reality in three words – '*Ex oriente – Nox*' [from the east – darkness]. That is one view of the ethnological future. For us it is a gloomy one . . .

Source: K.B. Aikman 'Race Mixture', read before the Eugenics Society, London, 20 June 1933, reproduced in *The Eugenics Review*, 25 (1933/4), p. 165.

Document 17   THE GERMAN STERILIZATION LAW

Law for the Prevention of Hereditarily Diseased Offspring

§1   (i)   Anyone who has a hereditary illness can be rendered sterile by a surgical operation if, according to the experience of medical science, there is a strong probability that his/her offspring will suffer from serious hereditary defects of a physical or mental nature.

(ii)   Anyone is hereditarily ill within the meaning of this law who suffers from one of the following illnesses: (a) congenital feeble-mindedness (b) schizophrenia (c) manic depression (d) hereditary epilepsy (e) Huntington's chorea (f) hereditary blindness (g) hereditary deafness (h) serious physical deformities.

(iii)   In addition, anyone who suffers from chronic alcoholism can be sterilised.

§2   An application for sterilisation can legitimately be made by the person to be sterilised. In the case of persons who are either not legally responsible or have been certified because of mental deficiency or have not yet reached their nineteenth birthday, the legal guardian is so entitled . . .

Reasons for the Law: Since the National Uprising public opinion has become increasingly preoccupied with questions of population policy and the continuing decline in birthrate. However, it is not only the decline in population which is the cause of serious concern but equally the increasingly evident genetic make-up of our people. Whereas the hereditarily healthy families have for the most part adopted a policy of having only one or two children, countless numbers of inferiors and those suffering from hereditary ailments are reproducing unrestrainedly while their sick and asocial offspring are a burden on the community . . .

Source: J. Noakes and G. Pridham (eds) (1986) *Documents on Nazism. Volume 2: State, Economy and Society 1933–1939* (University of Exeter Press, Exeter), pp. 263–4.

Document 18   THE OVER-SEXED GIRL

Sex-delinquency in women is a mode of misconduct fairly well defined; it is common in its incidence as it is baffling in its response to treatment. It seems, then, to be a social problem which calls, perhaps more urgently than any other, for intensive study . . . The passion for a particular man, or for male company, is an obvious consequence of the girl who is over-sexed; and leads easily to prostitution. Often, however, the chief motive is simply a passion for some selfish form of pleasure or the sheer absence of any ennobling passion whatsoever.

One deplorable characteristic, all but universal among these girls, is their narrow range of interests and incapacity for strong and permanent attachments. Most of them seem almost impotent to form steady sentiments whether for persons or for ideals . . . Among the youngest the chief interests that they acquire lie generally in the direction of the crudest pleasures – particularly, as I have already noted, the pleasure of eating; the blind instinct for sweet things develops quickly into a conscious passion for sweets or cake or fruit. With those who are a little older the chief interest is a craving for cheap amusement – for the cinema to begin with, later on for the music-hall or the theatre, for dancing or for restaurant life. At and after adolescence the passion for dress and personal adornment comes overwhelmingly to the fore.

Source: Cyril Burt (1926) 'The causes of sex-delinquency in girls', *Health and Empire*, 1, pp. 231, 268–9. (Burt was Professor of Education in the University of London.)

THE END OF THE ENLIGHTENMENT   **Document 19**

Thus there gradually became established that philosophy into whose realm all but the youngest of us were born. Man's faith in reason was so abundantly confirmed that it was hardly possible for him to doubt in the universal saving power of rational thought.

Such was the mental situation in Europe as recently as half a generation ago. Since then, however, a change has come over the spirit of our dream. To-day a revolt against reason has become general. That which was our greatest pride, is now contemned. Instead of worshipping reason, people incline to glorify whatever is unreasonable, contra-reasonable – the irrational, the instinctive, the elemental.

Blood, force, myth, race, nation; these are to-day the prevailing catch-words; these concepts, we are told, must guide us in developing the new social and political systems. States have been established whose leading principle is not the pursuit of a rational aim, and whose laws are not in conformity with the outlook of rational humanity and democracy. They proclaim their faith in the irrational powers of feeling, in impulses which, until recently, were unanimously looked upon as prejudices, as fallacies which had neither been proved nor were capable of proof.

Contemporary Europe regards this revolt against reason with astonishment not untinged with sympathy. Everywhere we see deserters from the camp of those who believe in reason, go over with banners flying and drums beating to swell the ranks of the rebels against reason.

Indeed, it is no exaggeration to say that for the majority, to-day, the ideas of their parents and grandparents concerning the possibility of general progress under the sign of reason, the brotherhood of man, universal humanity and democracy, have lost convincing force. The flame of these ideas no longer burns brightly; their truth seems questionable, their sublimity has become dubious.

The new rebels sing a siren's song, which to many seems much more alluring than the promises of the children of the rationalist Enlightenment. They proclaim a wonder-world of mythical experience; they trumpet the glories of action, of dynamic, the power of the instincts.

Source: René Fülöp-Miller (1935) 'The new revolt against Reason', *The Hibbert Journal*, 34, p. 181.

Document 20   THE PSYCHOLOGICAL DILEMMA OF MODERN MAN

Psychic life always found expression in a metaphysical system of some sort. But the conscious, modern man, despite his strenuous and dogged efforts to do so, can no longer refrain from acknowledging the might of psychic forces. This distinguishes our time from all others. We can no longer deny that the dark stirrings of the unconscious are effective powers – that psychic forces exist which cannot, for the present at least, be fitted with our rational world-order. We have even enlarged our study of these forces to a science . . . The revolution in our conscious outlook, brought about by the catastrophic results of the World War, shows itself in our inner life by the shattering of our faith in ourselves and in our own worth. We used to regard foreigners – the other side – as political and moral reprobates; but the modern man is forced to recognize that he is politically and morally just like anyone else. Whereas I formerly believed it to be my bounden duty to call other persons to order, I now admit that I need calling to order myself. I admit this the more readily because I realize only too well that I am losing my faith in the possibility of a rational organization of the world, that old dream of the millennium, in which peace and harmony should rule, has grown pale. The modern man's scepticism regarding all such matters has chilled his enthusiasm for politics and world-reform; more than that, it does not favour any smooth application of the psychic energies to the outer world . . . If he turns away from the terrifying prospect of a blind world in which building and destroying successively tip the scale, and if he then turns his gaze inward upon the recesses of his own mind, he will discover a chaos and darkness there which he would gladly ignore. Science has destroyed even the refuge of the inner life. What was once a sheltering haven has become a place of terror.

Source: Carl Jung (1936) 'The spiritual problem of modern man' in *Modern Man in Search of a Soul* (Kegan Paul, London), pp. 234–6. (Jung was a Swiss psychotherapist, who became, together with Freud, the most influential psychologist of his generation.)

DESCENT INTO BARBARISM   Document 21

One thing is clear: the nations are playing with fire to-day. The endurance of the peoples is nearly at an end. That is not to say that the people will rise, as the nineteenth-century optimists imagined, sweep away effete governments and found a new order. The outlook would not be so grave could we, beyond the smoke of the explosion, see the new order about to arise. The danger is that the anarchic immorality may spread to the ruled. Instead of states rising to the moral standards now expected of individuals, the individuals may be dragged down to the level of the states . . . There is something worse than the most frightful of revolutions as there is something more deadly than the most violent of eruptions, that is the cold of complete despair and the breaking, in man, through persistent betrayal, of his power to sacrifice himself for anything any more. Then all men of understanding flee the world and the only men remaining are worse than animals. The petty brigand and the gangster are the appointed successors of national leaders who use the brigand's methods till they have broken down the body of civilisation to the level at which these smaller putrefactive bacteria can reduce it to complete decomposition.

It is clear, then, that another war must be avoided at any price. The only consequence of it must be either a direct descent into brigandage or a descent via a dictatorship which, after a wretched delay, must deliquesce into the same barbarism.

Source: Gerald Heard (1935) 'And suppose we fail? After the next war' in *Challenge to Death* (Constable, London), p. 170. (Heard was a well-known author and peace campaigner.)

THE 'GOLDEN AGE' OF FREE TRADE   Document 22

. . . The nineteenth century formulated and applied a way of life which while retaining the basic principles of the eighteenth century tried to combine them with the new system of production resulting from the industrial revolution. During that glorious period of expansion, which really lasted down to the World War, the European continent was divided politically, but it functioned nevertheless as a unified civilization of a race everywhere recognized as superior and worthy to lead. There also existed an economic system which, originating in Europe and more particularly in England, extended its benefits to all Europeans and, in a general way, to all white humanity. Though not consciously so, it was in essence an international system and a liberal system. At any rate it was international and liberal in comparison with the system that the twentieth century is putting in its place. This is a matter of personal experience for my generation. As a boy I saw the nineteenth-century system in operation without realizing that it was something quite exceptional in history, and that before long we would be mourning its passing. Today I look back upon it with something of the nostalgia that the people of the Middle Ages felt for the Roman Empire, or that touched Talleyrand when he talked of 'the comfortable living' under the Old Regime.

In those days when one left the shores of Europe one entered a sort of international mercantile republic. It operated under the British flag; but by virtue of a principle called 'fair play' any white person, of whatever country, could take advantage of it. Economic management on a world-wide basis actually existed. Europe devised it and Europe largely benefited by it. The phenomenal development of the United States was not to come till later. It was a management of an exceedingly delicate and an exceedingly intelligent sort – nothing like the dictatorial 'planned economies' of today. It made money-changing, freightage and travelling very easy. Boats and trains were not so fast as they are now, but one was considerably surer of getting where one wanted to go. Bureaucratic difficulties were reduced to a shadow. One could rely on a general stability in almost everything. Tariffs and duties were stable under long-term treaties. National credits were stable – the word of any one of the great countries seemed as trustworthy as the existence of the country itself. Currencies had a value in gold and they were interchangeable at only slight fluctuations in price. There was the greatest freedom as regards the movement of persons. Emigration and immigration were virtually free. Investigations and examinations at frontiers were matters of perfunctory routine. I can see that enormous advances have been made since those days in technical equipment; but I cannot help seeing just as clearly that civilization has gone backward . . .

Source: A. Siegfried, 'War for our world', *Foreign Affairs*, vol. 18, 1939/40, pp. 415–16. (Siegfried was a French writer and economist.)

LIVING WITH INFLATION   **Document 23**

a)   15 November 1923 – Berlin

The value of the mark continues to drop to unbelievable figures, astronomical figures. When you go shopping you have to carry your banknotes in suitcases. Savings accounts have been absolutely wiped out. In order to mail a letter inside Germany I had to pay several million marks for a stamp. Germany's money is worth less than a scrap of paper. Foreigners can buy anything in Germany for a microscopic sum of their gold-backed currency.

Before I left Kitzingen I called on one of Mother's old friends, an old lady who had been one of the wealthiest women in that part of the country. I found the huge house stone-cold. All the rooms were practically empty. I found the old lady, shivering in blankets, by the fireplace in the only heated room in the house.

'For heaven's sake, Aunt Paula!' I exclaimed. 'Where are your rugs, your pictures, your furniture?'

'All gone, child,' she said. 'All gone to an antique shop in Munich, piece by piece. I used to have an income. That is no longer worth anything, and my furniture and pictures have gone for bread, week by week. When the last of it goes . . .' she shrugged her shoulders hopelessly.

Source: B. Fromm (1943) *Blood and Banquets: A Berlin Social Diary* (Geoffrey Bles, London), p. 20. (Bella Fromm was a high-society journalist in Berlin, who fled to America in the 1930s because she was Jewish.)

b)   The printing presses of the government could no longer keep pace. They were still printing ten-thousand-mark bills when one dollar had gone into the millions of marks. You could see mail carriers on the streets with sacks on their backs or pushing baby carriages before them, loaded with paper money that would be devaluated [sic] the next day. Life was madness, nightmare, desperation, chaos . . . The Middle Ages came back. Communities printed their own money, based on goods, on a certain amount of potatoes, or rye, for instance. Shoe factories paid their workers in bonds for shoes which they could exchange at the bakery for bread or the meat market for meat . . .

Before I tell you, however, of the 'happy time of solid money and prosperity' that lay before us, let us once more look back at the battlefield of inflation and the Republic. For a battle it was, this inflation, fought out with financial means. The cities were still there, the houses not yet bombed and in ruins, but the victims were millions of people. They had lost their fortunes, their savings; they were dazed and inflation-shocked and did not understand how it had happened to them and who the foe was who had defeated them. Yet they had lost their self-assurance, their feeling that they themselves could be the masters of their own lives if only they worked hard enough; and lost, too, were the old values of morals, of ethics, of decency.

Source: Erna von Pustau in conversation with Pearl Buck, in P.S. Buck (1947) *How it Happens: Talk about the German People, 1914–1933* (John Day, New York), pp. 201–3.

Document 24   TIME ON THEIR HANDS

Cut off from their work and deprived of contact with the outside world, the workers of Marienthal have lost the material and moral incentives to make use of their time. Now that they are no longer under any pressure, they undertake nothing new and drift gradually out of an ordered existence into one that is undisciplined and empty. Looking back over any period of this free time, they are unable to recall anything worth mentioning.

For hours on end, the men stand around in the street, alone or in small groups, leaning against the wall of a house or the parapet of the bridge. When a vehicle drives through the village they turn their heads slightly; several of them smoke pipes. They carry on leisurely conversations for which they have unlimited time. Nothing is urgent anymore; they have forgotten how to hurry.

Toward noon, when the traffic in Marienthal reaches its modest peak, the movements of the people in the roughly three-hundred meters' stretch of the village's main street presented the following picture, when we counted (for one hundred of them) the number of times they stopped on their way:

Stops on Main Street	Men	Women	Total
3 or more	39	3	42
2	7	2	9
1	16	15	31
0	6	12	18
Total	68	32	100

Almost two-thirds of the men interrupted their walk at least twice; only one out of every ten walked to his destination without stopping. The women presented a strikingly different picture: only about one-sixth of them stopped on two or more occasions. As we shall see later, they have considerably less time on their hands.

From our concealed position at a window we also attempted, watch in hand, to gauge the speed of movement on this leisurely village street. Here are the walking speeds of the fifty people who were observed while covering a reasonable distance without stopping:

Speed of walking miles per hour	Men	Women	Total
3	7	10	17
2½	8	3	11
2	18	4	22
Total	33	17	50

Since for every 100 persons walking in the street there were always about thirty simply standing around, the average speed of movement was extremely low. Once someone trotted past; it turned out to be the village idiot.

Time in Marienthal has a dual nature: it is different for men and women. For the men, the division of the days into hours has long since lost all meaning. Of one hundred men, eighty-eight were not wearing a watch and only thirty-one of these had a watch at home. Getting up, the midday meal, going to bed, are the only remaining points of reference. In between, time elapses without anyone really knowing what has taken place.

Source: M. Jahoda, P. Lazarsfeld and H. Zeisel, *Marienthal: The Sociography of an Unemployed Community* (Transaction Publications, 2002; reprinted from *Die Arbeitslosen von Marienthal*, 1933).

Document 25

THE 'COLLECTIVE' ECONOMY

The world's economic mechanism has lost its self-adjusting quality. And never was it so much needed. New process succeeds new process; the public taste and demand alter incalculably; and every improvement in the transmission of news and in transport increases both the range and the rapidity of the reactions of every change. The mechanism which adjusts production to new demands; which corrects sporadic excesses of supply; which moves capital where it is needed; which stops, or directs or expands enterprise; which adapts every activity to this shifting environment, needs to be flexible and rapid. And everywhere we see that it is precisely these qualities which it has been losing.

We can perhaps, here and there, restore the frictionless self-adjusting quality of the old freely working competitive system. But in every sphere which we have examined we find that this alone will not suffice. We need to supplement it by planned direction, by a regulative control. In the sphere of money and gold, for example, we may perhaps remove some of the impediments to the traditional working of the gold standard, such as the sudden imposition of new tariffs – but we can never have a tolerable medium of world trade unless Governments and Central Banks pursue the agreed objective of a stable general price level through deliberate and co-operative action. In the credit system we may gradually re-establish the confidence of the investor, but we can never avoid the disasters entailed by ill-judged loans unless there is at least a recognized standard of conduct and some accepted basis of policy by the great issue houses. Programmes of industrial production again need obviously to be based upon collective estimates, and to be subject, where necessary, in their execution to some collective influence. And tariff policies will clearly lead to disaster if they continue to be the outcome of the competitive pressure of sectional interests, and to be unrelated to the world situation or even to a general national policy.

The defects of the capitalist system have been increasingly robbing it of its benefits. They are now threatening its existence. A period of depression and crisis is one in which its great merit, the expansion of productive capacity under the stimulus of competitive gain, seems wasted; and its main defect, an increasing inability to utilise productive capacity fully and to distribute what it produces tolerably, is seen at its worst. And, in the mood of desperation caused by impoverishment and unemployment, the challenge of another system becomes more formidable. No one can expect that even if we now get through without disaster, we can long avoid social disintegration and revolution on the widest scale if we have only a prospect of recurring depressions, perhaps of increasing violence.

We have indeed before us only the alternatives of collective leadership, collective control, or chaos – not indeed quite mutually exclusive; for in practice we shall have something of all three. We must do our best to eliminate the third, and make the best mixture we can of the first two. For this is no simple choice between two alternatives: 'Hands off industry by the politician' or 'Leave it to the Government'; 'private enterprise' or 'state control'; 'Capitalism' or 'Communism'. We evade our intricate and complex task if we think it can be solved by slogans instead of reason.

Source: A. Salter (1933) *Recovery: The Second Effort* (G. Bell & Sons, Ltd, London), pp. 208–10. (Salter was a prominent British economist.)

Document 26   LENIN REJECTS DEMOCRACY

To decide once every few years which member of the ruling class is to repress and crush the people through parliament – this is the real essence of bourgeois parliamentarism, not only in parliamentary-constitutional monarchies, but also in the most democratic republics . . .

The way out of parliamentarism is not, of course, the abolition of representative institutions and the elective principle, but the conversion of the representative institutions from talking shops into 'working' bodies. 'The Commune was to be a working, not a parliamentary, body, executive and legislative at the same time' [Marx].

'A working, not a parliamentary, body' – this is a blow straight from the shoulder at the present-day parliamentarians and parliamentary 'lap dogs' of Social-Democracy! Take any parliamentary country, from America to Switzerland, from France to Britain, Norway and so forth – in these countries the real business of 'state' is performed behind the scenes and is carried on by the departments, chancelleries, and General Staffs. Parliament is given up to talk for the special purpose of fooling the 'common people'. This is so true that even in the Russian republic, a bourgeois-democratic republic, all these sins of parliamentarism came out at once, even before it managed to set up a real parliament. The heroes of rotten philistinism have even succeeded in polluting the Soviets after the fashion of the most disgusting bourgeois parliamentarism, in converting them into mere talking shops. In the Soviets, the 'socialist' Ministers are fooling the credulous rustics with phrasemongering and resolutions. In the government itself a sort of permanent shuffle is going on in order that, on the one hand, as many Socialist-Revolutionaries and Mensheviks [the main social-democratic parties in Russia in 1917] as possible may in turn get near the 'pie', the lucrative and honourable posts, and that, on the other hand, the 'attention' of the people may be 'engaged'. Meanwhile the chancelleries and army staffs 'do' the business of 'state'.

Source: V.I. Lenin (1949) *The State and Revolution* in *Collected Works* (State Publishing House, Moscow), vol. 25.

FRENCH POLITICS IN CRISIS, 6 FEBRUARY 1934   **Document 27**

On February 6th, the Daladier Government, with its 'heavy record of blunders', was making its first appearance before the Chamber of Deputies; having dismissed Chiappe [the Paris Prefect of Police] it was now practically certain of having obtained the support of the Socialists; and the mere thought that this Government would be approved by the majority of the elected representatives of the French people had a maddening effect on the 'Reactionaries'. This anger against the Government was shared by many other people who were not really reactionaries, but who were simply bewildered by Daladier's eccentric and muddle-headed behaviour. Without being necessarily in love with Chiappe a very large proportion of the people of Paris felt that Daladier had made a hopelessly bad start, and that the anger he had aroused among the 'Reactionaries' was, to say the least, understandable and excusable; and great was the number of Parisians that day who were sick of the Chamber . . . The Solidarité Française published in the *Ami du Peuple* of February 6th the following appeal:

> 'France for the French!
> Take your brooms and sweep out this rubbish!
> We have had enough of this!'

. . . A more coherent appeal appeared in the *Action Française* of February 6th:

> 'CONTRE LES VOLEURS, CONTRE LE REGIME
> ABJECT
> TOUS, CE SOIR, DEVANT LA CHAMBRE!'

Below this gigantic headline, the following appeal was published:

> **To the People of Paris*
> Called to power in the hope that they would restore justice and order, Messrs Frot and Daladier began their work by chasing out the policemen. They have given free rein to Socialist anarchy, and want to save the Masonic crooks.
>
> In trying to force this abject regime on us, in trying to smother the voice of public opinion, MM Daladier and Frot are hurling violent threats at decent people.
>
> The people of France will respond to these acts of defiance. With the regime falling to pieces, they will assert their own rights. After the closing of the factories and offices they will meet before the Chamber to-night and crying Down with the Thieves! they will tell the Government and its parliamentary supporters that they have had enough of this putrid regime.

Source: A. Werth (1934) *France in Ferment* (Jarrold, London), pp. 142–4. (Werth was a British foreign correspondent in Paris, and an eyewitness of the riots on 6 February.)

Document 28   MUSSOLINI DEFINES FASCISM

Anti-individualistic, the Fascist conception of life stresses the importance of the State and accepts the individual only insofar as his interests coincide with those of the State, which stands for the conscience and universal will of man as a historic entity. It is opposed to classical liberalism which arose as a reaction to absolutism and exhausted its historical function when the State became the expression of the conscience and will of the people. Liberalism denied the State in the name of the individual; Fascism reasserts the rights of the State as expressing the real essence of the individual. And if Liberty is to be the attribute of living men and not of abstract dummies invented by individualistic liberalism, then Fascism stands for liberty, and for the only liberty worth having, the liberty of the State and of the individual within the State. The Fascist conception of the State is all-embracing; outside of it no human or spiritual values can exist, much less have value. Thus understood, Fascism is totalitarian, and the Fascist State – a synthesis and a unit inclusive of all values – interprets, develops, and potentiates the whole life of a people.

No individuals or groups (political parties, cultural associations, economic unions, social classes) outside the State. Fascism is therefore opposed to Socialism to which unity within the State (which amalgamates classes into a single economic and ethical reality) is unknown, and which sees in history nothing but the class struggle. Fascism is likewise opposed to trade-unionism as a class weapon. But when brought within the orbit of the State, Fascism recognizes the real needs which gave rise to socialism and trade-unionism, giving them due weight in the guild or corporative system in which divergent interests are co-ordinated and harmonized in the unity of the State.

Grouped according to their several interests, individuals form classes; they form trade-unions when organized according to their several economic activities; but first and foremost they form the State, which is no mere matter of numbers, the sum of the individuals forming the majority. Fascism is therefore opposed to that form of democracy which equates a nation to the majority, lowering it to the level of the largest number; but it is the purest form of democracy if the nation be considered – as it should be – from the point of view of quality rather than quantity, as an idea, the mightiest because the most ethical, the most coherent, the truest, expressing itself in a people as the conscience and will of the few, if not, indeed, of one, and tending to express itself in the conscience and the will of the mass, of the whole group ethically moulded by natural and historical conditions into a nation, advancing, as one conscience and one will, along the self-same line of development and spiritual formation. Not a race, nor a geographically defined region, but a people, historically perpetuating itself; a multitude unified by an idea and imbued with the will to live, the will to power, self-consciousness, personality.

Source: Benito Mussolini (1935) 'Fascism: doctrine and institutions', in C.F. Delzell (ed.) (1971), *Mediterranean Fascism 1919–1945* (Macmillan, London), pp. 93–5.

————◀●▶————

THE DEMOCRATIC CRISIS   **Document 29**

I will try once more to make it more intelligible to you why we could not regard the German Republic, the 'Weimar system', as an effective first step in

German democracy. I can only do it with a few indications, and I am afraid that it may not convince you. We look back now on those years from a time of such confusion that they are bound to seem to us to be simply transfigured . . .

Carry yourself back to those years after the Armistice. You were in Germany soon after the conclusion of peace. You remember our anxieties. There were the acute ones – the peace treaty, some of the terms of which were hardly endurable; Reparations; the intrinsic weakness of our political life; then, later, unemployment, the agrarian crisis, and those internecine conflicts of parties with no political tradition and not even an established routine. There was the decay of the state as the guardian of public order, its capitulation to the mob, and, on the other side, the continual extension of the sphere of the state into new regions.

There were the disturbing signs of a new time – the masses, the growing collectivism, the growing primitiveness, the decline in spiritual standards, the *sequelae* [consequences] of the more and more radical technical revolution, the change in men, the mechanization of life, the growth of gigantic industrial organizations . . . Finally there was the progressive spiritual decay, the destruction of all accepted valuations and standards. There emerged plainly out of the loss of authority of all standards a new epoch, a post-Christian age. Christianity had lost its position of authority. Amid this spiritual change everything became subject to challenge – political tradition, the constitutional order, social solidarity, and positive legality. Science and art became problematical. An immense revolution seemed to be breaking out, and a large part of the world seemed to be ready to throw itself into its arms in a passion of destruction and iconoclasm . . .

That was our anxiety, Prelude to total dissolution and paralysis? Or prelude to a total centralization and uniformity? It was not we who wanted an era of tyranny. But that seemed to us the logical and inevitable consequence of mass-democracy.

Source: H. Rauschning (1941) *The Conservative Revolution* (G.P. Putnam's Sons, New York), pp. 158–60, 162. (Rauschning was a prominent Danzig Nazi, who later denounced Nazism and moved to America.)

Document 30   POPULAR ENTHUSIASM FOR HITLER

A far more powerful factor in the New Germany than the appeal of Hitler's doctrine, however, was the appeal of Hitler himself. Many Germans believed that Hitler was actually endowed with superhuman qualities. I remember

Frau Fleischer telling Jules Sauerwein and myself that in Germany there was no need for people to have opinions; they had the Führer's opinions and the Führer was 'inspired.'

Certainly the idea of the superman was encouraged by the vast displays in Nuremberg. Everything that was done was done on a gigantic scale. The power of the spectacles lay not so much in their ingeniousness but in their immensity. The keynote was always repetition and uniformity. Instead of a few gilt eagles there were hundreds; instead of hundreds of flags there were thousands; instead of thousands of performers there were hundreds of thousands.

At night the mystic quality of the ritual was exaggerated by huge burning urns at the top of the stadium, their orange flames leaping into the blackness, while the flood-lighting effect of hundreds of powerful searchlights played eerily against the sky. The music had an almost religious solemnity, timed by the steady beat of drums that sounded like the distant throb of tom-toms.

One night I went to the stadium with Jules Sauerwein to hear an address Hitler was making to Nazi political leaders gathered from all over Germany. The stadium was packed with nearly 200,000 spectators. As the time for the Führer's arrival drew near, the crowd grew restless. The minutes passed and the wait seemed interminable. Suddenly the beat of the drums increased and three motor-cycles with yellow standards fluttering from their windshields raced through the gates. A few minutes later a fleet of black cars rolled swiftly into the arena: in one of them, standing in the front seat, his hand outstretched in the Nazi salute, was Hitler.

The demonstration that followed was one of the most extraordinary I have ever witnessed. Hitler climbed to his box in the Grand Stand amid a deafening ovation, then gave a signal for the political leaders to enter. They came, a hundred thousand strong, through an opening in the far end of the arena. In the silver light they seemed to pour into the bowl like a flood of water. Each of them carried a Nazi flag and when they were assembled in mass formation, the bowl looked like a shimmering sea of swastikas.

Then Hitler began to speak. The crowd hushed into silence, but the drums continued their steady beat. Hitler's voice rasped into the night and every now and then the multitude broke into a roar of cheers. Some of the audience began swaying back and forth, chanting 'Sieg Heil' over and over again in a frenzy of delirium. I looked at the faces around me and saw tears streaming down people's cheeks. The drums had grown louder and I suddenly felt frightened. For a moment I wondered if it wasn't a dream; perhaps we were really in the heart of the African jungle. I had a sudden feeling of claustrophobia and whispered to Jules Sauerwein, asking if we couldn't leave. It was a silly question, for we were hemmed in on all sides, and there was nothing to do but sit there until the bitter end.

At last it was over. Hitler left the box and got back in the car. As soon as he stopped speaking the spell seemed to break and the magic vanish. That was the most extraordinary thing of all: for when he left the stand and climbed back into his car, his small figure suddenly became drab and unimpressive. You had to pinch yourself to realize that this was the man on whom the eyes of the world were riveted; that he alone held the lightning in his hands.

Source: V. Cowles (1941) *Looking for Trouble,* reproduced in *Decade 1931–1941: A Commemorative Anthology* (Hamish Hamilton, London), pp. 126–8. (Cowles was an American foreign correspondent.)

Document 31   BUILDING THE SOVIET SUPERPOWER

It is sometimes asked whether it is not possible to slow down the tempo a bit, to put a check on the movement. No, comrades, it is not possible! The tempo must not be reduced! On the contrary, we must increase it as much as is within our powers and possibilities. This is dictated to us by our obligations to the workers and peasants of the USSR. This is dictated to us by our obligations to the working class of the whole world.

To slacken the tempo would mean falling behind. And those who fall behind get beaten! But we do not want to be beaten. No, we refuse to be beaten! One feature of the history of old Russia was the continual beatings she suffered for falling behind, for her backwardness. She was beaten by the Mongol khans. She was beaten by the Turkish beys. She was beaten by the Swedish feudal lords. She was beaten by the Polish and Lithuanian gentry. She was beaten by the British and French capitalists. She was beaten by the Japanese barons. All beat her – for her backwardness, for political backwardness, for cultural backwardness, for agricultural backwardness. She was beaten because to do so was profitable and could be done with impunity. Do you remember the words of the pre-revolutionary poet: 'You are poor and abundant, mighty and impotent, Mother Russia.' These words of the old poet were learned by those gentlemen. They beat her, saying: 'You are abundant,' so one can enrich oneself at your expense. They beat her, saying: 'You are poor and impotent,' so you can be beaten and plundered with impunity. Such is the law of the exploiters – to beat the backward and the weak. It is the jungle law of capitalism. You are backward, you are weak, therefore you are wrong; hence you can be beaten and enslaved. You are mighty – therefore you are right; hence we must be wary of you.

That is why we must no longer lag behind.

In the past we had no fatherland, nor could we have one. But now that we have overthrown capitalism and power is in the hands of the working class, we have a fatherland, and we will defend its independence. Do you want our fatherland to be beaten and to lose its independence? If you do not want this you must put an end to its backwardness in the shortest possible time and develop genuine Bolshevik tempo in building up its Socialist system of economy. There is no other way. That is why Lenin said during the October Revolution: 'Either perish, or overtake and outstrip the advanced capitalist countries.'

We are fifty or a hundred years behind the advanced countries. We must make good this distance in ten years. Either we do it, or they crush us.

Source: 'The tasks of business executives', speech delivered by Stalin before the First All-Union Conference of Managers, 4 February 1931, in J. Stalin (1947), *Problems of Leninism* (State Publishing House, Moscow), pp. 355–6.

JAPAN, THE 'HAVE-NOT' STATE   **Document 32**

Behind Japan's urge to expansion are a number of impelling forces. There is the explosive pressure of rapidly increasing population in a land that is already overcrowded. There is the feeling of being unfairly treated in the world distribution of territory and raw materials. There is the exceptionally strong position of the fighting services *vis-à-vis* the civil authorities. There is the high-flown sense of nationalism, which for many Japanese has all the force of religious conviction. There is the mystical idea of Japan's Pan-Asian mission, very popular with retired army officers and nationalist theoreticians, which envisages Japan as the leader of an Asia from which 'white imperialism' has been banished. Finally, there is the great difficulty, not to say impossibility, of turning back from the imperial road on which the country has started, no matter how great may be the difficulties and obstacles which may be encountered . . .

Japan may be regarded, along with Germany and Italy, as one of the three major dissatisfied 'have-not' powers of the world. It was in Italian Fascist intellectual circles that the idea first found expression that there could just as logically be a 'class struggle' between rich and poor nations as between the 'bourgeoisie' and the 'proletariat' in a single nation. German National Socialist leaders have displayed an increasing tendency to attribute their country's economic difficulties largely to the lack of colonial sources of essential raw materials. Japan sees itself confronted with a similar problem, despite the acquisition of Manchukuo. So the spokesman of the Foreign Ministry, Mr Amau, recently remarked:

Unfortunately the territories which now feed Japan's population are too small. We are advised to practise birth control, but this advice comes too late, since the population of the Japanese Empire is already about 100,000,000. Japanese work harder and longer than people in Western countries; their opportunities in life are more restricted. Why? We need more territory and must cultivate more resources if we are to nourish our population.

The belief that overpopulation (in relation to available natural resources) is the root cause of Japan's difficulties runs like a red thread through almost all Japanese publications on social and economic subjects. Even liberal and radical professors and publicists who are outspokenly or cautiously critical of the high-handed methods of the country's military leaders are quick to point out that the world-wide restrictions on Japanese immigrants and Japanese goods greatly accentuate the strains within the Japanese social order and play into the hands of the advocates of violent courses.

Source: W.H. Chamberlin (1938) *Japan over Asia* (Duckworth, London), pp. 17–19. (Chamberlin was Tokyo correspondent for the *Christian Science Monitor*, and author of a number of books on inter-war Japan.)

Document 33   HITLER'S IDEA OF 'LIVING SPACE'

Yet the regulation of the relation between population and territory is of tremendous importance for a nation's existence. Indeed, we can justly say that the whole life struggle of a people in truth consists in safeguarding the territory it requires as a general prerequisite for the sustenance of the increasing population. Since the population grows incessantly, and the soil as such remains stationary, tensions perforce must gradually arise which at first find expression in distress, and which for a certain time can be balanced through greater industry, more ingenious production methods or special austerity. But there comes a day when these tensions can no longer be eliminated by such means. Then the task of the leaders of a nation's struggle for existence consists in eliminating the unbearable conditions in a fundamental way, that is in restoring a tolerable relation between population and territory.

In the life of nations there are several ways for correcting the disproportion between population and territory. The most natural way is to adapt the soil, from time to time, to the increased population. This requires a determination to fight and the risk of bloodshed. But this very bloodshed is also the only one that can be justified to a people. Since through it the necessary space is won for the further increase of a people, it automatically finds manifold compensation for the humanity staked on the battlefield. Thus the bread of freedom grows from the hardships of war. The sword was the path-breaker for the plough . . .

Hence every healthy, vigorous people sees nothing sinful in territorial acquisition, but something quite in keeping with nature . . . The present distribution of world space in a one-sided way turns out to be so much in favour of individual nations that the latter perforce have an understandable interest in not allowing any further changes in the present distribution of territories. But the overabundance of territory enjoyed by these nations contrasts with the poverty of the others, which despite the utmost industry are not in a position to produce their daily bread so as to keep alive. What higher rights would one want to oppose against them if they also raise the claim to a land area which safeguards their sustenance?

No. The primary right of the world is the right to life, so far as one possesses the strength for this. Hence on the basis of this right a vigorous nation will always find ways of adapting its territory to its population size . . . For this, however, a nation needs weapons. The acquisition of soil is always linked with the employment of force.

Source: Hitler's Secret Book (1961) (Grove Press, New York), pp. 14–16. (Hitler dictated this sequel to *Mein Kampf* in the summer of 1928, and then placed it in a safe in Nazi Party headquarters with orders for it not to be published until after his death. It was captured by the Americans in 1945, and authenticated in 1958.)

FACE TO FACE WITH HITLER

Document 34

November 19th. After a day in Berlin I was taken off to Berchtesgaden which we reached after a night in the special train, and were driven by what I assumed to be storm-troopers straight up to Hitler's chalet. Snow was on the ground and a path had been swept up the steep steps to the house. As I looked out of the car window, on eye level, I saw in the middle of this swept path a pair of black trousered legs, finishing up in silk socks and pumps. I assumed this was a footman who had come down to help me out of the car and up the steps, and was proceeding in leisurely fashion to get myself out of the car when I heard Von Neurath [German Foreign Minister] or somebody throwing a hoarse whisper at my ear of 'Der Führer, der Führer'; and then it dawned upon me that the legs were not the legs of a footman, but of Hitler. And higher up, the trousers passed into khaki tunic with swastika armlet complete. He greeted me politely and led me up to the house and to his study, which was very overheated, but with a magnificent mountain view from immense windows . . .

One had a feeling all the time that we had a totally different sense of values and were speaking a different language. It was not only the difference between a totalitarian and democratic state. He gave me the impression of feeling that, whilst he had attained to power only after a hard struggle with present-day realities, the British Government was still living comfortably in a world of its own making, a fairy-land of strange, if respectable, illusions. It clung to shibboleths – 'collective security', 'general settlement', 'disarmament', 'non-aggression pacts' – which offered no practical prospect of a solution of Europe's difficulties. He regards the whole conception embodied in a League of States equal in their rights of sovereignty as unreal, based on no foundation of fact; and consequently does not believe that discussions between large numbers of nations, with varying interests and of quite unequal value, can lead anywhere. Hence his preference for dealing with particular problems in isolation. With this goes the distrust of democratic method, to him inefficient, blundering, paralysed by its love of talk, and totally unsuited to the rough world, constantly changing, in which we have to live.

All this is naturally disturbing to us and makes approaches difficult. An explorer who has overcome countless perils in a savage land returns home to find his family unaware of his achievements and still immersed in local politics and problems. Their meeting is friendly, but he feels they are living in a wholly different world. The analogy is not perfect but it will serve to illustrate Hitler's attitude towards a meeting with a representative of the British Government.

Source: Diary entry for 19 November 1937, reproduced in the memoirs of Lord Halifax (1957) *Fulness of Days* (Collins, London), pp. 184–5, 189–90. (Halifax was Chamberlain's personal emissary to visit Hitler. He became Foreign Minister in February 1938.)

Document 35   THE DESTRUCTION OF GUERNICA

After four there were farm carts coming into Gernika [sic], rolling on solid wooden wheels and drawn by oxen whose heads were shaded under fleeces of sheep. Basque peasants in their long puckered market smocks walked backwards in front of them, mesmerising the oxen to Gernika with their slim wands, with which they kept touching the horns and yoke gently. They talked to the oxen. Others were driving sheep to market. There was an assembly of animals near the parish church, a stately structure cavernous, tall and dark within, standing upon a flight of thin steps like leaves piled one upon the other.

It is improbable that anyone was thinking about the war when at four-thirty the church bell rang out loud. All over Spain a peal on a single bell is an air-raid warning. The population took cover, and the sheep in the square were left to their own devices . . .

Fifteen minutes passed, and the people were coming out of their shelters. A heavy drumming of engines was heard to the east. It was what we called in lighter moments the *tranvias* – the trams – the Junker 52's, who were so clumsy that they seemed to clang rather than to fly. These were the heaviest bombers that Germany had sent to Spain.

Over the town, whose streets were once more empty trenches, they dispersed their load a ton at a time. They turned woodenly over Gernika, the bombs fell mechanically in line as they turned. Then came the crack of the explosions; smoke stood up over Gernika like wool on a negro's head. Everywhere it sprouted, as more heavy bombers came.

Besides many fifty- and hundred-pound bombs, they dropped great torpedoes weighing a thousand. Gernika is a compact little town, and most of these hit buildings, tearing them to pieces vertically from top to bottom and below the bottom. They penetrated refuges. The spirit of the people had been good, but now they panicked.

An escort of Heinkel 51's, the same perhaps that had molested us that afternoon, were waiting for this moment. Till now they had been machine-gunning the roads round Gernika, scattering, killing or wounding sheep and shepherds. As the terrified population streamed out of the town they dived low to drill them with their guns . . . . The terrified people lay face down in ditches, pressed their backs against tree trunks, coiled themselves in holes, shut their eyes and ran across sweet green open meadow. Many were foolish and fled back before the aerial tide into the village. It was then that the heavy bombing of Gernika began.

It was then that Gernika was smudged out of that rich landscape, the province of Vizcaya, with a heavy fist.

Source: G.L. Steer (1938) *The Tree of Gernika: A Field Study of Modern War* (Hodder & Stoughton, London), pp. 237–8. (Steer was a war correspondent who arrived in Guernica a few hours after the first bombing of the town.)

Document 36   THE CLASH OF IDEALS

'Either We or They'

The future existence of civilization depends upon an immense mobilization of new thought and energy. Many of the old ideals, surviving from a pre-industrial age, do not fit an environment fabricated by colossal trusts, combines, bureaucracies, agencies of propaganda, international movements of labour, and imperialistic aggregations of capital. Political control is still largely modelled upon a prescientific pattern; an economy of scarcity persists in an age of potential abundance; morals have not kept pace with the furious tempo of mechanical advancement; religion is powerless to stem the savagery of war or the ruthlessness of economic struggle. Technological change has been extraordinarily rapid but social institutions have remained relatively static; the consequence is a fundamental disharmony at the very heart of modern civilization. Men would like to rely upon the old moralizing agencies – the family, the Church, the neighbourhood, and the community; but these institutions are perhaps more insecure and ineffective than ever before in history. Hence the might of new ideals and institutions must be enlisted to curb the battalions of disaster. What I say is trite, but so long as millions persist in folly, the facts must be re-emphasized.

In view of the evidence in the present volume, we cannot look to Fascism for the salvaging of Western culture. The Fascist dictatorships, we can safely conclude, do not provide the mentality which is so desperately needed; they instead constitute the supreme threat to civilization – the expression of irrational and unbridled power upon a grand scale. Millions are wondering if tomorrow they shall not be called upon to fight and perhaps to die in a war brutally instigated by irresponsible dictators. By the time this page is read, another vast war may be reaping its ghastly harvest. Even if war is temporarily averted, the threat of world calamity is so great and so sinister that it can be checked only by the resolute and concerted action of all men of good will. Mankind has never faced a greater crisis.

The intellectual essence of this crisis can now be briefly summarized. The world is confronted by a clash between two irreconcilable ideals: humanism and anti-humanism. The humanistic ideal, which underlies the greatest achievements of Western culture, is based upon the Greek ideal of intellectual aristocracy and the Christian idea of democratic sharing. Science put to the service of human welfare; life 'motivated by love and guided by knowledge' – here is an ideal as old as civilization and as new as the perpetually shifting horizon of experience. The anti-humanistic ideal, which revives as nations plunge downward towards barbarism, is but the ancient code of tribalism rendered now more deadly by the hellish efficiency of lethal instruments and the pitiless dictatorship of the Power State . . . Mussolini was but stating a sober fact when he declared in his famous Palazzo Venezia speech on October 8 1921: 'The struggle between the two worlds can permit no compromise . . . Either We or They!'

Source: Reprinted with the permission of Scribner, an imprint of Simon & Schuster Adult Publishing Group, from NO COMPROMISE: CONFLICT BETWEEN TWO WORLDS by Melvin M. Rader. Copyright © 1939 by The Macmillan Company; copyright renewed © 1967 by Melvin M. Rader. All rights reserved. (Rader was Professor of Philosophy at the University of Washington, Seattle.)

Bibliography

CONTEMPORARY SOURCES, MEMOIRS

Carr, E.H. (1939) *The Twenty Years' Crisis*, Macmillan.

Caudwell, C. (1949) *Studies and Further Studies in a Dying Culture*, Dodd Mead.

Decade: A Commemorative Anthology, 1931–1941, (1941) Hamish Hamilton.

Decugis, H. (1936) *Le destin des races blanches*, Librarie de France.

Ford, H. (1931) *Moving Forward*, Heinemann.

Freud, S. (1953–74) *Collected Works*, 24 vols, Hogarth Press.

Hitler, A. (1961) *Hitler's Secret Book*, ed. T. Taylor, Grove Press.

Hitler, A. (1969) *Mein Kampf*, ed. D.C. Watt, Hutchinson.

Hodson, H.V. (1938) *Slump and Recovery 1929–1937: A Survey of World Economic Affairs*, Oxford University Press.

Joussain, A. (1939) 'La crise de la civilisation européene', *L'Année Politique: française et étrangère*, 14.

Jung, C. (1936) *Modern Man in Search of a Soul*, Kegan Paul.

Koestler, A. (1954) *Arrow in the Blue*, William Collins.

Kolnai, A. (1938) *The War Against the West*, Victor Gollancz.

Nordau, M. (1895) *Degeneration*, William Heinemann.

Ortega y Gasset, J. (1932) *The Revolt of the Masses*, George Allen and Unwin.

Rader, M. (1939) *No Compromise: The Conflict between Two Worlds*, Victor Gollancz.

Rees, R. (ed.) (1962) *Simone Weil: Selected Essays, 1934–1943*, Oxford University Press.

Schwarzschild, L. (1943) *World in Trance*, Hamish Hamilton.

Schweitzer, A. (1923) *The Decay and Restoration of Civilization: Part I*, Black.

Spengler, O. (1932) *The Decline of the West: Perspectives on World History*, 2 vols, George Allen and Unwin.

Stoddard, L. (1922) *The Revolt Against Civilization: The Menace of the Under-Man*, Chapman and Hall.

Wells, H.G. (1921) *The Salvaging of Civilisation*, London.

REVOLUTION AND COUNTER-REVOLUTION

Bessel, R. (1990) 'State and society in Germany in the aftermath of the First World War' in Lee, W.R. and Rosenhaft, E. (eds) *The State and Social Change in Germany 1880–1980*, Berg.

Brovkin, V. (1998) *Russia after Lenin: Politics, Culture and Society 1921–1929*, Routledge.

Carsten, F. (1972) *Revolution in Central Europe*, Temple Smith.

Cohen, S. (1985) *Rethinking the Soviet Experience: Politics and History since 1917*, Oxford University Press.

Ferro, M. (1980) *October 1917: A Social History of the Russian Revolution*, Routledge.

Figes, O. (1996) *A People's Tragedy: The Russian Revolution 1891–1924*, Jonathan Cape.

Figes, O. and Kolonitskii, B. (1999) *Interpreting the Russian Revolution: The Language and Symbols of 1917*, Yale University Press.

Fowkes, B. (1984) *Communism in Germany under the Weimar Republic*, Macmillan.

Geary, R. (1991) *European Labour Politics from 1880 to the Depression*, Macmillan.

Graziosi, A. (2000) *A New, Peculiar State: Explorations in Soviet History, 1917–1937*, Praeger.

Kochan, L. (1967) *Russia in Revolution 1890–1918*, Weidenfeld.

Maier, C. (1975) *Recasting Bourgeois Europe: Stabilization in France, Germany and Italy in the Decade after World War I*, Princeton University Press.

Rosenthal, B.G. (2002) *New Myth, New World: From Nietzsche to Stalinism*, Pennsylvania State University.

Ryder, A.J. (1967) *The German Revolution*, Cambridge University Press.

Service, R. (1979) *The Bolshevik Party in Revolution*, Macmillan.

Shlapentokh, D. (1999) *The Counter-Revolution in Revolution*, Macmillan.

Snowden, F. (1986) *Violence and the Great Estates in the South of Italy 1900–1922*, Cambridge University Press.

Tampke, J. (1979) *The Ruhr and Revolution, 1914–1919*, Croom Helm.

MODERNIZATION AND CRISIS

Affron, M. and Antliss, M. (eds) (1997) *Fascist Visions: Art and Ideology in France and Italy*, Princeton University Press.

Bailes, K. (1978) *Technology and Society under Lenin and Stalin, 1917–1941*, Princeton University Press.

Barnouw, D. (1988) *Weimar Intellectuals and the Threat of Modernity*, Indiana University Press.

Ben-Ghiat, R. (2001) *Fascist Modernities: Italy 1922–1945*, University of California Press.

Burleigh, M. and Wippermann, W. (1991) *The Racial State: Germany 1933–1945*, Cambridge University Press.

Childers, T. (ed.) (1986) *The Formation of the Nazi Constituency, 1919–1933*, Croom Helm.

Dickinson, E.R. (2004) 'Biopolitics, fascism, democracy: some reflections on our discourse about "modernity"', *Central European History*, 37.

Fischer, C. (ed.) (1996) *The Rise of National Socialism and the Working Classes in Weimar Germany*, Berghahn.

Gill, G. (1979) *Peasants and Government in the Russian Revolution*, Macmillan.

Herf, J. (1985) *Reactionary Modernism: Technology, Culture and Politics in Weimar and the Third Reich*, Cambridge University Press.

Hoffman, D. and Kotsonis, Y. (eds) (2000) *Russian Modernity: Politics, Knowledge, Practices*, Macmillan.

Kelikian, A. (1986) *Town and Country under Fascism: The Transformation of Brescia 1915–1926*, Oxford University Press.

Lewin, M. (1985) *The Making of the Soviet System: Essays in the Social History of Inter-War Russia*, Methuen.

Maier, C. (1970) 'Between Taylorism and technocracy: European ideologies and the vision of industrial productivity in the 1920s', *Journal of Contemporary History*, 5.

Malefakis, E. (1970) *Agrarian Reform and Peasant Revolution in Spain: Origins of the Civil War*, Yale University Press.

Mühlberger, D. (ed.) (1987) *The Social Bases of European Fascist Movements*, Croom Helm.

Müller, K.-J. (1976) 'French fascism and modernization', *Journal of Contemporary History*, 11.

Paxton, R. (1997) *French Peasant Fascism: Henry Dorgères's Greenshirts and the Crisis of French Agriculture*, Oxford University Press.

Peris, D. (1998) *Storming the Heavens: The Soviet League of the Militant Godless*, Cornell University Press.

Rinderle, W. and Norling, B. (1993) *The Nazi Impact on a German Village*, University Press of Kentucky.

Roseman, M. (1996) 'Modernization and fascism' in Bessel, R. (ed.), *Fascist Italy and Nazi Germany: Comparisons and Contrasts*, Cambridge University Press.

Shearer, D. (2004) 'Elements new and alien: passportization, policing and identity in the Stalinist state 1932–1952', *Journal of Modern History*, 76.

Stern, F. (1961) *The Politics of Cultural Despair: A Study in the Rise of the German Ideology*, University of California Press.

Stites, R. (1989) *Revolutionary Dreams: Utopian Visions, Experimental Life in the Russian Revolution*, Oxford University Press.

Turner, H.A. (1975) 'Fascism and modernization' in idem (ed.) *Reappraisals of Fascism*, Franklin Watts.

Viola, L. (1996) *Peasant Rebels under Stalin: Collectivization and the Culture of Peasant Resistance*, Oxford University Press.

A CRISIS OF CIVILIZATION

Bair, D. (2003) *Jung: A Biography*, Little, Brown.

Dean, C.J. (2000) *The Frail Social Body: Pornography, Homosexuality and Other Fantasies in Interwar France*, University of California.

Farrell, J. (1996) *Freud's Paranoid Quest: Psychoanalysis and Modern Suspicion*, New York University Press.

Hawkins, M. (1997) *Social Darwinism in European and American Thought 1860–1945: Nature as Model and Nature as Threat*, Cambridge University Press.

Hughes, H.S. (1952) *Oswald Spengler: A Critical Estimate*, Charles Scribner.

Ilič, M. (1999) *Women Workers in the Soviet Interwar Economy*, Macmillan.

Ilič, M. (ed.) (2001) *Women in the Stalin Era*, Macmillan.

Ipsen, C. (1996) *Dictating Demography: The Problem of Population in Fascist Italy*, Cambridge University Press.

Joshi, V. (2003) *Gender and Power in the Third Reich: Female Denouncers and the Gestapo 1933–1945*, Macmillan.

Kotkin, S. (1995) *Magnetic Mountain: Stalinism as Civilization*, University of California.

Miller, M.A. (1999) *Late Modernism: Politics, Fiction, and the Arts between the World Wars*, University of California Press.

Peel, R.A. (ed.) (1998) *Essays in the History of Eugenics*, Galton Institute.

Pick, D. (1993) *War Machine: The Rationalization of Slaughter in the Modern Age*, Yale University Press.

Proctor, R. (1988) *Racial Hygiene: Medicine under the Nazis*, Harvard University Press.

Roazen, P. (1968) *Freud: Political and Social Thought*, Knopf.

Spektorowski, A. and Mizrachi, E. (2004) 'Eugenics and the welfare state in Sweden', *Journal of Contemporary History*, 39.

Stibbe, M. (2003) *Women in the Third Reich*, Arnold.

Stites, R. (1989) *Revolutionary Dreams: Utopian Vision and Experimental Life in the Russian Revolution*, Oxford University Press.

Weikart, R. (2004) *From Darwin to Hitler: Evolutionary Ethics, Eugenics and Racism in Germany*, Macmillan.

Weindling, P. (1989) *Health, Race and German Politics between National Unification and Nazism 1870–1945*, Cambridge University Press.

Wilson, P. (ed.) (2004) *Gender, Family and Sexuality: The Private Sphere in Italy 1860–1945*, Macmillan.

THE INTER-WAR ECONOMY

Aldcroft, D. (1977) *From Versailles to Wall Street*, Allen Lane.

Badger, A.J. (1989) *The New Deal: The Depression Years 1933–1940*, Macmillan.

Balderston, T. (2002) *Economics and Politics in the Weimar Republic*, Cambridge University Press.

Barkai, A. (1990) *Nazi Economics: Ideology, Theory and Policy*, Berg.

Buchheim, C. (2001) 'The Nazi boom: an economic cul-de-sac' in Mommsen, H. (ed.) *The Third Reich between Vision and Reality: New Perspectives on German History 1918–1945*, Oxford University Press.

Buxton, N. and Aldcroft, D. (eds) (1979) *British Industry between the Wars: Instability and Industrial Development, 1919–1939*, Scolar Press.

Capie, F. (1994) *Tariffs and Growth: Some Insights from the World Economy 1850–1940*, Manchester University Press.

Clavin, P. (1991) 'The World Economic Conference 1933: The failure of British internationalism', *Journal of European Economic History*, 20.

Clavin, P. (2000) *The Great Depression in Europe 1929–1939*, Macmillan.

Eichengreen, B. (1992) 'The origins and nature of the Great Slump revisited', *Economic History Review*, 2nd ser., 45.

Feldman, G. (1994) *The Great Disorder: Politics, Economics and Society in the German Inflation, 1914–1924*, Oxford University Press.

Foreman-Peck, J. (1984) *A History of the World Economy: International Economic Relations since 1850*, Wheatsheaf.

Holtfrerich, C. (1988) *The German Inflation*, De Gruyter.

Jackson, J. (1985) *The Politics of Depression in France 1932–1936*, Cambridge University Press.

James, H. (1986) *The German Slump: Politics and Economics 1924–1936*, Oxford University Press.

Kindleberger, C. (1973) *The World in Depression 1929–1939*, Allen Lane.

Overy, R.J. (1994) *War and Economy in the Third Reich*, Oxford University Press.

Overy, R.J. (2001) 'The German economy 1919–1945' in Panayi, P. (ed.) *Weimar and Nazi Germany: Continuities and Discontinuities*, Arnold.

Saint-Etienne, C. (1984) *The Great Depression 1929–1938: Lessons for the 1980s*, Hoover Institution Press.

Schuker, S. (1988) *American 'Reparations' to Germany 1919–1933: Implications for the Third World Debt Crisis*, Princeton University Press.

Stachura, P. (ed.) (1986) *Unemployment and the Great Depression in Germany*, Macmillan.

Tooze, A. (2006) *The Wages of Destruction: The Making and Breaking of the Nazi Economy*, Allen Lane.

DEMOCRACY AND DICTATORSHIP

Allen, W.S. (1975) 'The appeal of fascism and the problem of national disintegration' in Turner, H.A. (ed.) *Reappraisals of Fascism*, Franklin Watts.

Bessel, R. (2004) 'The Nazi capture of power', *Journal of Contemporary History*, 39.

Blinkhorn, M. (1988) *Democracy and Civil War in Spain, 1931–1939*, Routledge.

Buchanan, T. (2002) 'Anti-fascism and democracy in the 1930s', *European History Quarterly*, 32.

Davies, S. and Harris, J. (eds) (2005) *Stalin: A New History*, Cambridge University Press.

Evans, R.J. (2004) *The Coming of the Third Reich*, Allen Lane.

Fischer, C. (2002) *The Rise of the Nazis*, Manchester University Press.

Gentile, E. (2005) *The Origins of Fascist Ideology*, Enigma Books.

Getty, J. Arch (1985) *Origins of the Great Purges: The Soviet Communist Party Reconsidered, 1933–1938*, Cambridge University Press.

Getty, J. Arch and Manning, R. (eds) (1993) *Stalinist Terror: New Perspectives*, Cambridge University Press.

Gill, G. (1990) *Stalinism*, Macmillan.

Griffin, R. (ed.) (1998) *International Fascism: Theories, Causes and the New Consensus*, Arnold.

Jackson, J. (1988) *The Popular Front in France: Defending Democracy*, Cambridge University Press.

Jones, L.E. (1988) *German Liberalism and the Dissolution of the Weimar Party System, 1918–1933*, North Carolina University Press.

Kershaw, I. (1987) *The 'Hitler Myth': Image and Reality in the Third Reich*, Oxford University Press.

Kershaw, I. (1998–2000) *Hitler: Volume I, Hubris. Volume II, Nemesis*, Allen Lane.

Kershaw, I., Lewin, M. (eds) (1990) *Weimar: Why Did Democracy Fail?*, Oxford University Press.

Linehan, T. (2000) *British Fascism 1918–1939: Parties, Ideology and Culture*, Manchester University Press.

Luebbert, G. (1991) *Liberalism, Fascism and Social Democracy: Social Classes and the Political Origins of Regimes in Interwar Europe*, Oxford University Press.

Luzzato, E. (2005) *The Body of il Duce: Mussolini's Corpse and the Future of Italy*, Henry Holt.

Lyttleton, A. (1988) *The Seizure of Power: Fascism in Italy 1919–1929*, Princeton University Press.

Melograni, P. (1976) 'The cult of the Duce in Mussolini's Italy', *Journal of Contemporary History*, 11.

Molony, J. (1977) *The Emergence of Political Catholicism in Italy: Partito popolare 1919–1926*, Croom Helm.

Moore, B. (1973) *The Social Origins of Dictatorship and Democracy*, Penguin.

Noakes, J. (2004) 'Leaders of the people? The Nazi Party and German society', *Journal of Contemporary History*, 39.

Nolte, E. (1969) *Three faces of Fascism*, Mentor.

Overy, R.J. (2004) *The Dictators: Hitler's Germany and Stalin's Russia*, Allen Lane.

Paxton, R. (2004) *The Anatomy of Fascism*, Allen Lane.

Payne, S. (1995) *A History of Fascism 1914–1945*, UCL Press.

Polonsky, A. (1972) *Politics in Independent Poland 1921–1939*, Oxford University Press.

Preston, P. (1984) *Revolution and War in Spain 1931–1939*, Methuen.

Renton, D. (2001) *This Rough Game: Fascism and Anti-Fascism*, Sutton.

Sternhell, Z. (1986) *Neither Right nor Left: Fascist Ideology in France*, Princeton University Press.

Szejnmann, C.-C. (1999) *Nazism in Central Germany: The Brownshirts in 'Red' Saxony*, Berghahn Books.

Thatcher, I. (2004) 'Stalin and Stalinism', *Europe–Asia Studies*, 56.

Winkler, H.-A. (1976) 'German society, Hitler and the illusion of restoration', *Journal of Contemporary History*, 11.

Woolf, S. (ed.) (1968) *European Fascism*, Weidenfeld.

THE INTERNATIONAL CRISIS

Adamthwaite, A. (1995) *Grandeur and Misery: France's Bid for Power in Europe, 1914–1940*, Arnold.

Bell, P.M. (1986) *The Origins of the Second World War in Europe*, Longman.

Betts, R.F. (1990) *France and Decolonisation 1900–1960*, Macmillan.

Bialer, U. (1980) *The Shadow of the Bomber: The Fear of Air Attack and British Politics, 1932–1939*, Royal Historical Society.

Boyce, R. (ed.) (1989) *Paths to War: Essays on the Origins of the Second World War*, Macmillan.

Boyce, R. and Maiolo, J.A. (eds) (2003) *The Origins of World War Two: The Debate Continues*, Macmillan.

Dallek, R. (1979) *Franklin D. Roosevelt and American Foreign Policy 1932–1945*, Oxford University Press.

Gorodetsky, G. (1999) *Grand Delusion: Stalin and the German Invasion of Russia*, Yale University Press.

Harrison, M. (1985) *Soviet Planning in Peace and War 1938–1945*, Cambridge University Press.

Imlay, T.C. (2003) *Facing the Second World War: Strategy, Politics and Economics in Britain and France 1938–1940*, Oxford University Press.

Kaiser, D. (1980) *Economic Diplomacy and the Origins of the Second World War*, Princeton University Press.

Leitz, C. (2004) *Nazi Foreign Policy 1933–1941: The Road to Global War*, Routledge.

Macdonald, C.A. (1981) *The United States, Britain and Appeasement, 1936–1939*, Macmillan.

Mack Smith, D. (1976) *Mussolini's Roman Empire*, Longman.

Macmillan, M. (2001) *Peacemakers: The Paris Peace Conference of 1919 and the Attempt to End War*, John Murray.

Marks, S. (1979) *The Illusion of Peace: International Relations in Europe 1918–1933*, Macmillan.

Mommsen, W. and Kettenacker, L. (eds) (1983) *The Fascist Challenge and the Policy of Appeasement*, George Allen and Unwin.

Nekrich, A. (1997) *Pariahs, Partners, Predators: German-Soviet Relations 1922–1941*, New York.

Northedge, F.S. (1986) *The League of Nations: Its Life and Times*, Leicester University Press.

Overy, R.J. and Wheatcroft, A. (1989) *The Road to War*, Macmillan.

Porter, B. (1975) *The Lion's Share: A Short History of British Imperialism*, Longman.

Ragsdale, H. (2004) *The Soviets, the Munich Crisis and the Coming of World War II*, Cambridge University Press.

Samuelson, L. (2000) *Plans for Stalin's War Machine: Tukhachevskii and Military and Economic Planning*, Macmillan.

Steiner, Z. (2005) *The Lights that Failed: European International History 1919–1933*, Oxford University Press.

Thomas, M. (2005) 'Economic conditions and the limits of mobilization in the French empire 1936–1939', *The Historical Journal*, 48.

Watt, D.C. (1989) *How War Came: The Immediate Origins of the Second World War 1938–1939*, Heinemann.

Young, R.J. (1978) *In Command of France: French Foreign Policy and Military Planning 1933–1939*, Harvard University Press.

GENERAL BOOKS

Biddiss, M. (1977) *The Age of the Masses: Ideas and Society in Europe since 1870*, Penguin.

Brendon, P. (2000) *The Dark Valley: A Panorama of the 1930s*, Jonathan Cape.

Ferro, M. (1973) *The Great War 1914–1918*, Routledge.

Kennedy, P. (1988) *The Rise and Fall of the Great Powers*, Unwin Hyman.

Koch, R. and Smith, C. (2006) *Suicide of the West*, Continuum.

Mazower, M. (1998) *Dark Continent: Europe's Twentieth Century*, Allen Lane.

Teich, M. and Porter, R. (eds) (1990) *Fin de Siècle and its legacy*, Cambridge University Press.

Winter, J. and Braggett, D. (1990) *The Great War and the Shaping of the Twentieth Century*, New York.

Index

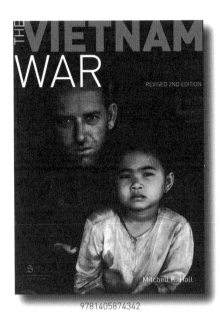

THE VIETNAM WAR
REVISED 2ND EDITION
Mitchell K. Hall

9781405874342

SEMINAR STUDIES
IN HISTORY

THE ARAB-ISRAELI CONFLICT
Kirsten E. Schulze

9780582771895

AND STALINISM
Martin McCauley

9781405874366

THE CIVIL RIGHTS MOVEMENT
Bruce J. Dierenfield

9781405874359

THE SECOND WORLD WAR ON THE EASTERN FRONT
Les Baker

9781405840637

ORIGINS OF THE FIRST WORLD WAR
Gordon Martel

9781405874311

RUSSIA AMERICA AND THE COLD WAR 1949–1991
Martin McCauley

9781405874304

THE SECOND WORLD WAR IN EUROPE
P. Mackenzie

9781405846998

CHINA IN TRANSFORMATION 1900–1949
Colin Mackerras

9781405840583

ORIGINS OF THE COLD WAR 1941–1949

9781405874335

ORIGINS OF THE SECOND WORLD WAR

9781405824699

MUSSOLINI AND ITALIAN FASCISM
Giuseppe Finaldi

9781405812535

SEMINAR STUDIES
IN HISTORY